First World War
and Army of Occupation
War Diary
France, Belgium and Germany

63 (ROYAL NAVAL) DIVISION
188 Infantry Brigade
2 Royal Marine Battalion
1 June 1916 - 28 April 1918

WO95/3110/2

The Naval & Military Press Ltd
www.nmarchive.com
Published in association with The National Archives

Published by

The Naval & Military Press Ltd

Unit 10 Ridgewood Industrial Park,

Uckfield, East Sussex,

TN22 5QE England

Tel: +44 (0) 1825 749494

www.naval-military-press.com

www.nmarchive.com

Contents

Document type	Place/Title	Date From	Date To
Heading	WO95/3110-2		
Heading	63rd Division 188th Infy Bde 2nd Bn Royal Marines Jun 1916-Apr 1918		
Heading	War Diary of 2nd. Royal Marines. from 1st. June to 30th June Inclusive		
War Diary	Hersin	01/06/1916	20/06/1916
War Diary	Trenches	21/06/1916	23/06/1916
War Diary	Fresnicourt Q.19	24/06/1916	30/06/1916
Operation(al) Order(s)	Operation Order No 3 By Lieut Colonel A.R.H. Hutchison R.M.L.I. Comdg 2nd Royal Marine Battalion	22/06/1919	22/06/1919
Heading	War Diary of 2nd. Royal Marines From 1st. July 1916 to 31st, July 1916		
War Diary	Fresnicourt Q.19	01/07/1916	12/07/1916
War Diary	Hersin	13/07/1916	13/07/1916
War Diary	Bully-Grenay R.H.A	14/07/1916	19/07/1916
War Diary	Angres II Sub-Section	20/07/1916	31/07/1916
Operation(al) Order(s)	Training Order No. 1	06/07/1916	06/07/1916
Operation(al) Order(s)	Operation Order No. 4 By Major C.E.C Eagles R.M.L.I. Comdg 2nd Royal Marines	12/07/1916	12/07/1916
Operation(al) Order(s)	Operation Order No. 5 By Lieut Colonel A.R.H. Hutchison R.M.L.I. Comdg 2nd Royal Marine Battalion	13/07/1916	13/07/1916
Map	Appendix IV War Diary July 1916 2nd Royal Marines.		
Operation(al) Order(s)	Operation Order No. 6 By Lieut Colonel A.R.H. Hutchison R.M.L.I. Comdg 2nd Royal Marine Battalion	16/07/1916	16/07/1916
Operation(al) Order(s)	Operation Order No. 7 By Lieut Colonel A.R.H. Hutchison R.M.L.I. Comdg 2nd Royal Marine Battalion	19/07/1916	19/07/1916
Operation(al) Order(s)	Operation Order No 8 By Lieut Colonel A.R.H. Hutchison R.M.L.I. Comdg 2nd Royal Marine Battalion	14/07/1916	14/07/1916
Operation(al) Order(s)	Operation Order No. 9 By Lieut Colonel A.R.H. Hutchison R.M.L.I. Comdg 2nd Royal Marine Battalion	25/07/1916	25/07/1916
Operation(al) Order(s)	Operation Order No 10 By Lieut Colonel A.R.H. Hutchison R.M.L.I. Comdg 2nd Royal Marine Battalion	26/07/1916	26/07/1916
Operation(al) Order(s)	Operation Orders No. 11 By Lieut Colonel A.R.H. Hutchison R.M.L.I. Commanding 2nd Royal Marines	28/07/1916	28/07/1916
Heading	War Diary Volume 3 Of 2nd, Royal Marines From 1st, August 1916 To 31st, August 1916		
War Diary	Angres II Sub Section	01/08/1916	02/08/1916
War Diary	Fosse 10c Bully	03/08/1916	05/08/1916
War Diary	Angres II Sub Section	06/08/1916	09/08/1916
War Diary	Fosse 10 & Bully	10/08/1916	13/08/1916
War Diary	Angre II Sub Section	14/08/1916	17/08/1916
War Diary	Bully	18/08/1916	21/08/1916
War Diary	Angres II Sub Section	22/08/1916	25/08/1916
War Diary	Bully	26/08/1916	29/08/1916
War Diary	Angres II Sub Section	30/08/1916	31/08/1916
Operation(al) Order(s)	Operation Order No. 12 By Lieut Colonel A.R.H. Hutchison R.M.L.I. Commanding 2nd Royal Marines	01/08/1916	01/08/1916
Operation(al) Order(s)	Operation Order No. 13 By Lieut Colonel A.R.H. Hutchison R.M.L.I. Commanding 2nd Royal Marines	09/08/1916	09/08/1916

Operation(al) Order(s)	Operation Order No. 14 By Lieut Colonel A.R.H. Hutchison R.M.L.I. Commanding 2nd Royal Marines	15/08/1916	15/08/1916
Operation(al) Order(s)	Operation Order No. 15 By Lieut Colonel A.R.H. Hutchison R.M.L.I. Commanding 2nd Royal Marines	13/08/1916	13/08/1916
Operation(al) Order(s)	Operation Order No. 16 By Lieut Colonel A.R.H. Hutchison R.M.L.I. Commanding 2nd Royal Marines	17/08/1916	17/08/1916
Operation(al) Order(s)	Operation Order No. 17 By Lieut Colonel A.R.H. Hutchison R.M.L.I. Commanding 2nd Royal Marines	17/08/1916	17/08/1916
Operation(al) Order(s)	Operation Order No. 18 By Lieut Colonel A.R.H. Hutchison R.M.L.I. Commanding 2nd Royal Marines	21/08/1916	21/08/1916
Operation(al) Order(s)	Operation Order No. 19 By Lieut Colonel A.R.H. Hutchison R.M.L.I. Commanding 2nd Royal Marines	25/08/1916	25/08/1916
Operation(al) Order(s)	Operation Order No. 20 By Lieut Colonel A.R.H. Hutchison R.M.L.I. Commanding 2nd Royal Marines	29/08/1916	29/08/1916
Heading	Volume.4 War Diary of 2nd, Royal Marines From 1st. September 1916 To 30th. September 1916.		
War Diary	Angres II Sub-Section	01/09/1916	02/09/1916
War Diary	Fosse 10 & Bully	03/09/1916	06/09/1916
War Diary	Angres II	07/09/1916	13/09/1916
War Diary	Fosse 10 & Bully Angres II Sub Section	14/09/1916	14/09/1916
War Diary	Angres II Sub Section	15/09/1916	18/09/1916
War Diary	Fosse 10	19/09/1916	20/09/1916
War Diary	Beugin	21/09/1916	27/09/1916
War Diary	Monchy-Breton	27/09/1916	30/09/1916
Operation(al) Order(s)	Operation Orders No.21 By Lieut Colonel A.R.H. Hutchison R.M.L.I. Commanding 2nd Royal Marines	02/09/1916	02/09/1916
Operation(al) Order(s)	Operation Orders No.22 By Lieut Colonel A.R.H. Hutchison R.M.L.I. Commanding 2nd Royal Marines	06/09/1916	06/09/1916
Operation(al) Order(s)	Operation Orders No.23 By Lieut Colonel A.R.H. Hutchison C.M.G. R.M.L.I. Commanding 2nd Royal Marines	10/09/1916	10/09/1916
Operation(al) Order(s)	Operation Order No. 24 By Lieut Colonel A.R.H. Hutchison C.M.G. R.M.L.I. Commanding 2nd Royal Marines	14/09/1916	14/09/1916
Heading	War Diary of 2nd. Royal Marines From 1st. October 1916 To 31st, October 1916 Volume 5		
War Diary	Monchy-Breton	01/10/1916	05/10/1916
War Diary	Engelbelmer	06/10/1916	08/10/1916
War Diary	Hedauville	09/10/1916	21/10/1916
War Diary	Engelbelmer	22/10/1916	30/10/1916
War Diary	Hedauville	31/10/1916	31/10/1916
Operation(al) Order(s)	Operation Orders No.30 By Lieut Colonel A.R.H. Hutchison C.M.G. R.M.L.I. Commanding 2nd Royal Marines	03/10/1916	03/10/1916
Operation(al) Order(s)	Operation Orders No.31 By By Major C.E.C. Eagles R.M.L.I. Commanding 2nd Royal Marines	08/10/1916	08/10/1916
Heading	War Diary of 2nd Royal Marines. From 1st, November 1916 To 30th, November 1916.		
War Diary	Hedauville	01/11/1916	05/11/1916
War Diary	Puchevillers	06/11/1916	07/11/1916
War Diary	Hedauville	08/11/1916	11/11/1916
War Diary	Englebelmer	12/11/1916	15/11/1916
War Diary	Hedauville	16/11/1916	16/11/1916
War Diary	Puchevillers	17/11/1916	17/11/1916
War Diary	Gezaincourt	18/11/1916	18/11/1916
War Diary	Bernaville	19/11/1916	21/11/1916

War Diary	Cramont	22/11/1916	22/11/1916
War Diary	Brailly	23/11/1916	23/11/1916
War Diary	Forest L'Abbaye	24/11/1916	24/11/1916
War Diary	Romaine	25/11/1916	30/11/1916
Miscellaneous	Medical Arrangements 2nd Royal Marines		
Operation(al) Order(s)	Operation Orders No.32 By Lieut Colonel A.R.H. Hutchison C.M.G. R.M.L.I. Commanding 2nd Royal Marines	23/10/1916	23/10/1916
Operation(al) Order(s)	Operation Orders No.33 By Lieut Colonel A.R.H. Hutchison C.M.G. R.M.L.I. Commanding 2nd Royal Marines	23/10/1916	23/10/1916
Heading	War Diary of 2nd. Royal Marines From 1st December To 31st, December 1916 Volume 6		
War Diary	Romaine	01/12/1916	12/12/1916
War Diary	Rue	13/12/1916	18/12/1916
War Diary	Vron	19/12/1916	31/12/1916
Operation(al) Order(s)	Operation Orders No.34 by Major L.W. Miller R.M.L.I. Commdg 2nd Royal Marines	11/12/1916	11/12/1916
Operation(al) Order(s)	Operation Orders No.35 by Major L.W. Miller R.M.L.I. Commdg 2nd Royal Marines	17/12/1916	17/12/1916
Heading	Volume 8 War Diary of 2nd, Royal Marines From 1st, January 1917 To 31st, January 1917		
War Diary	Vron	01/01/1917	13/01/1917
War Diary	Le Titre	14/01/1917	14/01/1917
War Diary	Fontaine	15/01/1917	15/01/1917
War Diary	Autheux	16/01/1917	17/01/1917
War Diary	Raincheval	18/01/1917	18/01/1917
War Diary	Englebelmer	19/01/1917	19/01/1917
War Diary	St Pierre Divion	20/01/1917	25/01/1917
War Diary	Englebelmer	26/01/1917	31/01/1917
Operation(al) Order(s)	Operation Order No. 36 By Lieut Colonel A.R.H. Hutchison C.M.G. R.M.L.I. Commanding 2nd Royal Marines	11/01/1917	11/01/1917
Operation(al) Order(s)	Operation Order No. 37 By Lieut Colonel A.R.H. Hutchison C.M.G. R.M.L.I. Commanding 2nd Royal Marines	13/01/1917	13/01/1917
Operation(al) Order(s)	Operation Order No. 38 By Lieut Colonel A.R.H. Hutchison C.M.G. R.M.L.I. Commanding 2nd Royal Marines	14/01/1917	14/01/1917
Operation(al) Order(s)	Operation Order No. 39 By Lieut Colonel A.R.H. Hutchison C.M.G. R.M.L.I. Commanding 2nd Royal Marines	16/01/1917	16/01/1917
Operation(al) Order(s)	Operation Order No. 40 By Lieut Colonel A.R.H. Hutchison C.M.G. R.M.L.I. Commanding 2nd Royal Marines	17/01/1917	17/01/1917
Operation(al) Order(s)	Operation Order No. 41 By Lieut Colonel A.R.H. Hutchison C.M.G. R.M.L.I. Commanding 2nd Royal Marines	18/01/1917	18/01/1917
Operation(al) Order(s)	Operation Order No. 42 By Lieut Colonel A.R.H. Hutchison C.M.G. R.M.L.I. Commanding 2nd Royal Marines	20/01/1917	20/01/1917
Operation(al) Order(s)	Operation Order No. 43	23/01/1917	23/01/1917
Operation(al) Order(s)	Operation Order No. 44 By Lieut Colonel A.R.H. Hutchison C.M.G. D.S.O. R.M.L.I. Commanding 2nd Royal Marines	23/01/1917	23/01/1917

Operation(al) Order(s)	Operation Order No. 45 By Lieut Colonel A.R.H. Hutchison C.M.G. D.S.O. R.M.L.I. Commanding 2nd Royal Marines	25/01/1917	25/01/1917
Operation(al) Order(s)	Operation Order No. 46 By Lieut Colonel A.R.H. Hutchison C.M.G. D.S.O. R.M.L.I. Commanding 2nd Royal Marines	26/01/1917	26/01/1917
Heading	Volume 9 War Diary of 2nd, Royal Marines From 1st, Feb, 1917 To 28th. Feb.1917		
War Diary	S.Pierre Divion	01/02/1917	10/02/1917
War Diary	Martinsart	11/02/1917	15/02/1917
War Diary	Beaucourt	15/02/1917	21/02/1917
War Diary	Engelbelmer	22/02/1917	28/02/1917
Operation(al) Order(s)	Operation Order No. 47 By Lieut Colonel A.R.H. Hutchison C.M.G. D.S.O. R.M.L.I. Commanding 2nd Royal Marines	01/02/1917	01/02/1917
Operation(al) Order(s)	Operation Order No. 48 By Lieut Colonel A.R.H. Hutchison C.M.G. D.S.O. R.M.L.I. Commanding 2nd Royal Marines	03/02/1917	03/02/1917
Operation(al) Order(s)	Operation Order No. 49 By Lieut Colonel A.R.H. Hutchison C.M.G. D.S.O. R.M.L.I. Commanding 2nd Royal Marines	04/02/1917	04/02/1917
Operation(al) Order(s)	Operation Order No. 50 by Major L.W. Miller R.M.L.I Commanding 2nd Royal Marines	05/02/1917	05/02/1917
Operation(al) Order(s)	Operation Order No. 51 by Major L.W. Miller R.M.L.I Commanding 2nd Royal Marines	08/02/1917	08/02/1917
Operation(al) Order(s)	Operation Order No. 52 by Major L.W. Miller R.M.L.I Commanding 2nd Royal Marines	10/02/1917	10/02/1917
Heading	War Diary of 2nd, Royal Marines From 1st, March 1917 To 31st, March 1917 Volume 10		
War Diary	Bouzincourt	01/03/1917	19/03/1917
War Diary	Rubempre	20/03/1917	20/03/1917
War Diary	Gezaincourt	21/03/1917	21/03/1917
War Diary	Rebreuve	22/03/1917	22/03/1917
War Diary	Siracourt	23/03/1917	24/03/1917
War Diary	Cauchy	25/03/1917	25/03/1917
War Diary	St Hilaire	26/03/1917	26/03/1917
War Diary	Calonne	27/03/1917	27/03/1917
War Diary	Fouquieres	28/03/1917	29/03/1917
War Diary	Sailly La Bourse	30/03/1917	31/03/1917
Operation(al) Order(s)	Operation Orders No.53 by Major C.E.C. Eagles D.S.O. R.M.L.I. Commanding 2nd Royal Marines	18/03/1917	18/03/1917
Operation(al) Order(s)	Operation Orders No.54 by Major C.E.C. Eagles D.S.O. R.M.L.I. Commanding 2nd Royal Marines	18/03/1917	18/03/1917
Operation(al) Order(s)	Operation Orders No.55 by Major C.E.C. Eagles D.S.O. R.M.L.I. Commdg 2nd Royal Marines	18/03/1917	18/03/1917
Operation(al) Order(s)	Operation Orders No.56 by Major C.E.C. Eagles D.S.O. R.M.L.I. Commanding 2nd Royal Marines	19/03/1917	19/03/1917
Miscellaneous	Operation Orders No.56 by Major C.E.C. Eagles D.S.O. R.M.L.I. Commanding 2nd Royal Marines	10/03/1917	10/03/1917
Operation(al) Order(s)	Operation Orders No.57 by Major C.E.C. Eagles R.M.L.I. Comdg 2nd Royal Marines	21/03/1917	21/03/1917
Operation(al) Order(s)	Operation Orders No.58 by Major C.E.C. Eagles D.S.O. R.M.L.I. Commanding 2nd Royal Marines	23/03/1917	23/03/1917
Operation(al) Order(s)	Operation Orders No.59 by Major C.E.C. Eagles D.S.O. R.M.L.I. Commanding 2nd Royal Marines	24/03/1917	24/03/1917

Operation(al) Order(s)	Operation Orders No.60 by Major C.E.C. Eagles D.S.O. R.M.L.I. Commanding 2nd Royal Marines	25/03/1917	25/03/1917
Operation(al) Order(s)	Operation Orders No.61 by Major C.E.C. Eagles D.S.O. R.M.L.I. Commanding 2nd Royal Marines	26/03/1917	26/03/1917
Operation(al) Order(s)	Operation Orders No.62 by Major C.E.C. Eagles D.S.O. R.M.L.I. Commanding 2nd Royal Marines	28/03/1917	28/03/1917
Operation(al) Order(s)	Operation Orders No.63 by Major C.E.C. Eagles D.S.O. R.M.L.I. Commanding 2nd Royal Marines	28/03/1917	28/03/1917
Heading	War Diary of 2nd Bn Royal Marine Light Infantry From 1st, April 1917 To 30th, April 1917. Volume II		
War Diary	Sailly-Labour (I.1)	01/04/1917	10/04/1917
War Diary	Ourton	11/04/1917	14/04/1917
War Diary	Ecoivres	15/04/1917	21/04/1917
War Diary	Trenches	22/04/1917	25/04/1917
War Diary	Gavrelle Trenches	26/04/1917	30/04/1917
Operation(al) Order(s)	Operation Order No. 61 by Lieut Colonel A.R.H. Hutchison C.M.G. D.S.O. R.M.L.I. Commanding 2nd Bn Royal Marines Light Infy.	13/04/1917	13/04/1917
Heading	War Diary of 2nd Battalion Royal Marine Light Infantry From 1st May To 31st May Volume 12		
War Diary	Ecoivres To Frevillers	01/05/1917	07/05/1917
War Diary	Ecoivres A26b6.1.	08/05/1917	10/05/1917
War Diary	A28a96	11/05/1917	18/05/1917
War Diary	H3.d.3.9	19/05/1917	29/05/1917
War Diary	B.30.a.&.c. H.6.a	30/05/1917	31/05/1917
Operation(al) Order(s)	Operation Order No. 62 by Lieut Colonel A.R.H. Hutchison C.M.G. R.M.L.I. Commanding 2nd Bn Royal Marine Light Infantry	07/05/1917	07/05/1917
Operation(al) Order(s)	Operation Order No. 63 by Lieut Colonel A.R.H. Hutchison C.M.G. D.S.O. R.M.L.I. Commanding 2nd Bn Royal Marine Light Infantry	08/05/1917	08/05/1917
Operation(al) Order(s)	Operation Order No. 64 by Lieut Colonel A.R.H. Hutchison C.M.G. D.S.O. R.M.L.I. Commanding 2nd Bn Royal Marine Light Infantry	28/05/1917	28/05/1917
Operation(al) Order(s)	Operation Order No. 65 by Major L.W. Miller R.M.L.I Commanding 2nd Bn Royal Marine Lt Infy		
Heading	Volume 13 War Diary of 2nd Bn. Royal Marine Light Infantry From 1st June 1917 To 30th June 1917.		
War Diary	In The Trenches (Close Support)	01/06/1917	09/06/1917
War Diary	Roclincourt	10/06/1917	10/06/1917
War Diary	Maroeuil	11/06/1917	22/06/1917
War Diary	A30c5.5	23/06/1917	30/06/1917
Operation(al) Order(s)	Operation Order No. 66 by Major L.W. Miller R.M.L.I Commanding 2nd Bn Royal Marine Lt Infy	08/06/1917	08/06/1917
Miscellaneous	Addendum To Operation Order No. 66	09/06/1917	09/06/1917
Operation(al) Order(s)	Operation Order No. 67 by Major L.W. Miller R.M.L.I Commanding 2nd Bn Royal Marine Lt Infy	21/06/1917	21/06/1917
Heading	War Diary (Vol. XIV) Of 2nd Battn. Royal Marine Light Infantry. From 1st July 1917 To 31st July 1917.		
War Diary	In Camp (Camp.51.B.N.W. A.30.c.5.5)	01/07/1917	02/07/1917
War Diary	In The Trenches (Close Support)	03/07/1917	07/07/1917
War Diary	Front Line	08/07/1917	11/07/1917
War Diary	Close Support	12/07/1917	14/07/1917
War Diary	In The Trenches	14/07/1917	14/07/1917
War Diary	Front Line	15/07/1917	17/07/1917
War Diary	Reserve	18/07/1917	23/07/1917

War Diary	Front Line in Mcshare Support	24/07/1917	24/07/1917
War Diary	In The Trenches	25/07/1917	25/07/1917
War Diary	Front Line	26/07/1917	30/07/1917
War Diary	Wakefield Camp A.28.a	31/07/1917	31/07/1917
Operation(al) Order(s)	Operation Order No. 68 by Major L.W. Miller R.M.L.I Commanding 2nd Bn Royal Marine Light Infantry	02/07/1917	02/07/1917
Operation(al) Order(s)	Operation Order No. 69 by Major L.W. Miller R.M.L.I Commanding 2nd Bn Royal Marine Light Infy	01/07/1917	01/07/1917
Operation(al) Order(s)	Operation Order No. 70 by Major L.W. Miller R.M.L.I Commanding 2nd Bn Royal Marine Light Infantry	11/07/1917	11/07/1917
Operation(al) Order(s)	Operation Order No. 71 by Lieut Colonel L.W. Miller R.M.L.I Commanding 2nd Bn Royal Marine Light Infantry	13/07/1917	13/07/1917
Operation(al) Order(s)	Operation Order No. 72 by Lieut Colonel L.W. Miller R.M.L.I Commanding 2nd Bn Royal Marine Light Infy	16/07/1917	16/07/1917
Operation(al) Order(s)	Operation Order No. 73 by Lieut Colonel L.W. Miller R.M.L.I Commanding 2nd Bn Royal Marine Light Infantry	22/07/1917	22/07/1917
Operation(al) Order(s)	Operation Order No. 74 by Lieut Colonel L.W. Miller R.M.L.I Commanding 2nd Bn Royal Marine Light Infy	29/07/1917	29/07/1917
Heading	War Diary (Vol. XV) Of 2nd Battn. Royal Marine Light Infantry. From 1st August 1917 To 31st August 1917.		
War Diary	Wakefield Camp (Div Reserve) A 28a	01/08/1917	07/08/1917
War Diary	In The Trenches	08/08/1917	08/08/1917
War Diary	In Support To Front Line	09/08/1917	15/08/1917
War Diary	Bde Reserve	16/08/1917	19/08/1917
War Diary	Front Line	20/08/1917	24/08/1917
War Diary	Wakefield Camp	25/08/1917	31/08/1917
Operation(al) Order(s)	Operation Order No. 75 by Lieut Colonel L.W. Miller R.M.L.I Commanding 2nd Bn Royal Marine Light Infantry	07/08/1917	07/08/1917
Operation(al) Order(s)	Operation Order No. 76 by Lieut Colonel L.W. Miller R.M.L.I Commanding 2nd Bn Royal Marine Light Infantry	10/08/1917	10/08/1917
Operation(al) Order(s)	Operation Order No. 77 by Lieut Colonel L.W. Miller R.M.L.I Commanding 2nd Bn Royal Marine Light Infantry	14/08/1917	14/08/1917
Operation(al) Order(s)	Operation Order No. 78 by Major G.C. Wainwright R.M.L.I Commanding 2nd Bn Royal Marine Light Infantry	12/08/1917	12/08/1917
Operation(al) Order(s)	Operation Order No. 79 by Major G.C. Wainwright R.M.L.I Commanding 2nd Bn Royal Marine Light Infantry	23/08/1917	23/08/1917
Heading	War Diary (Vol. XV.) 2nd Battn. Royal Marine Light Infantry. From 1st. September 1917 To 30th September 1917		
War Diary	Wakefield Camp Rolincourt Res	01/09/1917	01/09/1917
War Diary	In The Trenches	02/09/1917	06/09/1917
War Diary	Bde Res	07/09/1917	08/09/1917
War Diary	Front Line	09/09/1917	17/09/1917
War Diary	Div Res.	18/09/1917	20/09/1917
War Diary	Aeg	21/09/1917	21/09/1917
War Diary	Frevillers	22/09/1917	30/09/1917
Operation(al) Order(s)	Operation Orders No.80 by Major G.C. Wainwright R.M.L.I Commanding 2nd Bn Royal Marine Light Infantry	01/09/1917	01/09/1917

Operation(al) Order(s)	O.O. No.81	05/09/1917	05/09/1917
Operation(al) Order(s)	Operation Order No. 82 by Major G.C. Wainwright R.M.L.I Commanding 2nd Bn Royal Marine Light Infantry	08/09/1917	08/09/1917
Operation(al) Order(s)	Operation Order No. 83 by Lieut Colonel G.C. Wainwright R.M.L.I.	12/09/1917	12/09/1917
Operation(al) Order(s)	Operation Order No. 84 by Major G.C. Wainwright R.M.L.I Commanding 2nd Bn Royal Marine Lt Infy	16/09/1917	16/09/1917
Operation(al) Order(s)	Operation Order No. 85 by Major G.L. Parry R.M.L.I. Commanding 2nd Bn Royal Marine Light Infantry	19/09/1917	19/09/1917
Operation(al) Order(s)	Operation Order No. 86 by Major G.L. Parry R.M.L.I. Commanding 2nd Bn Royal Marine Light Infantry	20/09/1917	20/09/1917
War Diary	Frevillers	01/10/1917	01/10/1917
War Diary	Tincques	03/10/1917	03/10/1917
War Diary	Brown Camp	04/10/1917	05/10/1917
War Diary	Nouveau Monde	06/10/1917	23/10/1917
War Diary	Canal Bank	24/10/1917	24/10/1917
War Diary	Irish Farm	25/10/1917	25/10/1917
War Diary	Front Line	26/10/1917	27/10/1917
War Diary	Irish Farm	28/10/1917	28/10/1917
War Diary	Dambre Camp	29/10/1917	31/10/1917
Operation(al) Order(s)	Operation Orders No.87 by Lieut Colonel G.C. Wainwright R.M.L.I Commanding 2nd Bn Royal Marine Light Infantry	02/10/1917	02/10/1917
Operation(al) Order(s)	Operation Orders No.88 by Lieut Colonel G.C. Wainwright R.M.L.I Commanding 2nd Bn Royal Marine Light Infantry	05/10/1917	05/10/1917
Operation(al) Order(s)	Addendum to Operation Orders No.90	24/10/1917	24/10/1917
Operation(al) Order(s)	Operation Orders No.89 by Lieut Colonel G.C. Wainwright R.M.L.I Commanding 2nd Bn Royal Marine Light Infantry	22/10/1917	22/10/1917
Operation(al) Order(s)	Operation Orders No.91 by Major G.L. Parry R.M.L.I. Commanding 2nd Bn Royal Marine Light Infantry	25/10/1917	25/10/1917
War Diary	Dambre Camp	01/11/1917	05/11/1917
War Diary	Front Line	06/11/1917	07/11/1917
War Diary	Irish Camp	08/11/1917	08/11/1917
War Diary	School Camp	09/11/1917	12/11/1917
War Diary	Winnezeele	13/11/1917	13/11/1917
War Diary	Steenbrugge	14/11/1917	22/11/1917
War Diary	Reigersburg	23/11/1917	30/11/1917
Operation(al) Order(s)	Operation Orders No.92 by Major G.L. Parry R.M.L.I. Commanding 2nd Bn Royal Marine Light Infy	04/11/1917	04/11/1917
Miscellaneous	Operation Orders No.92/1 by Major G.L. Parry R.M.L.I. Comdg 2nd Bn Royal Marine Lt Infy	07/11/1917	07/11/1917
Miscellaneous	Operation Orders No.92/1 by Major G.L. Parry R.M.L.I. Commanding 2nd Bn Royal Marine Light Infy	06/11/1917	06/11/1917
Operation(al) Order(s)	Operation Orders No.93 by Major G.L. Parry R.M.L.I. Commanding 2nd Bn Royal Marine Light Infy	11/11/1917	11/11/1917
Operation(al) Order(s)	Operation Orders No.94 by Major G.L. Parry R.M.L.I. Commanding 2nd Bn Royal Marine Light Infy	12/11/1917	12/11/1917
Operation(al) Order(s)	Operation Orders No.96 by Major G.L. Parry R.M.L.I. Commanding 2nd Bn Royal Marine Light Infy	19/11/1917	19/11/1917
Operation(al) Order(s)	Addenda No 1 Operation Orders No.98	14/12/1917	14/12/1917
Operation(al) Order(s)	Addenda Operation Orders No.95 by Lieut Colonel G. Ll. Parry R.M.L.I. Commanding 2nd Bn Royal Marine Light Infy	21/11/1917	21/11/1917

Heading	War Diary (Vol. XIX) of 2nd Battn. Royal Marines Light Infantry. From 1st December 1917 To 31st December 1917		
War Diary	Reigersburg Camp	01/12/1917	06/12/1917
War Diary	School Camp	07/12/1917	09/12/1917
War Diary	Achiet-Le-Grand	10/12/1917	10/12/1917
War Diary	Beaulencourt	11/12/1917	14/12/1917
War Diary	Rocquigny	15/12/1917	15/12/1917
War Diary	Etricourt	16/12/1917	17/12/1917
War Diary	Metz	18/12/1917	22/12/1917
War Diary	Front Line	23/12/1917	26/12/1917
War Diary	Metz	27/12/1917	31/12/1917
Miscellaneous	Addendum Operation Order No. 94		
Miscellaneous	Operation Orders No. 94 by Lieut Colonel G. Ll. Parry R.M.L.I. Commanding 2nd Bn Royal Marine Light Infantry	05/12/1917	05/12/1917
Operation(al) Order(s)	Operation Orders No. 97 by Lieut Colonel G. Ll. Parry R.M.L.I. Commanding 2nd Bn Royal Marine Light Infantry	08/12/1917	08/12/1917
Operation(al) Order(s)	Operation Orders No. 98 by Lieut Colonel G. Ll. Parry R.M.L.I. Commanding 2nd Bn Royal Marine Light Infy	13/12/1917	13/12/1917
Operation(al) Order(s)	Operation Orders No.99 by Lieut Colonel G. Ll. Parry R.M.L.I. Commanding 2nd Bn Royal Marine Light Infantry	14/12/1917	14/12/1917
Operation(al) Order(s)	Operation Orders No.100 by Lieut Colonel G. Ll. Parry R.M.L.I. Commanding 2nd Bn Royal Marine Light Infantry	17/12/1917	17/12/1917
Operation(al) Order(s)	Operation Orders No.101 by Lieut Colonel G. Ll. Parry R.M.L.I. Commanding 2nd Bn Royal Marine Light Infantry	21/12/1917	21/12/1917
Operation(al) Order(s)	Operation Orders No.102 by Lieut Colonel G. Ll. Parry R.M.L.I. Comdg 2nd Bn Royal Marine Lt Infy		
Miscellaneous	Amendment To Operation Orders No.103 issued 30th December 1917	31/12/1917	31/12/1917
Heading	War Diary (Vol. XIX) 2nd Battn. Royal Marine Light Infantry. From 1st January 1918 To 31st January 1918.		
War Diary	Front Line	01/01/1918	04/01/1918
War Diary	Support	05/01/1918	08/01/1918
War Diary	Front Line	09/01/1918	10/01/1918
War Diary	Support	11/01/1918	12/01/1918
War Diary	Metz	13/01/1918	16/01/1918
War Diary	Front Line	17/01/1918	20/01/1918
War Diary	Support	21/01/1918	22/01/1918
War Diary	Front Line	23/01/1918	23/01/1918
War Diary	Havrincourt Wood	24/01/1918	24/01/1918
War Diary	Rocquigny	25/01/1918	31/01/1918
Operation(al) Order(s)	Operation Orders No.104 by Lieut Colonel G. Ll. Parry R.M.L.I. Commanding 2nd Bn Royal Marine Light Infantry	03/01/1918	03/01/1918
Operation(al) Order(s)	Operation Orders No.105 by Lieut Colonel G. Ll. Parry R.M.L.I. Commanding 2nd Bn Royal Marine Light Infantry	07/01/1918	07/01/1918
Operation(al) Order(s)	Operation Orders No.106 by Lieut Colonel G. Ll. Parry R.M.L.I. Comdg 2nd Bn Royal Marine Light Infantry	09/01/1918	09/01/1918

Operation(al) Order(s)	Operation Orders No.107 by Lieut Colonel G. Ll. Parry R.M.L.I. Commanding 2nd Bn Royal Marine Light Infantry	12/01/1918	12/01/1918
Operation(al) Order(s)	Operation Orders No.108 by Lieut Colonel G. Ll. Parry R.M.L.I. Commanding 2nd Bn Royal Marine Light Infantry	15/01/1918	15/01/1918
Operation(al) Order(s)	Operation Order No. 109 by Major C.G. Farquharson R.M.L.I. Commanding 2nd Bn Royal Marine Light Infantry	17/01/1918	17/01/1918
Operation(al) Order(s)	Operation Orders No.110 by Major C.G. Farquharson M.C. R.M.L.I. Commanding 2nd Bn Royal Marine Light Infantry	19/01/1918	19/01/1918
Operation(al) Order(s)	Operation Orders No.111 by Major C.G. Farquharson M.C. R.M.L.I. Commanding 2nd Bn Royal Marine Light Infantry	21/01/1918	21/01/1918
Operation(al) Order(s)	Operation Orders No.112 by Major C.G. Farquharson M.C. R.M.L.I. Commanding 2nd Bn Royal Marine Light Infantry	22/01/1918	22/01/1918
Miscellaneous	Addendum Operation Orders No.112	23/01/1918	23/01/1918
Heading	War Diary (Vol. XX) 2nd Battn. Royal Marine Light Infantry. From 1st February, 1918 To 28th February,1918		
War Diary	Rocquigny	01/02/1918	15/02/1918
War Diary	Vallulart Wood	16/02/1918	18/02/1918
War Diary	In The Line Collviet Wood	19/02/1918	21/02/1918
War Diary	Vallulart Wood	22/02/1918	23/02/1918
War Diary	In The Line Plesquieres	24/02/1918	27/02/1918
War Diary	Eastwood Camp	28/02/1918	28/02/1918
Operation(al) Order(s)	Operation Orders No.113 by Lieut Colonel C.G. Farquharson R.M.L.I. Commanding 2nd Bn Royal Marine Light Infantry	14/02/1918	14/02/1918
Operation(al) Order(s)	2nd Bn Royal Marine Light Infantry Operation Orders No.114	17/02/1918	17/02/1918
Operation(al) Order(s)	2nd Bn Royal Marine Light Infantry Operation Orders No.115	20/02/1918	20/02/1918
Operation(al) Order(s)	2nd Bn Royal Marine Light Infantry Operation Orders No.116	22/02/1918	22/02/1918
Operation(al) Order(s)	2nd Bn Royal Marine Light Infantry Operation Orders No.117	27/02/1918	27/02/1918
Heading	188th Brigade 63rd Division. 2nd Battalion Royal Marine Light Infantry March 1918		
Heading	War Diary of 2nd Bn. Royal Marine Light Infy Volume From March 1st 1918 To March 31st 1918		
War Diary	Eastwood Camp	01/03/1918	03/03/1918
War Diary	Support	04/03/1918	07/03/1918
War Diary	Front Line	08/03/1918	11/03/1918
War Diary	Eastwood Camp	12/03/1918	15/03/1918
War Diary	Front Line	16/03/1918	19/03/1918
War Diary	Support	20/03/1918	21/03/1918
War Diary	Front Line	22/03/1918	22/03/1918
War Diary	Havrincourt Wood	23/03/1918	23/03/1918
War Diary	Front Line	24/03/1918	24/03/1918
War Diary	Support	25/03/1918	25/03/1918
War Diary	Front Line	26/03/1918	26/03/1918
War Diary	Martinsart	27/03/1918	27/03/1918
War Diary	Aveluy Wood	28/03/1918	28/03/1918

War Diary	Forceville	29/03/1918	31/03/1918
Operation(al) Order(s)	2nd Bde R.M.L.I. Operation Order No. 118	07/03/1918	07/03/1918
Operation(al) Order(s)	2nd Bn R.M.L.I. Operation Orders No.119	10/03/1918	10/03/1918
Operation(al) Order(s)	2nd Bn Royal Marine Light Infantry Operation Orders No.120	14/03/1918	14/03/1918
Operation(al) Order(s)	2nd Bn Royal Marine Light Infantry Order No. 121	18/03/1918	18/03/1918
Miscellaneous	Not For Visitors		
Heading	War Diary of 2nd Bn. Royal Marine Light Infy Volume 22 From April 1st 1918 To April 30th 1918.		
War Diary	Forceville	01/04/1918	02/04/1918
War Diary	Toutencourt	03/04/1918	03/04/1918
War Diary	Engelbelmur	04/04/1918	06/04/1918
War Diary	Aveluy Wood	07/04/1918	07/04/1918
War Diary	Forceville	08/04/1918	09/04/1918
War Diary	Aveluywood	10/04/1918	11/04/1918
War Diary	Forceville	12/04/1918	14/04/1918
War Diary	Arqueves	15/04/1918	28/04/1918
Operation(al) Order(s)	2nd Battalion Royal Marine Light Inf Operation Orders No.130	01/04/1918	01/04/1918
Operation(al) Order(s)	2nd Battalion Royal Marine L.I. Operation Orders No.131	03/04/1918	03/04/1918
Operation(al) Order(s)	2nd Battalion Royal Marine L.I. Operation Orders No.132	06/04/1918	06/04/1918
Operation(al) Order(s)	2nd Battalion Royal Marine L Inf Operation Orders No.133	07/04/1918	07/04/1918
Operation(al) Order(s)	2nd Battalion Royal Marine L Inf Operation Orders No.134	09/04/1918	09/04/1918
Operation(al) Order(s)	2nd Bn Royal Marine Light Infantry Operation Orders No.135	11/04/1918	11/04/1918
Operation(al) Order(s)	2nd Battalion Royal Marine L.I. Operation Orders No.136	13/04/1918	13/04/1918

WO 95/3110 (2)

WO 95/3110 (2)

63RD DIVISION
188TH INFY BDE

2ND BN ROYAL MARINES

JUN 1916-APR 1918

ABSORBED BY 1 BN 1918 APR

3rd Brigade Royal Naval Division

Later 190 Brigade

2 Marines Vol 1

"CONFIDENTIAL"

Headquarters,
2nd., Royal Marines.

2nd., July 1916

WAR DIARY

of

2nd. Royal Marines.

from

1st., June

to

30th., June

inclusive.

To:- The A.G's Office,
3rd., Echelon.

A.R.H. Hutchison

Lieut., Colonel R.M.L.I.

Comdg., 2nd. Royal Marines.

1

Instructions regarding War Diaries and Intelligence Summaries are contained in F. S. Regs., Part II. and the Staff Manual respectively. Title pages will be prepared in manuscript.

WAR DIARY
or
~~INTELLIGENCE SUMMARY.~~
(Erase heading not required.)

Army Form C. 2118.

2nd Royal Marine Batt.

Place	Date	Hour	Summary of Events and Information	Remarks and references to Appendices
HERSIN	June 1st	–	Fatigues 300 in forenoon. Close order drill. Gas Helmet drill.	FRANCE
– " –	2nd	–	Clothing issued. Gas Helmet drill. Rapid loading etc. Night fatigues 350 burying cable.	36 b.
– " –	3rd	–	Drills etc. Inspection of 1/RMs & 1/ANSON by 1st Army Commander	
– " –	4th	–	1 Officer 3 ORs for P.T. & Bayonet Fighting, 2 Officers & 20 ORs for Light Trench Mortars, 2 Officers & 10 ORs for Lewis Gun Course all sent to PERNES	
– " –	"		4 Officers & 6 ORs to 47th Div. Bomb School PERNES, 1 Officer & 1 OR to 47th Div. Gas School.	
– " –	5th		300 fatigues in forenoon, Gas Helmet drill, Rapid Loading, Arm drill etc	
– " –	6th		350 " at night ditto ditto do	
– " –	7th		Lieut Slaughter and 45 ORs rejoined from ENGLAND. Railhead for R.N.D. altered to at BRUAY	
– " –	8th		Whole Battn. attended lecture on Gas at 23rd Div. Gas School in afternoon. Instruction as usual in forenoon	
– " –	9th		Drills as usual	
– " –	10th		Gas helmet drill. Night fatigues (digging in cable.	
– " –	11th		400 officers & men attended lecture by 1st Army Chemical Adviser. Night fatigues.	
– " –	12th		Lewis Gun crews formed. Lieut Andrews supervisor.	
– " –	13th		A & B Coys attached 18th & 19th London Regt in Angres Sector for instruction & supplied with trench helmets	
– " –	14th		a.m. Drill Gas helmet & close order. P.m. night fatigues (carrying parties).	
– " –	15th		P.m. Drill	

T2134. Wt. W708—776. 500000. 4/15. Sir J. C. & S.

Instructions regarding War Diaries and Intelligence Summaries are contained in F. S. Regs., Part II. and the Staff Manual respectively. Title pages will be prepared in manuscript.

WAR DIARY

or

~~INTELLIGENCE SUMMARY.~~

(*Erase heading not required.*)

Army Form C. 2118.

Place	Date	Hour	Summary of Events and Information	Remarks and references to Appendices
	1916 June			
HERSIN	16	.	C&D Coys attached 23rd & 24th London Regts respectively for instruction relieving A & B Coys.	France 36B. CCL
— " —	17th		A & B Coys bathed at 47th Div Baths. 1 Off 8 OR sent to Bde. Stokes Battery	CCL
— " —	18th		Drill and refitting A & B Coys.	CCL
— " —	19th	.	Received orders to relieve 7th London Regt on 20/21st in Souchez sector. C & D Coys returned.	CCL
— " —	20th		am. C & D Coys bathed. p.m. Proceeded to trenches & relieved 7th London Regt	CCL M 32. 1. M 32. 2.
Trenches	21st		a.m. Quiet. Heavy bombardment by enemys trench mortars 3 – 4 15 pm. – 3K. 9 W.	CCL
— " —	22nd		2nd Lieut Somerville killed about 3.15 p.m. by trench mortar. Issued orders for relief by HOWE Bn. RND.	CCL Appendix I
— " —	23rd		Pm. Heavy rain all night. Relieved by HOWE Bn and marched to billets in FRESNICOURT	CCL
FRESNICOURT	24th	1.0 a.m. to 9.15 a.m.	Battn arrived by companies on relief and were billeted in Huts	[illegible]
Q. 19	25th		Kit inspection to obtain deficiencies and replace damaged clothing etc	[illegible]
— " —	26th		4th Corps Comr inspected Battn at work. The following Battn Classes were started, each under an Officer & NCOs trained at the Schools. Bombing, Wiring, Physical Training & Bayonet Fighting, Lewis Gun. A & B Coys commenced course of Musketry. Scouts under Scout Officer. Signal Class under Signal Sergt. Remainder of Battn close order, gas & rapid loading drill.	[illegible]

3

Instructions regarding War Diaries and Intelligence Summaries are contained in F. S. Regs., Part II. and the Staff Manual respectively. Title pages will be prepared in manuscript.

WAR DIARY

or

~~INTELLIGENCE SUMMARY~~.

(Erase heading not required.)

Army Form C. 2118.

Place	Date	Hour	Summary of Events and Information	Remarks and references to Appendices
FRESNICOURT	June 27th	a.m.	Training Classes as usual. Remainder at drill. "D" Coy at Baths	FRANCE
Q 19		p.m.	Battn. Medical Inspection. "C" Coy at Baths [initials]	36 b
	28th		Training Classes. "A" & D Coys Route March. Transport inspected. [initials]	
	29th		— ditto — [initials]	
	30th	a.m.	— ditto — "D" Coy disinfected all clothing and blankets.	
		p.m.	— ditto — "C" —— ditto —— [initials]	

A. R. H. Hutchison.

30th June 1916

Lieut Colonel
Comdg 2nd Royal Marine Battn

T2134. Wt. W708—776. 500000. 4/15. Sir J. C. & S.

Copy No. 10.

Appendix I (War Diary)

S E C R E T...........OPERATION ORDER NO......3

BY LIEUT., COLONEL A.R.H. HUTCHISON R.M.L.I.

COMDG., 2ND., ROYAL MARINE BATTALION.

:-:-:-:-:-:-:-:-:-:-:-:-:-:-:-:-:-:-:

Reference Map 36B 1/40,000   22nd. June 1916

1 ....The 2nd. R.M.Bn., will be relieved by "HOWE" Bn., on night of 23/24th. June. and march into billets at FRESNICOURT P 21 a.

2.........O.C. Co's will detail Platoon Guides to parade at Orderly Room at 8-45 p.m. under command of Lieut., Sanders. Guides will meet relieving Battalion at FRENCH DUMP at 11-0 p.m and lead relieving Platoons to their places. Lieut., Sanders will rejoin his Co., on relief at FRENCH DUMP.
"D" Co., will make its own arrangements for Guides.

3.........Battalion Bombers and Lewis Guns will be relieved at 4-0 p.m. Bomb Officer and Lewis Gun Officer will send Guides to the Orderly Room at this time. Limber for Lewis Guns will be at AIX-NOULETTE at 6-0 p.m.

These two parties will march independently to FRESNICOURT via HERSIN and join their Co's on arrival.

4.........On relief Companies will march independently to FRESNICOURT. O.C. Co's will report completion of relief by runner to Bn., Headquarters.

5.........Battalion Sergeant Major, Co., Sergeant Majors and Signallers will arrive at Orderly Room at 6-0 p.m. to take over Bn., and Co., Stores, they are to be met on arrival by corresponding details.

6.........Headquarter Mess Cart will be at COLONELS HOUSE at 11-0 p.m.

7.........The Quartermaster will arrange to transfer all Stores and baggage to FRESNICOURT during the day.

8.........O.C. Co's will detail one N.C.O. each as advance billeting party, to report to Captain Farquharson at HERSIN at noon.

Copy No. 1 retained.
" 2 O.C. "A" Co.,
" 3 O.C. "B" Co.,
" 4 O.C. "C" Co.,
" 5 O.C. "D" Co.,
" 6 Quartermaster.
" 7 Transport Officer.
" 8 O.C. "Howe" Bn.,
" 9 Captain Farquharson.
" 10 War Diary.

C. Eagles
Captain and Adjutant,
2nd. R.M.Bn.,

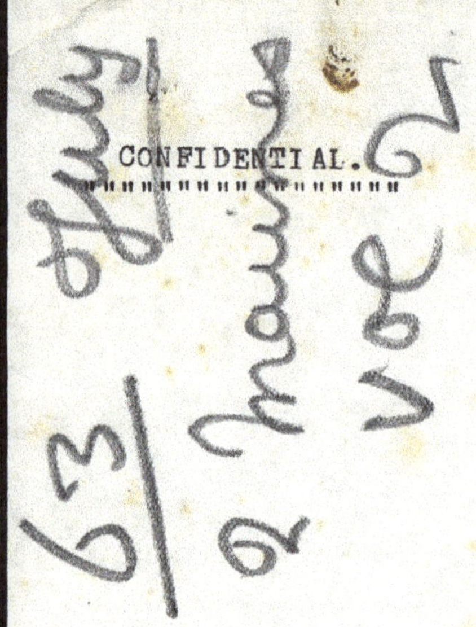

CONFIDENTIAL.

""""""""""""""""""""""

Headquarters,

2nd., Royal Marines,

31st., July 1916

WAR DIARY

OF

2ND., ROYAL MARINES

from

1st., JULY 1916

to

31st., JULY 1916

""""""""""""""""""""""""""""""""

volume 2.

To:- Headquarters,

63rd., (R.N.) Division.

A.R.H. Hutchison

Lieut., Colonel R.M.L.I.
Commanding 2nd., Royal Marines.

""""""""""""""""""""""""""""""""""""""

1.

Army Form C. 2118.

Instructions regarding War Diaries and Intelligence Summaries are contained in F. S. Regs., Part II. and the Staff Manual respectively. Title pages will be prepared in manuscript.

WAR DIARY
or
INTELLIGENCE SUMMARY.
(*Erase heading not required.*)

2nd Royal Marines

Place	Date	Hour	Summary of Events and Information	Remarks and references to Appendices
FRESNICOURT	July 1st	a.m	Training Classes. Remainder close order & gas drill, rapid loading etc. B Coy disinfected all clothing & blankets	FRANCE
Q.19		p.m	— ditto — ——— do ——— A " ——— do ———	36.b.
	2nd		Parade Service & company inspections	
	3rd		{Commenced No 2 Bombing, Wiring & Physical Training Courses. No 3 Lewis Gun Course. Drills as usual {Lt. Colonel A R.H. Hutchison assumed command of the 3rd Bde. Major A. S. Tetley assumed command of 2nd Royal Marine Battn during absence on duty of Brig: Gen C. Trotman C.B.	
	4th	a.m.	Training Classes & Drill as usual	
		p.m.	Medical Inspection of Battn (weekly) 6 Other Ranks to Stokes Gun Course at Bde Trench Mortar School	
	5th		Training Classes & Drill. 1 Officer & 10 ORs to Bde Grenade School. 1 Officer & 2 Signalmen to BRUAY for instruction in "Contact" with aircraft	
			Commenced enteric innoculation of men not previously done. 20 men on alternate days	
	6th		Training Classes & Drill	
	7th		Battn Route March to Bde Training Ground. Rained very heavily from 10.45 a.m. on, so Battn had to return	{See Appendix} Orders.
			Lt Colonel ARH Hutchison resumed command of 2nd R.M. Battn. 3rd Bde changed to 1st Bde under Colonel F. J. Saunders	
			consisting of 1st Royal Marine Bn, 2nd Royal Marine Bn, "Howe" Bn and "Anson" Bn. Lieut J. E. Preston appd O.C. Laundry R.N.D.	
	8th		Training Classes & Drill. Capt Stapleton to PERNES for Lewis Gun Course at 4th Corps School. 2nd Lts Simpson &	
			Mitchell & 7 other ranks returned from 4th Corps School (P.T. & Bayonet Course)	
	9th		Divine Service and Company Inspections	
	10th		Commenced new courses of Bombing, Wiring, Signalling & Lewis Gun. Battn had use of baths during the day. Drill etc as usual Major A. S. Tetley R.M.L.I. left the Battn and assumed Command of the "Drake" Battn	

T2134. Wt. W708—776. 500000. 4/15. Sir J. C. & S.

2

Instructions regarding War Diaries and Intelligence Summaries are contained in F. S. Regs., Part II. and the Staff Manual respectively. Title pages will be prepared in manuscript.

WAR DIARY
or
~~INTELLIGENCE SUMMARY.~~
(Erase heading not required.)

2nd Royal Marines

Army Form C. 2118.

Place	Date	Hour	Summary of Events and Information	Remarks and references to Appendices
	1916 July			Map
FRESNICOURT	11th	10.0 a.m.	G.O.C. RND inspected the Battn at training, also the Transport. Lieut Colonel A.R.H. Hutchison Regt assumed command	FRANCE
		"	of 1st Bde during the temporary absence on duty of Colonel F.J. Stroud Regt. Major C.E.C. Eagles assumed command of	36. b.
		[illegible]	2nd Royal Marines. Training Classes & drill as usual. 1 Officer & 6 O.Rs returned from 3rd Army School. 4 O.R. from CAMIERES	
			M.G. School. 2 Officers & 85 O.Rs took part in Bombing exercise at Bde Grenade School	
	12th		Training Classes & drill. Lieut Colonel ARH Hutchison resumed command of Battn on return of Colonel F.J. Stroud. 12 Officers joined	
			from England bringing establishment up to 37 Officers out of 43 Officers. Received orders to proceed to HERSIN on 13th. 1 Officer to Fd Amb.	{Appendix II attaches orders}
HERSIN	13th	2.15 p.m.	Battn proceeded by route march to HERSIN. Billeted in Convent Q.6.c.1.5.	FRANCE 36B.NE2
BULLY-GRENAY R.11.a	14th	9.15 p.m.	Proceeded in accordance with Operation Order No 3 of 1st Bde RND to BULLY-GRENAY, 'B' & 'C' Coys billeted R.11.a. 'A' Coy CORONS D'AIX	{ORDERS Appendix III}
			Trench, D Coy MECHANICS TRENCH.	TRENCH MAP Appendix IV
	15th		'A' & 'D' Coys 4½ hours work improving BAJOLLE LINES during night of 14th - 15th.	— " —
	16th	p.m.	141st Infantry Bde carried out a small raid on the apex of enemy salient at M.32d.0.3. Smoke demonstration opposite salient M.26c	— " —
			by 1st Bde R.N.Divn proved a successful "blind", the enemy evidently expecting attack to come from there. This was proved	{ORDERS Appendix V}
			by enemy clearing his front line & opening "barrage" on it, then increasing his range to "No man's Land" and finally on to our	
	17th	a.m.	front line + support line. Raiding party found trenches empty & no dug-outs but brought back some rifles. [illegible]	
			Battn "stood to arms" during the raid preparatory to moving up to "Alarm Posts" via BAJOLLE LINES	
			2nd Lt Curtis & 4 O.Rs appointed Bde Scouts and left the Battn.	

3

Instructions regarding War Diaries and Intelligence Summaries are contained in F. S. Regs., Part II. and the Staff Manual respectively. Title pages will be prepared in manuscript.

WAR DIARY
or
~~INTELLIGENCE SUMMARY.~~
(Erase heading not required.)

2nd - Royal Marines

Army Form C. 2118.

Place	Date	Hour	Summary of Events and Information	Remarks and references to Appendices
	1916 July			
BULLY-GRENAY R 11 a	18th		R N Divl School opened at PERNES – 2 ORs to same. 119th INF BDE on our LEFT carried out Raid on enemy trenches at M15D3.5 at 12.15 a.m. 19th	(Map not issued 43 a)
	19th		Orders issued for relief of 1st Royal Marines in ANGRES SECTION II 'B&C' Coy bats. 19th RW Fusiliers on our LEFT, ANSON Battn on our RIGHT	{ORDERS Appendix 6}
ANGRES II Sub-Section	20th		Took over ANGRES II Sub-Section from 1st Royal Marines, Very quiet. Relief completed at 4.50 p.m. Mine exploded on our left at 9.15 p.m. Enemy fired 2 Green followed by 2 Red lights at 10.30 p.m. Artillery activity on both sides 10.30 p.m to 11.30 p.m. Our front & support lines shelled during these hours. Sergt Doran shot through knee and killed about 12.45 a.m. (21st) whilst out wiring. Wind N to NNW. fine	{Trench Map ANGRES II Sub-S Appendix IV}
	21st		3 enemy aeroplanes crossed our line about 7.30 a.m. but returned quickly, another attempt to cross at 11.0 a.m. was driven off by our machines. Enemy shelled our front & support lines from 8.30 a.m. to 9.15 a.m. We retaliated with 18 lbrs & L.T.Ms. Work done, recovering trench boards & clearing up trenches. We blew a Camouflet 30x from long arm of BULLY CRATER, R 26 a 1.9. The crater was reported by mining Officer to be negligable but on examination in daylight was found to be about 20x wide lips 4' high. No enemy barrage. Wind N to NNE fine	
	22nd		Day quiet. We tried to level out crater of mine R 26 a 1.9 with medium T.Ms but without success. Very heavy Artillery bombardment heard continuously from the SOUTH also at times from the NORTH. Enemy shelled junction of BULLY ALLEY & front line to PYRENEES about 3.20 p.m. Casualties O.Rs 4 killed 3 wounded. 1 of our Lewis guns knocked out. "Crater jumping" party connected long arm of BULLY CRATER to new crater and partially consolidated near lip of same. Wind N to NNW fine, colder at night. R. W Fusiliers relieved by 13th E. SURREYS on our LEFT	
	23rd		Intermittent bombardment during the afternoon in which our guns easily had the upper hand. Continued consolidating new crater and also both arms of BULLY CRATER at night. Wiring parties on rest of front. Wind N to NNW fine. wounded O.R one	
	24th		Trench Mortars and some artillery activity between 10.15 a.m. to 11.0 a.m. Minenwerfers fired between 5.45 p.m. & 6 p.m. we replied [with	

4

Instructions regarding War Diaries and Intelligence Summaries are contained in F. S. Regs., Part II. and the Staff Manual respectively. Title pages will be prepared in manuscript.

WAR DIARY

or

~~INTELLIGENCE SUMMARY.~~

(Erase heading not required.)

Army Form C. 2118.

2nd Royal Marines

Place	Date	Hour	Summary of Events and Information	Remarks and references to Appendices
	1916 July			
ANGRES II	24th (continued)		with 4". 5" Howitzers & 18 prs, also with medium T-Ms during afternoon & between 6.0 p.m. & 7.3 p.m. Repaired damage done to their crater. Wind North fine	Trench Map ANGRES SECTION Appendix VI
Sub-Section	25th		Orders issued for relief by 1st Royal Marines and orders for Defence on arrival in BULLY. 1st RMs relieved. "C" Coy moved to MECHANICS, "B" Coy to CORONS D'AIX & CAP DE PONT, "A" & "D" Coys billetted in BULLY	Appendix VII orders for relief. Appendix VIII orders for defence
	26th		New clothing issued. Inspection of arms and Physical Training. Orders issued for combined Gas & Artillery Attack. Wind unsuitable attack postponed	Appendix IX Gas attack orders
	27th		Inspection of arms. Physical Training. Baths — do —	
	28th		— do — — do — About 12.30 a.m. Aircraft heard over BULLY and some bombs dropped. Slight artillery activity — do —	
	29th		Relieved 1st Royal Marines in ANGRES II Sub-Section, 19th Battn. R. W. Fusiliers on LEFT, ANSON Battn on our RIGHT. Very quiet during day. Heavy artillery bombardment by us at night. Germans did not reply very much. Gas attack postponed. Casualties nil. Wind N to NNE. Very hot	Appendix X orders for relief
	30th		Quiet until 5.0 p.m. Artillery & Trench Mortar duel on and off during the evening. Gas attack postponed. Casualties nil. Wind N. Calm & very hot	
	31st		Complete calm with the exception of a few Shrapnel at junction of FLAPPER ALLEY & PYRENEES in the morning	

A. R. H. Hutchison.
Lieut Colonel
Commanding 2nd Royal Marines
188th Bde, 63rd (RN) Divn.

Appendix 1
War Diary July 1916
2nd Royal Marines

Issued at 1.15 p.m.

Copy No. 9.

T R A I N I N G   O R D E R   NO. 1

BY LIEUT., COLONEL A.R.H. HUTCHISON R.M.L.I.

COMMANDING 2ND., ROYAL MARINES.

Reference Map 36B.

FRESNICOURT.
6th., July 1916

1...............The Battalion will parade at 8-30 a.m. on FRIDAY 7th., inst. and march via GAUCHIN-LE-GAL and HERMIN to the Brigade Training Ground P.20 c. Dress Marching Order.

2...............On arrival Companies will carry out Training, special attention being paid to extended order drill and company attack.
The 100 yards Rifle Range will be allotted to "A" Co., for the morning, to the Scouts and Lewis Guns for the afternoon. Targets to be prepared beforehand.

3...............Travelling Kitchens and Watercarts will accompany the Battalion. Dinners will be taken, Tea will be on return to Billets. The water being boiled on the line of march.

4...............The Transport Officer will detail 1 Limbered Wagon for Transport of LEWIS GUNS & 1 wagon for Bayonet Fighting & Bombing Stores

5...............The Battalion will march off to return to billets at 3-15 p.m. and march via REBREUVE and OLHAIN.

Copy No., 1 Retained.
" 2 O.C. "A" Co.,
" 3 O.C. "B" Co.,
" 4 O.C. "C" Co.,
" 5 O.C. "D" Co.,
" 6 Qr.Quartermaster.
" 7 Transport Officer.
" 8 Lewis Gun Officer.
" 9 War Diary.

signed. C.G. Farquharson.
Captain and Adjutant.
2nd. Royal Marines.

Issued at 3.30 p.m.

Appendix 2.
War Diary July 1916
2nd Royal Marines

SECRET

COPY NO. 11

OPERATION ORDER NO. 4

BY

MAJOR C.E.C. EAGLES R.M.L.I.

COMMANDING 2ND ROYAL MARINES.

Reference Map 36B FRANCE

1. MOVE ...... The Battalion will move from FRESNICOURT to HERSIN at 2-30 p.m. tomorrow and go into Billets.

2. BILLETING PARTY. Advanced Billeting Party of 1 N.C.O. per Coy. under Command of Lieut. Woolley will leave at 10-0 a.m. tomorrow and march to HERSIN by road. Reporting to the Town Major for billets. Interpreter will join this party at HERSIN at 12 Noon.

3. PARADE ... Coys. will parade at their ALARM POSTS at 2-15 p.m.

4. ORDER OF MARCH. Headquarter Details, "B" "C" "A" "D" Coys & Transport.

5. G.S. WAGONS ...1/2 G.S. Wagon is available for Coy. Stores. "A" and "B" Coys will use one and "C" and "D" the other. These will be loaded at Quartermaster's Stores by 1-0 p.m.

6. FATIGUE PARTY "A" Coy. will provide 1 N.C.O. and 12 Men as Fatigue Party. Parade at Quartermaster's Stores at 9-0 a.m.

7. TEA ...To be prepared on the March.

C.G. Farquharson

Captain and Adjutant,
2nd. Royal Marines.
12th July 1916.

Copies to
No. 1 Retained
" 2 O.C. "A" Co.
" 3 O.C. "B" Co.
" 4 O.C. "C" Co.
" 5 O.C. "D" Co.
" 6 Quartermaster
" 7 Transport Officer
" 8 Lieut. Woolley
" 9 Interpreter
" 10 Bn. Sergt. Major
" 11 War Diary

Issued at..7.0 p.m.   Copy No...............1.

Appendix 3
War Diary July
2nd Royal Marines
7

SECRET.

OPERATION ORDER NO......5

BY LIEUT COLONEL A.R.H. HUTCHISON R.M.L.I.

COMMANDING 2ND., ROYAL MARINES.

Hd., Qrs.,
13th., July 1916

Reference 36B., S.E. 1/20,000

1.....The 2nd., Royal Marines will relieve the 23rd., London Regt., in Support in ANGRES 2 Sector to-morrow.

2.....Headquarters, and "B" and "C" Co's will be in BULLY-GRENAY (R. 11 a 5. 5.) "A" Co., will be in CORONS D'AIX Trench, and "D" Co., in MECHANICS TRENCH.

3.....
The Battalion will parade at 9-15 a.m. and march off by platoons at 100 yards distance, in the following order :- Headquarters, "D" "A" "B" and "C" Co's."B"

4.....The cookers of "B" and "C" Co's will follow at same distances. On arrival the horses will return to Transport Lines at HERSIN.

5.....Platoon Guides of 23rd., London Regt., will meet Platoons at Battalion Headquarters in BULLY and conduct them to their positions.

6....Lewis Guns and Bomb Sections will remain in their Co's.,

7....1 Limbered Wagon for Lewis Guns will march between Headquarters and "D" Co., as far as BULLY. The guns of "D" and "A" Co., will then be carried by hand.

8....To-morrows rations will be carried on the man by "A" and "D" Co., in the cookers by "B" and "C" Co;s.,

9.....All Officers Valises are to be at Quartermasters Stores by 8-30 a.m.

10....Officers Mess Cart will be in Town Hall Square at 8-45 a.m. and will follow the Battalion as Far as BULLY.

11....On taking over Co's Billets in BULLY O.C. Co's will ensure that there is sufficient cellar accommodation for their Co's., and allot it to their men.

12....The Cookers of "B" and "C" Co's., will be located in the Courtyard of the MAIRIE.

13 On arrival "B" Co., will detail a guard of 1 N.C.O. and 6 Men to mount at Battalion Headquarters.

C.G. Farquharson
Captain and Adjutant.
2nd. , Royal Marines.

Copies. to :-
No. 1 Retained for War Diary. No. 5 "D"
" 2 O.C. "A" Co., No., 6 L.G.O.
" 3 O.C. "B" Co., No., 7 Q.M.
" 4 O.C. "C" Co., No., 8 T.O.

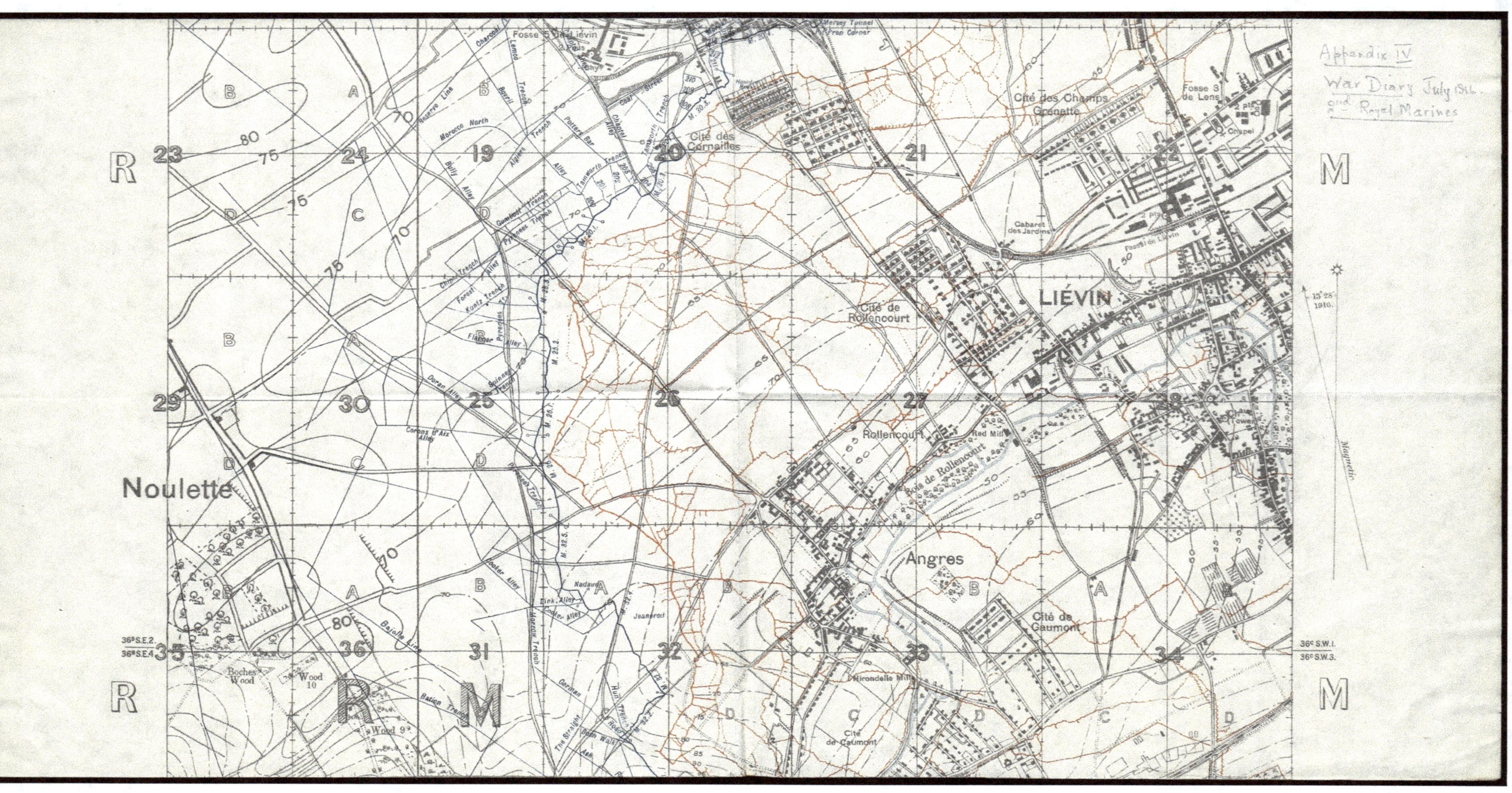

Appendix IV
War Diary July 1916
2nd Royal Marines
LIÉVIN
Noulette
Angres
Rollencourt
Cité de Rollencourt
Cité des Champs Grenette
Cité des Cornailles
Cité de Caumont
Cabaret des Jardins
Fosse 3 de Lens
Fosse 5 de Liévin
Bois de Rollencourt
Red Mill
Hirondelle Mill
Boches Wood
Wood 10
Wood 9
Mersey Tunnel
Reserve Line
Morocco North
Bully Alley
Lemco Trench
Bovril
Potters Bar
Chantel Alley
Coal Street
Tamworth Trench
Gumboot Trench
Pyrenees Trench
Kuntz Trench
Forest Alley
Flanner Alley
Spinney Trench
Doran Alley
Corons d'Aix Alley
Cooker Alley
Dink Alley
Nadaud
Jeanerot
Morrow Trench
Bajolle Line
Ration Trench
German
Hun Trench
The Straight
Magnetic
13°28' 1916.
36c S.W.1.
36c S.W.3.
36b S.E.2.
36b S.E.4.

Appendix V
War Diary July 1916
2nd Royal Marines

SECRET

"@"@"@"@"@"@"@"@"@"

ISSUED at 2.45 p.m. COPY NO. 1

OPERATION ORDER NO..6

BY LIEUT., COLONEL A.R.H. HUTCHISON R.M.L.I.

COMMANDING 2ND., ROYAL MARINES.

Reference Trench Map ANGRES SECTION (A)

Headquarters,
16th., July 1916.

1....The 141st., Infantry Brigade will carry out a small raid on the apex of enemy salient at M 32 d. 0. 3. to-night.

2....The First Brigade R.N. Divn., will demonstrate opposite salient M. 26 c. from zero for 40 minutes, by lighting smoke candles, if wind is favourable and by opening short bursts of machine gun and trench mortar fire on enemy's trenches.

3....Front line of ANGRES 1 & 2 is being held as lightly as possible during the operations.

4....The 2nd., Royal Marines will "stand to" and be ready to move at immediate notice to Alarm Posts.

5....The following code will be used :-

(i) Show cancelled ---- RAT.

(ii) Carry on. ---- FERRET.

(iii) Stop All firing- STOAT.

6....Zero time is 11.30 p.m. X

C. G. Farquharson

Captain and Adjutant,

2nd., Royal Marines.

Copies :-
No., 1 Retained for War Diary.
" 2 O.C. "A" Co.,
" 3 O.C. "B" Co.,
" 4 O.C. "C" Co.,
" 5 O.C. "D" Co.,
" 6 Lewis Gun Officer.

Note
X Afterwards this was changed to 1. 0. a.m 17-7-16
[initials]

Appendix No 6
War Diary July 1916
2nd Royal Marines

Issued at 2-30 p.m.
SECRET.   COPY NO. 8.......

""""""""""""""""""

OPERATION ORDER NO..7

BY LIEUT., COLONEL A.R.H. HUTCHISON R.M.L.I.

COMMANDING 2ND., ROYAL MARINES.

"-"-"-"-"-"-"-"-"-"-"-"-"-"-"-"-"-"-"

Reference Trench Map - ANGRES (A)   Headquarters,
19th., July 1916.

1....The 2nd., Royal Marines will relieve the 1st., Royal Marines in the front line to-morrow.

2...."A" and "D" Co's., will be in the front line and support, "B" and "C" Cos'., will be in Reserve.
O.C. Co's., will reconnoitre the positions of their Companies to-day.

3.....All Companies will move up BULLY ALLEY.
"A" Co., will lead and will enter the communication trench at 2-0 p.m Moving from its present position by Platoons at 100 yards distance. "B" and "C" Cos., will follow fifteen minutes later, by platoons at 100 yards distance. "D" Co., will 'Tail in' after "A" Co., after the latter has passed MECHANICS TRENCH.

4......Headquarters will start at 1-45 p.m. at which time present Headquarters will close and new one will be opened at P.C.5 at 3-0 p.m.

5......Transport Officer will send up the horses for the Cookers by 2-0 p.m. The Cookers and all Co., Cooks will return to HERSIN and report to the Quartermaster.

6......The Special Brigade Parties will be relieved by 1/R.M. at 9-0 a.m. and return to their Co's.,

7......The Guard Will dismount at 9-0 a.m.

8......1st., Brigade Trench Standing Orders Paras., 1,2,3,4 & 8 are to be read to all ranks before going up.

-_-_-_-_-_-_-_-_-_-_-_-_-_-

Copy No., 1 Retained.
" 2 O.C. 1/R.M.
" 3 O.C. "A" Co.,
" 4 O.C. "B" Co.,
" 5 O.C. "C" Co.,
" 6 O.C. "D" Co.,
" 7 Q.M. and T.O.
" 8 War Diary.

C.G. Farquharson
Captain and Adjutant,
2nd., Royal Marines,

S E C R E T

Issued at..10.15 a.m..... Copy No...8.........

Appendix 1
War Diary July 1916
2nd Royal Marines.

O P E R A T I O N   O R D E R   No...8

BY LIEUT., COLONEL A.R.H.HUTCHISON R.M.L.I.

COMMANDING 2ND., ROYAL MARINES.

:":":":":":":":":":":":":":":":":":":":

References.. Map 36B.
Trench Map (A) ANGRES SECTION.

Headquarters,
24th., July 1916.
....

1.........The 2nd., Royal Marines will be relieved by the 1st., Royal Marines on 25th., inst.,

2.........On relief "A" and "D" Co., will move via BOYRIE ALLEY to BULLY-GRENAY. "C" Co., will move via BULLY ALLEY to MECHANICS TRENCH. "B" Co., will move via CORONS D'AIX to METRO-CAP DE PONT, CORONS D'AIX.

3.........The Battalion will act as Support Battalion to the Brigade.

4.........O.C's "A" and "D" Co., will detail Platoon Guides to report at Battalion Headquarters at 8-15 p.m. O.C's "B" and "C" Co., will have Company Guides at the BULLY ALLEY entrances of their respective trenches.

5.........Cos'., will move off independently by Platoons on relief. O.C.C's reporting to Battalion Headquarters by runner when relief is completed.

6.........Trench Stores will be handed over to relieving Cos'., using Army Form W. 3408. Duplicate Copies in manuscript are to be rendered to Orderly Room by 10-0 a.m.

7.........2nd., Lieut., Walker will proceed to BULLY GRENAY "a.m." 25th., inst and take over the necessary Billets for Headquarters, and "A" and "D" Cos'.,

8.........Battalion Headquarters will close in trenches on completion of relief and re-open at BULLY @ R. 11.a.5.5.

9.........Transport Officer to arrange for Cookers of "A" and "D" Cos'., to be at BULLY by 2-0 p.m. Cooks of "B" and "C" Cos' to rejoin their Co's.,

"-"-"-"-"-"-"-"-"-"-"-"-"-"-"-"

C. G. Farquharson
Captain and Adjutant,
2nd., Royal Marines.

Copies to :-
1...Retained.
2...O.C. Bn., Royal Marines.
3...O.C. "A" Co.,
4...O.C. "B" Co.,
5...O.C. "C" Co.,
6...O.C. "D" Co.,
7...Q.M. and T.O.
8...War Diary.

Appendix VIII
War Diary July 1916
2nd Royal Marines

S E C R E T

Issued at. 12.45 pm   Copy No. 7......

OPERATION ORDER No. 9.
BY LIEUT., COLONEL A.R.H.HUTCHISON R.M.L.I.
COMMANDING 2ND., ROYAL MARINES.
"-"-"-"-"-"-"-"-"-"-"-"-"

Ref:- Trench Map
ANGRES Secn., (A)

Battalion Headquarters,
25-7-16.

1...When the Battalion moves into Brigade Support the Alarm Posts for Cos'., will be in BAJOLLE LINE as follows:-   5.2.

"B" Co., from R. 30a.2.x Southwards.
"C" Co., " R. 30 a.2.6., toR. 24.c.Central.
"D" Co., " R. 24 c. Central to R. 24 a.?.2.
"A" Co., " R. 24 a.2.2. Northwards.

2...All Company Officers and L.G.O. are to reconnoit this line.

3..."A" "C" and "D" Cos'., move in via BULLY ALLEY "B" Co., via CAP DE PONT.

4....Battalion Headquarters will be in MECHANICS.

[illegible]
Captain and Adjutant,
2nd., Royal Marines.

Copies.
1 Retained.
2. O.C. "A" Co.,
3 O.C. "B" Co.,
4 O.C. "C" Co.,
5 O.C. "D" Co.,
6. L.G.O.
7 War Diary.

Appendix to War Diary July 1916 2nd Royal Marines

SECRET

ISSUED AT 11.50 a.m. COPY NO 6

OPERATION ORDER NO. 10

BY LIEUT., COLONEL A.R.H.HUTCHISON R.M.L.I.

COMMANDING 2ND., ROYAL MARINES.

Reference Trench Map ANGRES SECTION "A" Bn., Headquarters, 26th., July 1916

1....The German position opposite the ANGRES SECTION will be attacked with gas to-night if the wind is suitable. The Gas attack will be accompanied by an artillery bombardment. No infantry assault will be made. The arrangements for starting the Gas is entirely in the hands of the O.C. "H" Co., Special R.E. who will fix Zero time

2...."B" and "C" Co's., will wear Gas Helmets rolled on the head.

3....All watches will be synchronised at 5-0 p.m. Zero time will be notified later.

4....O.C. "B" Co., will detail three carrying parties, each consisting of 1 Sergeant and 12 Privates to report to representative of "H" Co., Special R.E. at entrance ~~x2~~ to CORONS-D'AIX Communication Trench on BULLY-CORONS D'AIX ROAD at 3-0 p.m. this afternoon, to carry appliances to gas-proof dug-outs in the line.

5....2 Guides from 1st., Royal Marines will meet these parties at junction of CORONS-D'AIX and MECHANICS at 3-30 p.m. to conduct them via BULLY ALLEY to the selected dug-outs.

6....O.C. "A" Co., will detail a party of 1 Sergeant, 1 Corporal and 32 Privates to report at entrance of CORONS D'AIX Communication Trench on BULLY-CORONS D'AIX Road at 3-0 p.m. to carry Vermoral Sprayers into the line. Guides for this party will be provided by Special R.E.

7.~~xxx~~..All Carrying parties to carry rifles and bandoliers, and wear tin helmets if available.

8....From 8-0 p.m. till completion of operations all telephones are to be kept clear for use of special R.E. and Priority Infantry messages only.

9....No Working parties are to be out during the evening.

10....The following code words will be used :-

BERLIN = Attack postponed until to-morrow night.

VIENNA = Carry on.

LONDON = Conditions appear favourable.

Copies to:-
1..Retained.
2..O.C. "A" Co.,
3..O.C. "B" Co.,
4 O.C. "C" Co.,
5..O.C. "D" Co.,
6..War Diary.

C W Farquharson
Captain and Adjutant,
2nd., Royal Marines.

Appendix X
War Diary July 1916
2nd Royal Marines

SECRET

Copy No........

OPERATION ORDERS

Issued at 8.15.p.m.

NO....11

BY LIEUT., COLONEL A.R.H. HUTCHISON R.M.L.I.

COMMANDING 2ND., ROYAL MARINES.

"s"s"s"s"s"s"s"s"s"s"s"s"s"s"

Reference Trench Map
ANGRES SECTION "A"

Battalion Headquarters,

28th., July 1916.

1....The 2nd., Royal Marines will relieve the 1st., Royal Marines in the front line on 29th., inst.,

2....."B" Co., will occupy the right and "C" Co., the left of the front line. "A" Co., will occupy MOROCCO SOUTH, and "D" Co., MOROCCO NORTH.

3......"C" Co., will move from MECHANICS at 2-0 p.m. Headquarters will enter BULLY ALLEY at 1-45 p.m. followed by "B" "A" and "D" Cos'. in order. All Cos., will move by Platoons at a hundred yards distance.

4......"A" and "D" Cos., will each detail a Crater Jumping Party as laid down in Brigade Instructions No., 2. These parties will march at the head of their Companies.

5......Trench Helmets for "A" and "D" Cos'., will be left in MOROCCO SOUTH and NORTH respectively. The Senior N.C.O. of each Crater Jumping Party will see that each man of his party draws one as they pass these points.

6.......O.C. Co's., will report when relief is completed to Bn., H.Q. by runner.

7......Transport Officer will send up the horses for the Cookers and the Officers Mess Cart by 12-30 p.m. These will return to HERSIN accompanied by the Co., Cooks.

8 .....Present Headquarters will close at 1-30 p.m. and new ones opened at P.C. 5 at 2-30 p.m.

9......The Bn., Bombing Officer will arrange for the necessary Bombing Parties.

"-"-"-"-"-"-"-"-"-"-"-"-"-"-"

Copy
No., 1 Retained
No., 2 O.C. 1st., R.M.
No., 3 O.C. "A" Co.,
No., 4 O.C. "B" Co.,
No., 5 O.C. "C" Co.,
No., 6 "D" Co.,
No., 7 Q.M. and T.O.
No., 8 War Diary.

C.G. Hutchison
Captain and Adjutant,
2nd., Royal Marines.

" CONFIDENTIAL "

Headquarters,

2nd., Royal Marines.

1st., September 1916

WAR DIARY

VOLUME 3

OF

2ND., ROYAL MARINES

FROM

1ST., AUGUST 1916

TO

31ST., AUGUST 1916

A. R. H. Hutchison

Lieut., Colonel R.M.L.I.
Commanding 2nd., Royal Marines.

To :- A.G's Officer

3rd., Echelon.

The Base.

2nd Royal Marines

Army Form C. 2118.

1

WAR DIARY
or
~~INTELLIGENCE SUMMARY.~~

August 1916.

(*Erase heading not required.*)

Instructions regarding War Diaries and Intelligence Summaries are contained in F. S. Regs., Part II. and the Staff Manual respectively. Title pages will be prepared in manuscript.

Place	Date	Hour	Summary of Events and Information	Remarks and references to Appendices
	Aug: '16			
ANGRES II	1st	6 a.m.	Hostile aeroplane dropped two bombs on our right apparently in ANGRES I Sub-Section.	
Sub Section			2nd Lieut Yeldham and 10 other ranks to Bde Bomb School. Orders issued for relief by 1st Royal Marines. Day very quiet	Appendix I attached
		8.45 p.m. & 9.30 p.m.	Enemy Trench Mortars bombarded fairly intensely we retaliated with Stokes Light Trench Mortars and 18 pdrs. 11.30 p.m. light railway heard working behind German lines	
	2nd		During the early morning German in blue grey uniform with black hat with white cap round it, seen to jump into their trench	References
		10-10.15 a.m.	Enemy bombarded ALGIERS doing a certain amount of damage with 5.9" Howitzers. Hostile aeroplane tried to cross our line but driven back	Trench Map ANGRES
			by Anti-aircraft guns. Relieved by 1st RMs, relief completed by noon. Went into Bde Reserve, HQs and 2 companies at FOSSE 10	SECTION &
			2 companies billeted at BULLY.	FRANCE 36b
FOSSE 10 & BULLY.	3rd		Baths and medical inspection of Batt.	
	4th		Inspection of arms, close order drill, physical training and gas helmet inspection and drill	
	5th		— ditto — — do — — do — — do — Captain Burton-Fanning	
			rejoined from instructional duties at IV Corps School PERNES. Issued orders for relief	Appendix II attached
ANGRES II	6th		2nd Lt Yeldham & 10 ORs returned from and 2nd Lt Garnett & 10 ORs joined Bde Bomb School. Relieved 1st Royal Marines in ANGRES II	
Sub. Section			Sub-Section. Relief completed by 12.15 p.m. Very quiet. Enemy artillery active between 8.30 pm & 9.0 p.m. silenced by	
			our retaliation with 18 pdr & 4.5" Howitzers. From 11.0 p.m. onwards for 2 hours, heavy barrage by our artillery on VIMY RIDGE and North	
	7th	9.30 a.m. & 10 a.m.	Enemy shelled junction of FLAPPER ALLEY & PYRENEES with shrapnel and H.E. we replied with organised "Straffe B". Wind	
			between NE & E Gas alert on. 3.0 p.m. Gas alert off. Rest of day quiet except for Rifle Grenades & occasional TMs	

T2134. Wt. W708—776. 500000. 4/15. Sir J. C. & S.

2.

2nd Royal Marines

Army Form C. 2118.

Instructions regarding War Diaries and Intelligence Summaries are contained in F. S. Regs., Part II. and the Staff Manual respectively. Title pages will be prepared in manuscript.

WAR DIARY

or

~~INTELLIGENCE SUMMARY.~~

(Erase heading not required.)

August 1916

Place	Date	Hour	Summary of Events and Information	Remarks and references to Appendices
	Aug: 16			
ANGRES II Sub-Section	8th	8.30am	We blew a Camouflet on S edge of THOMPSONS CRATER. It did a certain amount of damage to enemy's wire and the near lip of crater slipped a bit. No barrage on either side. Enemy started digging vigorously in crater, we put over R.Gs, Medium & Light TMs which made him stop work. Wind variable between NE & SE, weather fine and warm. "Gas alert on". Enemy sent over a few 77mm shells between 5 & 6 pm and from 7.30pm to 8.15pm shelled with 4.2" & 5.9". Organised "Strafe" at 8.0pm. About 9.15pm one of our shells set fire to a dump about M36 a 3.9 in rear of enemy lines large flame + sparks observed. Captains T Edwards and TA Golding returned from Course at CONDETTE.	
		5pm		
	9th	2.30am to 3.30am	Our M & L TMs were very active and enemy retaliated vigorously with 4.2" & 5.9". Wind North weather fine and warm during day. Enemy fire 4.2" Shrapnel between FOREST ALLEY and HdQrs. Issued orders for relief. Organised "Strafe" at 7.30pm. "Gas alert off" at 6.0pm	Appendix III attached.
		11am to 12.30pm		
FOSSE 10 & BULLY.	10th		Relieved by 1st Royal Marines, went into Brigade Reserve, HdQrs & 2 companies at FOSSE 10, 2 companies at BULLY. Wind West, fine drizzle	
	11th		Baths and Medical inspection	
	12th		2nd Lt Woodhall returned with 2 ORs from Sniping Course at PERNES. 2nd Lt Wrangham left for Sniping Course. 2nd Lt Garnett & 10 ORs returned and 2nd Lt Stokes left with 10 ORs for Bde Bomb School. Issued new clothing	
			Inspection of men, ~~close~~ physical training etc fatigues	
	13th		Held Divine Service. Issued orders for relief	Appendix IV attached.
ANGRES II Sub Section	14th		Relieved 1st RMs in ANGRES II. Intermittent minenwerfer and R.G activity also some 4.2" shrapnel very quiet on the whole	

T2134. Wt. W708—776. 500000. 4/15. Sir J. C. & S.

3.

2nd Royal Marines

Army Form C. 2118.

Instructions regarding War Diaries and Intelligence Summaries are contained in F. S. Regs., Part II. and the Staff Manual respectively. Title pages will be prepared in manuscript.

WAR DIARY
or
~~INTELLIGENCE SUMMARY.~~
(Erase heading not required.)

August 1916

Place	Date	Hour	Summary of Events and Information	Remarks and references to Appendices
	Aug: 16			
ANGRES II Sub-Section	15th	11.30 a.m. to 12.30 p.m.	Trench mortar activity on both sides. Very quiet during the day and at night. Enemy attempted to put out wire in several places but dispersed by Lewis Gun fire. Our patrols and wiring parties out as usual	
	16th		Wind S.W. fine and clear. Enemy observation balloons up. Enemy shelled MECHANICS with about a dozen H.E. 5.9", a large working party was there at time but no casualties. B Company 7th Royal Fusiliers attached for instruction, 1 platoon to each company. Fokker crossed our lines but was driven back by our planes. We bombarded enemy salient at M26c between 6.0 p.m. & 6.20 p.m. with 63rd (RN) Divl. Arty and Corps Heavies. Very little reply by the enemy	
	17th	1.15 a.m.	Captain A.C. St Clair Morford wounded in the foot whilst out on patrol near THOMPSONS CRATER & evacuated to C.C.S. 3 Enemy aeroplanes over our lines at 10.30 a.m. Very quiet during the day and night, wind South. Orders for relief and defence	Appendix V & V A attached
BULLY	18th		Relieved by 1st Royal Marines by noon. Battn. went into Bde Support at BULLY	
	19th		Baths and Medical inspection. Fatigues at night	
	20th		2nd Lt Stokes and 10 other ranks returned from Bde Bomb School. Divine Service. Fatigues cancelled on account of wind being favourable for Gas. Let go gas and bombarded enemy in ANGRES Section at 10.30 p.m. Enemy retaliated on Mines and our front line.	
	21st		About 4 5.9" shells dropped in BULLY between 2.15 a.m. and 2.30 a.m. no damage. Inspection of arms and gas helmets 1 hours drill during forenoon. Enemy bombarded BULLY between 6.45 p.m. & 7.15 p.m. Casualties Killed 1, wounded 8 other ranks. Issued orders for relief	Appendix VI attached.

2nd Royal Marines
Army Form C. 2118.

Instructions regarding War Diaries and Intelligence Summaries are contained in F. S. Regs., Part II. and the Staff Manual respectively. Title pages will be prepared in manuscript.

4

WAR DIARY
or
~~INTELLIGENCE~~ SUMMARY.

August 1916

(Erase heading not required.)

Place	Date	Hour	Summary of Events and Information	Remarks and references to Appendices
	Aug:			
ANGRES II Sub Section	22nd	10.0 a.m.	Relieved 1st Royal Marines in ANGRES II. Enemy bombarded our front line between 11.30 a.m. & 12.30 p.m. with 5.9" "Hows", Heavy and Medium Trench Mortars, we retaliated with 18 pdrs, M.T-Ms and Stokes. Casualties for 24 hrs ending noon Other ranks Killed 1 wounded 9	
		7.30 p.m.	3 enemy aeroplanes crossed our lines but were driven back by anti-aircraft guns.	
			7th H.L.I. on our left carried out a successful raid at 10.40 p.m. A number of enemy killed and wounded and 1 prisoner taken. Our casualties slight. Enemy retaliated very heavily on ANGRES II Sub Section from 10.50 p.m to 11.30 p.m.	[initials]
	23rd		2nd Lt Stokes & 1 N.C.O. to Div. Gas School. Wire cutting by our M T-Ms from 6.15 a.m to 6.45 a.m. & " 3.0 p.m. to 3.30 p.m. Casualties for 24 hours other ranks 1 killed 3 wounded. Prearranged "Strafe" 4.23 p.m. to 4.38 p.m by 63rd (RN) Div. Art. and Corps "Heavies". Slight hostile Arty activity 8.15 p.m to 8.45 p.m	[initials]
	24th	10.a.m to 10.30 a.m	Enemy shelled FOREST ALLEY & PYRENEES with H.E and Shrapnel. Wire cutting by M T Ms between 2.30 p.m & 3.0 p.m. Enemys L T Ms & Rifle Grenades very active between 5.30 p.m & 6 p.m we replied successfully with Stokes. At 9.50 p.m enemy opened a sudden violent burst of Arty fire simultaneously with rapid rifle and M.G. fire for 7 minutes on left of ANGRES I after which all quiet.	[initials]
	25th	12.52 a.m	Our Arty bombarded enemy Salient opposite ANGRES I for 20 minutes, Very little retaliation. Issued orders for relief	[initials]
BULLY	26th	11.30 a.m	Relieved by 1st Royal Marines. Battn went into Bde Support. Fatigues carrying out gas cylinders 230 men, 6 officers	[initials] Appendix VII attached
	27th		Held Divine Service. Baths and Medical Inspection of Battn — ditto — — do —	[initials]
	28th		Inspection of arms, Close order drill etc — ditto — — do —	[initials]
	29th		— ditto — Carried out practice "Gas Helmet Alarm". Alarm received 7.49 p.m Battn ready to move by 8.20 p.m. Arrangements found inadequate for companies in BULLY on account of difficulty in passing alarm by word of mouth only. Issued orders for relief	[initials] Appendix VIII attached

2nd Royal Marines

Army Form C. 2118.

5

WAR DIARY

or

~~INTELLIGENCE SUMMARY~~.

(*Erase heading not required.*)

August 1916

Instructions regarding War Diaries and Intelligence Summaries are contained in F. S. Regs., Part II. and the Staff Manual respectively. Title pages will be prepared in manuscript.

Place	Date	Hour	Summary of Events and Information	Remarks and references to Appendices
	Aug: 16		D Company of 10th Royal Dublin Fusiliers attached, 1 section to each platoon	
ANGRES II	30th	11.30 a.m	Relieved 1st Royal Marines in ANGRES II. Very heavy rain had done a lot of damage to the trenches. Very	
Sub-Section			quiet indeed during the day and night. Wire cutting carried out by M.T-Ms from 2.45 p.m to 3.0 p.m but owing to	
			the strong wind this was not very satisfactory, it was also continued from 7.0 p.m to 7.45 p.m.	[initials]
	31st		Wire cutting by M.T-Ms 6.45 a.m to 7.30 a.m and 3.30 p.m to 4.15 p.m. Enemy replied with a few minenwerfers.	
			Very quiet day and night. Enemy appear to be less active both with Rifle grenades and Artl. No gaps discovered	
			by patrols or enemy patrols encountered	[initials]

A.R.H. Hutchison.

Lieut Colonel

Commanding 2nd Royal Marines

1st September 1916.

Appendix I
to August 1916 War Diary Vol III
of 2nd Royal Marines

SECRET.
""""""""""""""""""

ISSUED at 1.0 p.m.

COPY NO. 9

OPERATION ORDER NO....12

BY LIEUT., COLONEL A.R.H. HUTCHISON R.M.L.I.

COMMANDING 2ND., ROYAL MARINES.

"-"-"-"-"-"-"-" -"-"-"-"-"-"-"-"-"-"-"-"-"

Reference Map 36B FRANCE &
TRENCH MAP ANGRES Sect. "A"

Bn., Headquarters,
1st., August 1916.

1....The 1st., Royal Marines will relieve the 2nd., Royal Marines in the line to-morrow. Relief to commence at 2-0 p.m.

2.....On relief the Battalion will go into Brigade Reserve.

3....Headquarters, "B" and "C" Co's., will move to FOSSE 10 and "A" and "D" Co's to BULLY.

4....Platoon Guides from "B" and "C" Cos., will report at Battalion Headquarters at 2-0 p.m.

5....Co's will move off independently by Platoons on relief moving by BOVRIL ALLEY. O.C. Co's reporting to Battalion Headquarters by runner when relief is complete.

6....O.C. "D" Co., will detail one Officer to go to BULLY by 11-0 a.m. and O.C. "C" Co., one Officer to go to FOSSE 10 by same time ; These Officers to take over Billets tec., from 1st., Royal Marines. The Officer proceeding to FOSSE 10 will report at 1st., R.M. Battalion Headquarters and take over and sign for any documents that may be handed over.

7....Lewis Guns will be relieved to-day. Relief to be complete by 3-0 p.m L.G.O's conscerned making necessary arrangements.

8.....Trench Stores will be handed over to relieving Co's., using A.F.W. 3405. Duplicate copies in manuscript to be rendered to Orderly Room by 10-0 a.m.

9.....The Officers Mess Cart will be at BULLY at 3-0 p.m. to take Officers Mess Traps to FOSSE 10.

OVER

Operation Order No., 12 continued.

10.......Transport Officer to send Cookers of "B" and "C" Co., to FOSSE 10 and "A" and "D" Cos'., to BULLY by 3-0 p.m. Co., Cooks to proceed at same time.

11.......O.C. "D" Co., will detail a Sentry to prevent anyone moving down BULLY ALLEY after 1-15 p.m. until relief is complete.

12.......Battalion Headquarters will close at P.C. 25 on completion of relief and open at FOSSE 10 one hour and a half later.

"-"-"-"-"-"-"-"-"-"-"-"-"-"

C.G. Farquharson

Captain and Adjutant,
2nd., Royal Marines.

Copies to :-

1.....Retained.

2.....O.C. 1st., Royal Marines.

3.....O.C. "A" Co.,

4.....O.C. "B" Co.,

5.....O.C. "C" Co.,

6.....O.C. "D" Co.,

7.....Q.M. and T.O.

8.....L.G. Officer.

9.....War Diary.

Appendix IX to August 1916 War Diary Vol IX of 2nd Royal Marines

S E C R E T. COPY NO...9.......

-.-.-.-.-.-.-.-.-.-.-

Issued at.....NOON.

OPERATIONS ORDERS NO....17

BY LIEUT., COLONEL A.R.H. HUTCHISON R.M.L.I.

COMMANDING 2ND., ROYAL MARINES.

"-"

8th., August 1916

1....The 2nd., Royal Marines will relieve the 1st., Royal Marines in the front line to-morrow.

2...."A" Co., will occupy the right and "D" Co., the left of the front line. "B" Co., will be in MOROCCO SOUTH, "C" Co., in MOROCCO NORTH. Battalion Scouts will be accomodated in MOROCCO NORTH, in Dug-Out nearest BULLEY ALLEY.

3...."B" and "C" Co's., will provide the usual Crater Jumping Parties.

4....Companies will move up by Platoons at 100 yards distance. "A" Co., will move at 8-45 a.m. followed by "D" Co.; Headquarters and Scouts will move from FOSSE 10 at 9-45 a.m. followed by "B" and "C" Co's.,

5....O.C. Co's will report by runner when relief is complete.

6....Officers Baggage of "B" and "C" Co., to be dumped by "C" Co., Cookers by 9-0 a.m. "A" and "D" Co., outside "D" Co., Billets. Transport Officer to arrange for removal of same.

7....Officers Mess Cart will be at the Orderly Room at 9-15 a.m. to take Officers' Mess Traps as far as BULLY.

8....The Transport Officer will arrange to remove Co., Cookers and Water Carts back to HERSIN at 9-0 a.m.

9....To-Morrows rations will be carried on the men.

10...Lewis Guns will relieve to-day, relief to be complete by 3-0 p.m.

11...Headquarters will close at FOSSE 10 at 9-15 a.m. and reopen at P.C. 5 at 11-30 a.m.

"o"o"o"o"o"o"o"o"o"o"o"o"

Copies :-
No., 1 Retained.
No., 2 O.C. 1/R.M. No., 8 L.G.O.
No., 3 O.C. "A" Co. No., 9 War Diary.
No., 4 O.C. "B" Co.,
No., 5 O.C. "C" Co.,
No., 6 O.C. "D" Co.,
No., 7 Q.M. and T.O.

C.G. Farquharson

Captain and Adjutant,
2nd., Royal Marines

Appendix III of August 1916 War Diary Vol III of 2nd Royal Marines

SECRET....

Copy No. 11.......

ISSUED AT. 10.15 a.m.

OPERATION ORDER NO....14

BY LIEUT., COLONEL A.R.H. HUTCHISON R.M.L.I.

COMMANDING 2ND., ROYAL MARINES.

--*-*-*-*-*-*-*-*-*-*-*-*-*-*-*

9th., AUGUST 1916

Headquarters....2/R.M.

1.....The 1st., Royal Marines will relieve the 2nd., Royal Marines in the line to-morrow. Relief to commence at 10-0 a.m.

2.....On relief the Battalion will go into Brigade Reserve.

3.....Headquarters, "A" and "D" Cos'., will move to FOSSE 10. "B" and "C" Cos., to BULLY.

4.....Platoon Guides from "A" and "B" Cos., will report at Battalion Headquarters at 10-0 a.m.

5.....Cos., will move independently by Platoons on relief via BOVRIL ALLEY. O.C. Co's., reporting to Battalion Headquarters by runner when relief is complete.

6.....Captain Goldring will take over Billets at BULLY at 9-0 a.m. Captain Edwards will take over Billets at FOSSE 10 at same time, and sign for any documents that may be handed over by 1/R.M.

7.....Lewis Guns will be relieved to-day, relief to be complete by 5-0 p.m. Lewis Gun Officers making necessary arrangements.

8.....Trench Stores will be handed over to relieving Cos., using manuscript lists, duplicate copies to be rendered to Orderly Room by 6-30 a.m.

9.....O.C. "C" Co., will detail a sentry to prevent anyone moving down BULLY ALLEY after 9-15 a.m. until relief is complete.

10....The Officers Mess Cart and Medical Cart will be at BULLY at 11-30 a.m. , the former to convey Officers Mess Traps to FOSSE 10. One water cart to be at BULLY and one at FOSSE 10 by NOON. O.C. 2nd., in Cd., Adjt., and Med., Officers' chargers to be at BULLY at 11-45 a.m. Transport Officer to arrange for stabling at FOSSE 10 as before.

C Y E R.

No.....O.O. 14 continued.

11 ....Cookers of "A" and "D" Co's to be at FOSSE 10 and of "B" and "C" Co's., at BULLY by 10-0 a.m.
Breakfast ration only to be sent up to trenches to-night, dinners to be ready on arrival of Co's., in their billeting areas, Quartermaster to make necessary arrangements.

12....Battalion Headquarters will close at P.C. 5 on completion of relief, and open at FOSSE 10 one hour and a half later.

"o"o"o"o"o"o"o"o"o"o"o"o"o"

C.G. Farquharson
Captain and Adjutant,
2nd., Royal Marines.

Copies to :-

No., 1 Retained.
No., 2 O.C. 1/R.M.
No., 3 O.C. "A" Co.,
No., 4 O.C. "B" Co.,
No., 5 O.C. "C" Co.,
No., 6 O.C. "D" Co.,
No., 7 Lewis Gun Officer.
No., 8 Quartermaster and Transport Officer.
No., 9 Captain Edwards.
No., 10 Captain Goldring.
No., 11 War Diary.

Appendix IV
to August 1916 War Diary Vol. [illegible] of
2nd Royal Marines

S E C R E T.
-.-.-.-.-.-.-.-.-. C O P Y NO...8...

Issued at...12.45 pm.

OPERATION ORDERS NO....15

BY LIEUT., COLONEL A.R.H. HUTCHISON R.M.L.I.

COMMANDING 2ND., ROYAL MARINES.

"-"-"-"-"-"-"-"-"-"-"-"-"-"-"-"-"

19th., August 1916.

1.....The 2nd., Royal Marines will relieve the 1st., Royal Marines in the front line to-morrow.

2....."B" Co., will occupy the right and "C" Co., the left of the front line. "A" will be in MOROCCO SOUTH, "D" Co., in MOROCCO NORTH.
Battalion Scouts will be accomodated in MOROCCO NORTH, in dug-out nearest BULLY ALLEY.

3....."A" and "D" Co's., will provide the usual Crater Jumping Parties.

4.....Companies will move up by Platoons at 100 yards distance. "B" Co., will move at 9-45 a.m. followed by "C" Co., Headquarters and Scouts will move from FOSSE 10 at 9-45 a.m. followed by "A" and "D" Co's.,

5.....O.C. Co's., will report by runner when relief is complete.

6.....Officers Baggage of "A" and "D" Co., to be dumped by "D" Co., Cookers by 9-0 a.m. "B" and "C" Co., outside "B" Co., Billets. Transport Officer to arrange for removal of same, also ALL Orderly Room Boxes.

7.....Officers Mess Cart will be at the ORDERLY ROOM at 9-15 a.m. to take Officers Mess Traps as far as BULLY.

8.....Transport Officer will arrange to remove Co., Cookers and Water Carts back to HERSIN at 9-0 a.m.

9.....To-morrows rations will be carried on the men.

10....Lewis Guns will relieve to-day, relief to be complete by 3-0 p.m.

11.....Periscopes will be drawn from the Orderly Room by "B" and "C" Co's., at 6-0 p.m. to-day.
They will be returned to Battalion Sergeant Major as soon as possible after taking over Billets.

12.....O.C. Co's., will report to Battalion Headquarters as soon as possible after taking over, that all arrangements have been made for the operation laid down in O.O. 12 of 25th., JULY.

continued. over.

Continued.

13..........Headquarters will close at FOSSE 10 at 9-15 a.m. and re-open at P.C. 5 at 11-30 a.m.

"s"s"s"s"s"s"s"s"s"s"s"s"s"s"

C.G. Farquharson

Captain and Adjutant,

2nd., Royal Marines.

Copies to :-

No., 1 Retained.
No., 2 O.C. 1/R.M.

No., 3 O.C. "A" Co.,

No., 4 O.C. "B" Co.,

No., 5 O.C. "C" Co.,

No., 6 O.C. "D" Co.,

No., 7 Q.M. and T.O.

No., 8 War Diary.

-"s"s"s"s"s"s"s"s"s"s"s"s"s"s"s"s"s"s"s-

Appendix V
to August 1916 War Diary Vol III
of 2nd Royal Marines.

ISSUED AT 6-30 a.m. SECRET....... COPY NO....10........

OPERATION ORDERS NO...16

BY LIEUT., COLONEL A.R.H. HUTCHISON R.M.L.I.

COMMANDING 2ND., ROYAL MARINES.

Battalion Headquarters,

17th., AUGUST 1916.

1.........The 2nd., Royal Marines will be relieved by 1st., Royal Marines to-morrow, on relief Battalion will move into Brigade Support.

2.........On relief "B" and "C" Co's., will move via BOVRIL ALLEY to BULLY. "A" Co., will move via CORONS D'AIX to MECHANICS TRENCH. As soon as "A" Co., have moved "D" Co., will follow them via MOROCCO SOUTH and CORONS D'AIX to METRO CAP DE PONT, CORON D'AIX.

3.........Co's., will move off independently on relief by platoons. O.C. Co's reporting to Battalion Headquarters by runner when relief is completed.

4.........Trench Stores will be handed over to relieving Co's., using A.F.W. 3405. Duplicate copies in manuscript are to be rendered to Orderly Room by 6-30 a.m.

5.........Lewis Guns will be relieved to-day under arrangements by Lewis Gun Officers. Relief to be complete by 3-0 p.m.

6.........Captain Cutcher will take over the Billets and any documents from 1st., Royal Marines at 9-0 a.m. to-morrow.

7........."B" and "C" Cos., will hand over 85 Steel Helmets each to relieving Co's.,

8..........10 Water Cans per Co., and 3 per Crater Jumping Party are to be handed over FILLED.

9..........Transp ort Officer is to send Cookers of "B" and "C" Cos., and both Water Carts to BULLY also Headquarter, "B" and "C" Co., Officers Valises, Orderly Room Boxes and Bicycles. and Medical Gear.

OVER.

continued.

10.........Quartermaster will send up Breakfast Ration ONLY for "B" and "C" Co., to-night, Dinners for these Co's to be ready on arrival in Billets. Co., Cooks of "A" and "D" to join up with their Co's.,

11..........O. C. "D" Co., will detail a Guard of 1 Corporal (Long Service) and 6 Men to relieve 1st., R.M. Guard at Brigade Headquarters at 8-0 a.m. He will also arrange to relieve 1st., R.M. at the following two control Posts at the same time.:-

(a) West End of CORON D'AIX.

(b) CORON D'AIX Entrance to CAP DE PONT.

Lewis Gun Officer will detail a Guard of 1 N.C.O. and 3 Men to mount a t Battalion Headquarters at 10-0 a.m.

12 ....Batt alion Headquarters will close at P.C. 5 on. completion of relief and re-open at R. 11 a 6.4. BULLY.

", ", ", ", ", ", ", ", ", ", ", "

Captain and Adjutant,

2nd., Royal Marines.

Copies to

No., 1 Retained.

No., 2 O.C. 1st., R.M.

No., 3 O.C. "A" Co.,

No., 4 O.C. "B" Co.,

No., 5 O.C. "C" Co.,

No., 6 O.C. " D" Co.,

No., 7 Q.M. and T.O.

No., 8 Captain Cutcher.

No., 9 Lewis Gun Officer.

No., 10 War Diary.

Appendix V A
to August 1916 War Diary Vol VII of
2nd Royal Marines

Issued at 8.0 p.m. SECRET. COPY NO. 9

OPERATION ORDERS NO. 17

BY

LIEUT., COLONEL A.R.H. HUTCHISON R.M.L.I.

COMMANDING 2ND., ROYAL MARINES.

References { FRANCE 36B $\frac{1}{10,000}$
{ Trench Map ANGRES
{ Section "A"

Battalion Headquarters,

17th., August 1916

1..........When the Battalion moves into Brigade Support to-morrow the following are the positions which will be occupied on receipt of message " Occupy Alarm Post".
"A" Co., to garrison FORBES ALLEY from its junction with DAMASCETTE southwards.

BAJOLLE LINE.
("D" Co., from R. 30 a.3.7½ inclusive to R.24.c.5.7.
("B" Co., from R.24 c.5.7. to BULLY ALLEY exclusive.
("C" Co., from BULLY ALLEY inclusive to BOVRIL ALLEY.
(inclusive.

2..........Routes as follows :-

B "A" Co., BULLY ALLEY- DAMASCETTE.

C "D" Co., CORONS D'AIX.

A "B" Co., followed by "C" D Co., BULLY ALLEY.

3..........O.C. Co's are to reconnoitre lines they will have to occupy.

4..........Battalion Headquarters will be at MECHANICS.

Copies to :-
No., 1 Retained.
No., 2 O.C. "A" Co.,
No., 3 O.C. "B" Co.,
No., 4 O.C. "C" Co.,
No., 5 O.C. "D" Co.,
No., 6 L.G.O.
No., 7 Scout Officer.
No., 8 Bombing Officer.
No., 9 War Diary.

C.G. Farquharson
Captain and Adjutant,
2nd., Royal Marines.

Appendix VI to August 1916 War Diary Vol III of 2nd Royal Marines

SECRET

Issued at.. 2 pm...   Copy No..8.....

OPERATION ORDER NO.....10

BY LIEUT., COLONEL A.R.H. HUTCHISON R.M.L.I.

COMMANDING 2ND., ROYAL MARINES.

* * * * * * * * * * * * * * * *

Bn., Headquarters,
21st., August 1916.

1..........The 2nd., Royal Marines will relieve the 1st., Royal Marines in the front line to-morrow.

2..........."A" Co., will occupy the right and "D" Co., the Left of the Front Line. "B" Co., will be in MOROCCO SOUTH (less one platoon in CUMBERT) "C" Co., in MOROCCO NORTH. Battalion Scouts will be accommodated in MOROCCO NORTH in Dug-Out nearest BULLY ALLEY.

3.........."B" and "C" Cos., will provide the usual Crater Jumping Parties.

4...........Cos., will move up by SECTIONS at 100 yards distance "A" Co., will move out of MECHANICS by 10-0 a.m. "D" Co., will be at the entrance to BULLY ALLEY by 9-30 a.m. followed by Headquarters, "B" and "C" Cos.,

5...........104 Trench Helmets each for "B" and "C" Co., will be taken over from 1st., Royal Marines.

6...........O.C. Co's., will report to Battalion Headquarters by runner when relief is completed.

7...........Transport Officer will arrange to remove Cookers, Water Carts and Officers Valises, Orderly Room Boxes and Medical Officers Stores at 9-0 a.m.

8...........Periscopes for "A" and "D" Co., will be drawn from the Orderly Room at 6-0 p.m. to-day.

9...........To-morrow's rations will be carried on the men.

10..........Present Headquarters will close at 9-30 a.m. and re-open at P.C. 5 at 11-0 a.m.

"-"-"-" -"-"-" -"-"-"-"-"-"

Copies to :-
No., 1 Retained.
No., 2 O.C. 1st., R.M.
No., 3 O.C. "A" Co.,
No., 4 O.C. "B" Co.,
No., 5 O.C. "C" Co.,
No., 6 O.C. "D" Co.,
No., 7 Q.M. and T.O.
No., 8 War Diary.

C.G. Fogelsang [signature]
Captain and Adjutant,
2nd., Royal Marines.

Appendix VII to August 1916 War Diary Vol III of 2nd Royal Marines

Issued at 11 AM.... SECRET COPY NO. 9..

OPERATION ORDERS NO.....17

BY LIEUT., COLONEL A.R.H. HUTCHISON R.M.L.I.

COMMANDING 2ND., ROYAL MARINES.

Battalion Headquarters,

25th., August 1916.

1.........The 2nd., Royal Marines will be relieved by the 1st., Royal Marines on the 26th., inst., commencing at 10-0 a.m. On relief the 2nd., R.M. will move into Brigade Support.

2.........."A" and "D" Co's., will move via BOVRIL ALLEY to BULLY on relief. "B" Co., will move via CORON D'AIX to MECHANICS. As soon as "B" Co., has moved "C" Co., will follow them via MOROCCO SOUTH, CORON D'AIX to METRO, CAP DE PONT, CORONS D'AIX.

3..........Co's., will move off independently by Platoons on relief, O.C. Co's., reporting to Battalion Headquarters by runner when relief is completed.

4.........Trench Stores will be handed over to relieving Co's., using A.F.W. 3405, duplicate copies in manuscript are to be rendered to Orderly Room by 6-30 a.m. to-morrow.

5........."A" and "D" Co's., will dump 104 Trench Helmets each at junction of BULLY and GUMBOOT and junction of BOVRIL and ALGIERS respectively, leaving an N.C.O. at dump until relieved by N.C.O. from 1st., Royal Marines.

6.........Captain Staughton will take over the Billets in BULLY, and any documents from 1st., R.M. at 9-0 a.m. on day of relief.

7..........10 Water Cans per Co., and 3 per Crater Jumping Party and 4 Headquarters are to be handed over full.

8..........Transport Officer is to send Cookers of "A" and "D" Co's., and both Water Carts to BULLY, also Headquarters, ~~Officers Valises~~ "A" "C" and "D" Co., Officers Valises, and Orderly Room Box and Medical Officer's Stores.

9..........Quartermaster will arrange to send up breakfast ration ONLY for "A" and "D" Co., having their dinners ready on arrival in BULLY. "B" and "C" Co., Cooks to join up with their Co.,

10........."C" Co., will arrange to relieve 1st., R.M. at the following 2 Control Posts at 8-0 a.m.

(a) West End of CORON D'AIX.

(b) CORON D'AIX ENTRANCE to CAP DE PONT.

continued. P.T.O.

continued.

11.......Lewis Gun Officer will detail a Guard of :-
1 Junior N.C.O. and 3 Men
to mount at Battalion Headquarters at 10-0 a.m.
Also :-
& 1 Long Service Corporal &
3 Men
to mount at Brigade Headquarters at 8-0 a.m.

12......."A" and "D" Co's., will have their Periscopes and Verys Pistols returned to Orderly Room by 6-0 p.m. to-morrow.

13........Battalion Headquarters will close at P.C. 5 on completion of relief and re-open at R. 11 a. 6.4. BULLY.

"-"-"-"-"-"-"-"-"-"-"-"-"-"-"-"

Captain and Adjutant,
2nd., Royal Marines.

Copies to :-

No., 1 Retained.
No., 2 O.C. "A" Co.,
No., 3 O.C. "B" Co.,
No., 4 O.C. "C" Co.,
No., 5 O.C. "D" Co.,
No., 6 Q.M. and T.O.
No., 7 L.G.O.
No., 8 ~~Captain Staughton.~~ O.C. 1/RM
No., 9 War Diary.

Appendix VIII
to August 1916 War Diary Vol. II
of 2nd Royal Marines

ISSUED AT...2.0 p.m. SECRET. COPY NO....9.......

OPERATION ORDER NO......20

BY LIEUT., COLONEL A.R.H. HUTCHISON R.M.L.I.

COMMANDING 2ND., ROYAL MARINES.

Battalion Headquarters,

29th., AUGUST 1916.

1.........The 2nd., Royal Marines will relieve the 1st., Royal Marines in the Front Line to-morrow.

2.........."B" Co., will occupy the Right and "C" Co., the Left of the line. "A" Co., will be in MORROCCO SOUTH (less One Platoon in GUMBOOT) and "D" Co., in MOROCCO NORTH. Battalion Scouts will be accomodated in MOROCCO NORTH in dug-out nearest BULLY ALLEY.

3.........."A" and "D" Co's., will provide the usual Crater Jumping Parties.

4..........Cos., will move up by Sections at 100 yards distance. "B" Co., will move out of MECHANICS by 10-0 a.m. "C" Co., will be at the entrance to BULLY ALLEY by 9-45 a.m. followed by Headquarters, "A" and "D" Cos.,

5..........Periscopes for "B" and "C" Co's., will be drawn from the Orderly Room at 6-0 p.m. to-day.

6..........O.C. Co's., will report to Battalion Headquarters by runner when relief is completed.

7..........To-morrows rations will be carried on the man.

8.........."B" and "C" Cos., will take over sufficient Steel Helmets to complete from 1st., R.M. reporting number of same to Battalion Headquarters.

9..........O.C. Co's., will forward certificate to Battalion Headquarters by 6-0 p.m. to-morrow to the effect that " All occupied Dug-outs have a pick and shovel in them, which are never taken out".

10..........Transport Officer will arrange to remove Cookers, Watercarts and Officers Valises, Orderly Room Boxes and Medical Officers Stores at 9-0 a.m.

continued.

11........Present Headquarters will close at 9-30 a.m. and reopens at P.C. 5 on completion of relief.

"-"-"-"-"-"-"-"-"-"-"-"-"-"-"-"

C.G. Farquharson

Captain and Adjutant,
2nd., Royal Marines.

29-8-16.

Copies to :-

No., 1 Retained.
No., 2 O.C. 1st., R.M.
No., 3 O.C. "D" Co., 10th., Batt. R.D.F's.
No., 4 O.C."A" Co.,
No., 5 O.C. "B" Co.,
No., 6 O.C. "C" Co.,
No., 7 O.C. "D" Co.,
No., 8 Q.M. and T.Q.
No., 9 War Diary.

"CONFIDENTIAL"

Battalion Headquarters,

2nd., Royal Marines.

1st., OCTOBER 1916.

VOLUME... .4

WAR DIARY

of

2ND., ROYAL MARINES

from

1st., SEPTEMBER 1916

to

30th., SEPTEMBER 1916.

"-"-"-"-" -"-"-"-"-"

A.E. Eagles

Major R.M .L.I.
Commanding 2nd., Royal Marines.

TO/
The A.G's Office,

3rd., ECHELON.

j-------------------------j

Vol 4

2nd Royal Marines
Army Form C. 2118.

1.

Instructions regarding War Diaries and Intelligence Summaries are contained in F. S. Regs., Part II. and the Staff Manual respectively. Title pages will be prepared in manuscript.

WAR DIARY
or
~~INTELLIGENCE~~ SUMMARY.
(*Erase heading not required.*)

Volume IV
September 1916

Place	Date	Hour	Summary of Events and Information	Remarks and references to Appendices
	Sept			References
ANGRES II Sub-Section	1st		Howitzers fired on our left opposite CALONNE. Some good results were obtained, several explosions taking place, followed later by a large explosion and a fire which lasted several hours. Our Medium Trench Mortars carried out wire cutting from 12.15 p.m to 1.0 p.m. and from 6.0 to 6.45 p.m. Enemy retaliated with minenwerfers. Otherwise quiet.	FRANCE 36b 6 Trench Map ANGRES Sect
"	2nd		7.15 a.m to 8.0 a.m & 6.30 p.m to 7.15 p.m wire cutting by our M. T-Ms, very slight retaliation by enemy's mortars and 77 mm guns. Gas alert on at 3.25 p.m wind S-E. Quiet night on the whole, a few rifle grenades being put over by enemy and replied to at the rate of 6 to 1 by us. Lewis guns fired on gaps in the wire during the night. Orders for relief	Appendix I attached
FOSSE 10 & BULLY	3rd		Wire cutting by our M.T.Ms 7.15 a.m to 8.0 a.m. Relieved by 1st Royal Marines, went into Brigade Reserve — HdQrs & 2 companies at FOSSE 10, 2 companies at BULLY.	
"	4th		Inspection of arms, close order drill, helmet inspection & drill etc. Baths. 40 men inoculated against enteric	
"	5th		— ditto — — do — — do Medical Inspection.	
"	6th		— do — — do — G.O.C. 63rd (R.N) Divn presented Military Medal to No Ply/3582 Pte W Aldred for bravery & devotion to duty in SOUCHEZ II on 21st June. Orders for relief. 2nd Lt Garnett & 6 other ranks to Bde Bomb School	Appendix II attached
ANGRES II	7th		Relieved 1st Royal Marines with Battn less ½ company + D Coy 10th Battn Royal Dublin Fusiliers. Our medium T-Ms cut enemy wire from 12.15 p.m to 1.0 p.m. & 6.30 p.m to 7.15 p.m. Slight retaliation. Enemy's snipers active during the hours of darkness. Our Lewis guns fired a large number of rounds at gaps in wire and dispersed two enemy working parties	

T2134. Wt. W708—776. 500000. 4/15. Sir J. C. & S.

2nd Royal Marines

Army Form C. 2118.

Instructions regarding War Diaries and Intelligence Summaries are contained in F. S. Regs., Part II. and the Staff Manual respectively. Title pages will be prepared in manuscript.

2

WAR DIARY or ~~INTELLIGENCE SUMMARY.~~

Volume IV
September 1916

(*Erase heading not required.*)

Place	Date	Hour	Summary of Events and Information	Remarks and references to Appendices
ANGRES II Sub-Section	Sept 8th		2" Trench Mortars cut wire between 6.0 a.m & 6.45 a.m & also from 3.0 p.m to 3.45 p.m. At 11.45 a.m our Artillery bombarded enemy trenches at M26 a for about 5 minutes. No enemy retaliation. The enemy sent over a considerable number of Aerial Torpedoes and Minnenwerfers between 7.0 p.m & 9.0 p.m. Our Stokes Mortars retaliated. Lieut Young rejoined Battn from Base ETAPLES. Lieut H.N Pearse & 2nd Lt G.J. Richards joined Battn. 4 NCOs (2 senior 2 junior) to 63rd (RN) Div. School PERNES	[initials]
"	9th		2" T.Ms cut wire from 6.45 a.m to 7.20 a.m & 3.45 p.m to 4.30 p.m. No retaliation. Very quiet both during day & night. Enemys Snipers practically silent and very few Verys lights sent up	[initials]
"	10th		2" T.Ms cut wire from 7.20 a.m to 8.15 a.m & 4.15 p.m to 5.0 p.m. Slight retaliation on each occasion with 77 m.m shrapnel over FOREST ALLEY & PYRENEES. Enemys' Rifle grenades much less active due probably to our "8 rifle" Batty. Small Bombing raid carried out by ANSON Battn on our right. At Zero time our Artly put over an excellent barrage and raiding party jumped into Sap at M26 c 2.4. Three ~~[struck]~~ men ran towards trench & one was wounded and brought in, proving to be a Saxon. Raid was most successful several enemy being killed. Our own casualties 2 Officers & 1 O.R. slightly wounded. Orders for relief	[initials] Appendix III attached
	11th		Relieved by 1st Royal Marines, Battn went to Brigade Reserve, Hd Qrs & 2 companies at FOSSE 10 & 2 companies to BULLY. Lieut/Capt: A.C. St Clair Morford struck off Battn strength on evacuation to ENGLAND	[initials]
	12th		Inspection of arms, close order drill fatigues etc. Baths. 40 men inoculated against enteric. 2nd Lt Garnett & 6 O.Rs from Bde Bomb School	[initials]
	13th		– ditto – – do – – do. Medical Inspection. Lt Cook & 2 O.Rs to M.T.M Course CLARQUES. 2nd Lt Richards & 7 O.Rs to Bde Bomb School	[initials]

T2134. Wt. W708–776. 500000. 4/15. Sir J. C. & S.

2nd Royal Marines
Army Form C. 2118.

3

Instructions regarding War Diaries and Intelligence Summaries are contained in F. S. Regs., Part II. and the Staff Manual respectively. Title pages will be prepared in manuscript.

WAR DIARY or INTELLIGENCE SUMMARY.

Volume IV
September 1916

(*Erase heading not required.*)

Place	Date	Hour	Summary of Events and Information	Remarks and references to Appendices
	Sept			
FOSSE 10 &	14th		Inspection of arms, close order & physical drill, fatigues etc. 3 O.Rs to Lewis Gun Course at LE TOUQUET. Orders for relief	Appendix IV attached
BULLY ANGRES II Sub sector	15th		Relieved 1st Royal Marines. Enemy aeroplane attempted to cross our lines at 2.40 p.m. but was driven back by our anti-aircraft guns 3.30 p.m. Our artillery carried out 15 minutes practice Barrage on enemy's lines opposite our left limit followed by 12 minutes further practice. 30 other ranks, reinforcements joined the Battn. 2nd Lt Stokes to 4th Corps Hd Qrs for Signalling Course. We put Shrapnel over THOMPSONS CRATER for 3 minutes at 10.0 p.m. to try and catch working parties reported on previous night	
	16th		Lieut Colonel A.R.H. Hutchison C.M.G. appointed to command 190th Infy Bde during the absence of Brig Gen C. Trotman C.B. sick. Major C. F. C. Eagles appointed to command 2/RMs. Divl arty & T.Ms carried out bombardment of enemy Trench System in M 20 b & d, M21 c. at 2.30 p.m & 2.38 p.m.	
	17th	1.40 a.m	Enemy placed a barrage on our front line between BOVRIL & BULLY ALLEY which at 1.45 a.m. was lifted to round GUMBOOT & ALGIERS. About 200 rounds fired mostly 77 mm with a few 4.2" There were several blinds. Hostile aircraft approached our lines at 11.30 a.m but retired on being fired on by our A.A. guns. Enemy artillery very quiet. Snipers less active	
	18th		Extraordinarily quiet night 17th/18th. hardly a rifle fired, very few lights put up by enemy. Enemy sent over a few rifle grenades but we at once silenced him. Orders for relief by 8th East Lancashire Regt. 112th Bde.	Appendix V attached
FOSSE 10	19th		Relieved by 8th Battn. East Lancashire Regt. 112th Bde 37th Divn. proceeded to FOSSE 10	
	20th		63rd (R.N) Divn. changed its area. 2nd Royal Marines proceeded by route march to BEUGIN (P.1) and went into billets	

T2134. Wt. W708—776. 500000. 4/15. Sir J. C. & S.

2nd Royal Marines

Army Form C. 2118.

Instructions regarding War Diaries and Intelligence Summaries are contained in F. S. Regs., Part II. and the Staff Manual respectively. Title pages will be prepared in manuscript.

4.

WAR DIARY
or
~~INTELLIGENCE SUMMARY~~.
(*Erase heading not required.*)

Volume IV
September 1916

Place	Date	Hour	Summary of Events and Information	Remarks and references to Appendices
	Sept			
BEUGIN	21st		Day spent in cleaning up equipment and clothing and making good deficiencies. Officers sent out to reconnoitre training area South of MAGNICOURT. A hostile plane flew over the village about 11.30 a.m. but was driven back by our anti-aircraft guns. 5 other ranks sent to England on leave. Rev. Father T. J. Bradley C.F. R.C. joined the Battn.	
	22nd		Commenced Company training. Close order drill, bayonet fighting, extended order drill. The IVth Corps Commander presented the Conspicuous Gallantry Medal to Corpl Grindey & Pte Turner of the 2nd Royal Marines. 2 O.Rs to England on leave	
	23rd		Continued Company training. Platoon in attack, company in attack including advancing in artillery formation. Bayonet & physical training etc	
	24th		Continued Company training same programme as for 23rd	
	25th		Battn. training — Battn. in artillery formation getting quickly into extended order, building up the firing line etc. All done in slow time in order to correct mistakes.	
	26th		Battn. training. Exercise in attacking an entrenched position. One company (less one platoon at Musketry) occupied a defensive position and the 3 other companies carried out an attack commencing with Arty formation. 3 O.Rs to England on leave	
	27th		Bde training. Practiced advancing from trenches in 5 waves. 1st & 2nd wave {1 company each, 50 yards behind one another} attacked Red Line which represented Enemy's front line. 3rd wave (1 company) consolidating party advanced to Red line behind 1st and 2nd wave and remained there until 4th & 5th wave (½ company each 50 yards behind one another) had seized Blue line (representing Enemy's Support line). Then 3rd wave advanced and consolidated Blue line. After the exercise the 2nd Royal Marines marched to MONCHY-BRETON (0.31) and billeted there	
MONCHY-BRETON			Capt M E E Barton – Joining to England 12-9-16 & Lieut A.J. Simpson to England 8-9-16 struck off strength of Battn.	

T2134. Wt. W708—776. 500000. 4/15. Sir J. C. & S.

5.

2nd Royal Marines

Army Form C. 2118.

Instructions regarding War Diaries and Intelligence Summaries are contained in F. S. Regs., Part II. and the Staff Manual respectively. Title pages will be prepared in manuscript.

WAR DIARY
or
INTELLIGENCE ~~SUMMARY~~.
(Erase heading not required.)

Volume IV
September 1916.

Place	Date	Hour	Summary of Events and Information	Remarks and references to Appendices
MONCHY-BRETON {0.31}	Sept 28th		Bde Training. Open Attack practice. Howe Battn. & 2nd Royal Marines formed the Right & Left Front Battns respectively and delivered an attack on 1st Objective and consolidated. 1st Royal Marines afterwards attacked through the Battns holding 1st Objective onto 2nd Objective. Carried out signal communication with Observation Aeroplane. Signal was taken in by the aeroplane and passed on through the Bde to 63rd (RN) Divn. [initials]	
	29th		Divl Training. Carried out practically the same scheme as for 27th Sept viz attacking out of trenches in 5 waves. 190th Bde afterwards advanced through 188th Bde and seized a further objective. The whole scheme of advance of the various waves was done successfully by timing, the Barrage being represented by a line of men with white flags. [initials]	
	30th		Divl Route March. The whole ~~[illegible]~~ 63rd (RN) Divn carried out a route march (less Medium T.M. Battns, Divl Am. Col, Medical & Vet'y units). All Stores and 1st Line Transport were taken and move was exercised, the idea being to practice a move of the division as a whole to a new area. [initials]	

A. C. Eagles
Major Royal ?
Commanding ~~[illegible]~~ 2nd Royal Marines

Appendix 1 to Vol IV of War Diary 2nd Royal Marines

ISSUED AT..6.10pm.. SECRET COPY NO..10.....

OPERATION ORDERS NO.......21

BY LIEUT., COLONEL A.R.H. HUTCHISON R.M.L.I.

COMMANDING 2ND., ROYAL MARINES.

Battalion Headquarters,

2nd., September 1916.

1.........The 1st., Royal Marines will relieve the 2nd., Royal Marines in the line to-morrow. Relief to commence at 6-30 a.m.

2.........On relief Battalion will go into Brigade Reserve.

3.........Headquarters, "B" and "C" Co., will move to FOSSE 10. "A" and "D" Co., to BULLY.

4.........Cos., will move independently by Platoons on relief via BOVRIL ALLEY. O.C. Cos'., reporting to Battalion Headquarters by runner when relief is completed.

5.........Lieut., Cook will take over Billets at BULLY by 7-0 a.m. 2nd., Lieut., Walker will take over billets at FOSSE 10 by 5-30 a.m.

6.........."B" and "C" Co., will send Platoon Guides to Battalion Headquarters at 8-0 a.m.

7.........Trench Stores will be handed over to relieving Cos., using A.F.W. 3405, Duplicate copies in manuscript to be rendered to Orderly Room by 7-0 p.m. to-night.

8.........O.C. "A" Co., will detail a sentry to prevent anyone moving down BULLY ALLEY after 6-30 a.m. to-morrow.

9..........The Royal Dublin Fusiliers at present attached will move out with the Battalion and report to their Co., Commander in BULLY.

10.........Headquarter Officers Chargers and Mess Cart, also Medical Cart will be at BULLY at 9-0 a.m. Cookers of "A" and "D" Co., and one Water Cart will be sent to BULLY, "B" and "C" Co., and one Water Cart to FOSSE 10.
Officers Valises, Medical Stores and Orderly Room Boxes to be sent up by 9-0 a.m.

11.........Battalion Headquarters will close at P.C. 5 on completion of relief and reopen at FOSSE 10.

Copies to :-
No., 1 Retained.
No., 2 O.C. 1/R.M.
No., 3 O.C. "D" Co. R.D.F's.
No., 4 O.C. "A" Co.,
No., 5 O.C. "B" Co.,
No., 6 O.C. "C"Co.
No., 7 O.C. "D"Co.,
No., 8 O.C. "Howe"
No., 9 Q.M. & T.O.
No., 10 War Diary.

A.G. Farquharson
Captain and Adjutant,
2nd., Royal Marines.

Appendix II to Vol IV of War Diary 2nd Royal Marines

Issued at.......   S E C R E T.   COPY NO...2..

OPERATION ORDERS NO.....32

BY LIEUT., COLONEL A.R.H. HUTCHISON R.M.L.I.
COMMANDING 2ND., ROYAL MARINES.
"-"-"-"-"-"-"-"-"-"-"-"-"-"-"-"-"

Battalion Headquarters,
6th., September 1916 .

1........The 2nd., Royal Marines less half an Company plus "B" Co., 10th., Battalion Royal Dublin Fusiliers will relieve the 1st., Royal Marines in the Front Line to-morrow.

2........"B" Co., Royal Dublin Fusiliers will occupy the Right and "D" Co., 2nd., R.M. the left of the Front Line. "B" Co., will be in MOROCCO SOUTH, "C" Co., MOROCCO NORTH. Battalion Scouts of "B" and "C" Co., will be accomodated in MOROCCO NORTH in Dug-Out nearest BULLY ALLEY, those of "A" and "D" Co., will rejoin their Cos., after tea to-day.

3........Half "A" Co., will be accomodated in GUMBOOT and will supply left Crater Jumping Party, the remaining half will move into Billets vacated by "B" Co., 10th., Bn., Royal Dublin Fusiliers at FOSSE 10, and come under 1st., Royal Marines for Tactical and Brigade Fatigue purposes.

4........"D" Co., 2nd., Royal Marines will be at the entrance to BULLY ALLEY at 6-30 a.m. "B" Co., ~~xxxx~~ R.D.F's will leave FOSSE 10 at 6-0 a.m. and will be met by an Officer from "A" Co., at the entrance to BULLY. This Officer will assist O.C. "B" Co., R.D.F's in taking over the line.
Headquarters, Scouts, "B" and "C" Co., will leave FOSSE 10 at 6-30 a.m.

5..........Cos., will move by half platoons at 100 yards distance.

6.........O.C. Co's., will report to Battalion Headquarters by runner when relief is completed.

7.........Officers Baggage of "B" and "C" Co., to be dumped by "C" Co., Cookers by 6-0 a.m. "A" and "D" Co., outside "A" Co., Billets at same time, Transport Officer to arrange for removal of same, also for transport of half "A" Co., Officers Gear to FOSSE 10 from BULLY, details to be given to T.O. by O.C. "A" Co.,

8.........Officers Mess Cart will be at Orderly Room at 6-0 a.m. to take Officers Mess Trays as far as BULLY.

9.........Transport Officer will arrange to remove Co., Cookers, Water Carts, Orderly Room Boxes and Medical Officers Stores back to HERSIN at 6-0 a.m.

continued.

10.......To-morrows ration will be carried on the men.

11.......Headquarters will close at FOSSE 10 at 6-0 a.m. and re-open at P.C. 5 at 6-0 a.m.

"-"-"-"-"-"-"-"-"-"-"-"-"

L. A. Marshall

Lieut.& Assistant Adjutant,
2nd., Royal Marines.

Copies to :-

No., 1 Retained.
No., 2 O.C. 1st., R.M.
No., 3 O.C. "D" Sq., R.D.F's.
No., 4 O.C. "A" Co.,
No., 5 O.C. "B" Co.,
No., 6 O.C. "C" Co.,
No., 7 O.C. "D" Co.,
No., 8 Q.M. and T.O.
No., War Diary.

Appendix 10 to Vol IV of War Diary 2nd Royal Marines

Issued at 12-5 p.m.   S E C R E T.   Copy No. 9

OPERATION ORDERS NO.. 23

BY LIEUT., COLONEL A.R.H. HUTCHISON C.M.G. R.M.L.I.

COMMANDING 2ND., ROYAL MARINES.

"_"_"_"_"_"_"_"_"_"_"_"_"

Battalion Headquarters,

10th., September 1916

1.....The 1st., Royal Marines will relieve the 2nd., Royal Marines less half "A" Co., plus "D" Co., 10th., Battalion Royal Dublin Fusiliers on Monday 11th., inst., commencing at 6-0 a.m.

2.....On relief the Battalion will go into Brigade Reserve.

3 ....Headquarters, "D" and half "A" Co., will move to FOSSE 10, "B" Co., and "C" Co., to BULLY.

4.....Cos., will move independently by Platoons on relief via BOVRIL ALLEY, O.C. Co's reporting to Battalion Headquarters by runner when relief is completed. "D" Co., 10th., Bn., R.D.F's will move via BULLY ALLEY, MOROCCO NORTH and BOVRIL.

5.....O.C. Co's., will render to Battalion Headquarters Work Done, Operation and Intelligence Reports by 9-0 a.m.

6.....Lieut., Thomas will take over Billets at BULLY by 6-30 a.m. Lieut., Cook will take over Billets at FOSSE 10 by 7-30 a.m.

7.....Trench Stores will be handed over to relieving Cos., using A.F.W. 3406, Duplicate copies in manuscript to be rendered to Orderly Room by 7-0 p.m. to-night. 10 Water Cans per Co., 3 per Crater Jumping Party and 4 Battalion Headquarters will be handed over 'Filled'

8.....O.C. "C" Co., will detail a sentry to prevent anyone moving down BULLY ALLEY after 6-0 a.m. to-morrow.

9.....Transport Officer will make the usual arrangements for Officers Chargers, Co., Cookers etc., etc., Quartermaster will arrange for breakfast ration only to be sent up.

10....Battalion Headquarters will close at P.C. 5 on completion of relief, and re-open at FOSSE 10.

"_"_"_"_"_"_"_"_"_"_" _"_"_" _"

E.A. Marshall
Lieut., and Assistant Adjutant,
2nd., Royal Marines.

Copies No.
1 Retained.
2 O.C. 1st., R.M.
3 O.C. "D" Co., R.D.F's
4 O.C. "A" Co.,
5 O.C. "B" Co.,
No. 6 O.C. "C" Co.
No., 7 O.C. "D" Co.,
No., 8 Q.M. and T.O.
No. 9 War Diary

Appendix IV to Vol IV of War Diary 2nd Royal Marines

ISSUED AT. 2.0 p.m. S E C R E T COPY NO....8....

""""""""""""""""

OPERATION ORDER No 24

BY LIEUT., COLONEL A.R.H. HUTCHISON C.M.G. R.M.L.I.

COMMANDING 2ND., ROYAL MARINES.

"-"-"-"-" -" -"-"-"-" Bn., Headquarters
14th., September 1916

1....The 2nd., Royal Marines will relieve the 1st., Royal Marines in the front line to-morrow commencing at [illegible]-0 a.m.

2...."B" Co., will occupy the right and "C" Co., the left of the line. "A" Co., will be in MOROCCO SOUTH (less one Platoon in GUMBOOT) and "D" Co., in MOROCCO NORTH.

3...."A" and "D" Co., will provide the usual Crater Jumping Parties.

4....Cos., will move up by half platoons at 100 yards distance, "B" Co., will be at the entrance to BULLY ALLEY at [illegible]-0 a.m. followed by "C" Co., Headquarters, "A" and "D" Cos., will leave FOSSE 10 at [illegible]-0 a.m. in the order here stated.

5....Periscopes for "B" and "C" Co., will be drawn from the Orderly Room at 6-0 p.m. to-day.

6....O.C. Co's will report to Battalion Headquarters by runner when relief is completed.

7....To-morrows rations will be carried on the men.

8....Transport Officer will arrange to remove Cookers, Water Carts, and Officers Valises, Orderly Room Boxes and Medical Stores at [illegible]-0 a.m.

9....Officers Mess Cart will be at FOSSE 10 at 8-30 a.m. to take Officers Mess Traps as far as BULLY.

10....Headquarters will close at FOSSE 10 at 8-30 a.m. and reopen at P.C. 6 at 11-30 a.m.

"-"-"-"-"-"-"-"- "-"-"

Copies to :-

1 Retained.

2 O.C. "A" Co.,

3 O.C. 1st., R.M.

4 O.C. "B" Co.,

5 O.C. "C" Co.,

6 O.C. "D" Co.,

7 Q.M. and T.O.

8 War Diary.

C G Farquharson

Captain and Adjutant,

2nd., Royal Marines.

"CONFIDENTIAL"

Headquarters,

2nd., Royal Marines,

2nd., November 1916.

5

707

VOLUME.... 5
WAR DIARY

OF

2ND., ROYAL MARINES

FROM

1ST., OCTOBER 1916

TO

31ST., OCTOBER 1916

A. R. H. Hutchison

Lieut., Colonel R.M.L.I.

Commanding 2nd., Royal Marines

TO/ The A.G's Office,

3rd., ECHELON.

Instructions regarding War Diaries and Intelligence Summaries are contained in F. S. Regs., Part II. and the Staff Manual respectively. Title pages will be prepared in manuscript.

WAR DIARY or ~~INTELLIGENCE~~ SUMMARY.

October 1916

(Erase heading not required.)

Army Form C. 2118.

2nd Royal Marines

Place	Date	Hour	Summary of Events and Information	Remarks and references to Appendices
MONCHY-BRETON	1st		Church Parade. Capt. C.G. Farquharson left for 190th Bde. Lt Richards & 3 NCOs left for Gas Course at FERME-DESTRAYELLE.	CHA
	2nd		Coy training, 1 platoon A Coy musketry. Lt Col A R H Hutchison, CMG & Capt C.G. Farquharson rejoined from 190th Bde. Major L.W. Miller RMLI joined Bn.	CHA
	3rd		Arms inspection: heavy rain.	CHA
	4th		Bn marched to LIGNY-ST-FLOCHEL (T23d) station & entrained for ACHEUX. Lieuts Weeks & Cook to F.A. Detached parties rejoined Bn.	CHA Appendix I a 4th Reference France 57.D
	5th		Bn arrived ACHEUX (P13) detrained & marched to ENGELBELMER (O.12) & went in to billets.	CHA
ENGELBELMER	6th		Inspection of Arms, gas helmets etc. Lt Col A R H Hutchison left for 190th Bde. Major C E C Cagles assumed command. Officers reconnoitred roads alarm posts etc.	CHA
	7th		Inspection of Arms etc. Training. Transport lines moved to FORCEVILLE (P21). Officers reconnoitred trenches to firing line.	CHA
	8th		One officer, fifty six other ranks, guard on Reserve Army Prisoners at ACHEUX. Bn marched to HEDAUVILLE (P34) & went in to huts. Lieut G. Holloway rejoined Bn.	CHA Appendix II a 4th
HEDAUVILLE	9th		Working parties. Inspection of arms etc. Officers reconnoitred roads & trenches to Divn area.	CHA
	10th		Coy training. Officers reconnoitring trenches.	CHA
	11th		Coy training. Lt S.A. Walker rejoined from Hosp. Working parties.	CHA
	12th		Coy & Bn training. Working parties. Officers reconnoitred trenches.	CHA
	13th		Working parties.	CHA
	14th		Working parties. One other rank to Etaples, Lewis Gun course. Lieut D.L. Young and five other ranks returned from English leave	CHA

Instructions regarding War Diaries and Intelligence Summaries are contained in F. S. Regs., Part II. and the Staff Manual respectively. Title pages will be prepared in manuscript.

2

WAR DIARY
or
~~INTELLIGENCE SUMMARY.~~
(Erase heading not required.)

October 1916

Army Form C. 2118.

2nd Royal Marines

Place	Date	Hour	Summary of Events and Information	Remarks and references to Appendices
HEDAUVILLE	15th		Working parties. Lieut. S.A. Walker and 10 other ranks to Reserve Army Rest Camp at AULT	[illegible]
	16th		Working parties. Lieut. H.V. Scott-Wilcox to Bn, attached to L.T.M.Bty from Div. Train	[illegible]
	17th		Working parties. Coy training. Bn transport moved to HEDAUVILLE from FORCEVILLE	[illegible]
	18th		Working parties. Coy training. Lt Col. A.R.H. Hutchison D.M.G. R.M.L.I. from 190th Bde, assumed command. Major L.W. Miller R.M.L.I. appointed 2nd i/c	[illegible]
	19th		Working parties.	[illegible]
	20th		Working parties.	[illegible]
	21st		Bn moved to ENGELBELMER (Q25.B88) & went into tents & shelters. Officers reconnoitred trenches. Working parties night.	[illegible]
ENGELBELMER	22nd		Working parties	[illegible]
	23rd		Working parties	[illegible]
	24th		Working parties T/Lieut O.L. Young to Field Ambulance	[illegible]
	25th		Working parties T/Lieut S.A. Walker to Field Ambulance, Temp. Lieut D.B. Woolley struck off strength on transfer to Royal Flying Corps. Aircraft very active, several duels, one hostile machine seen to fall	[illegible]
	26th		Working parties. Temp. 2nd Lt Richards to Field Ambulance. Heavy rain	[illegible]
	27th		Working parties. Very heavy rain	[illegible]
	28th		Working parties. Shifted bivouac to a dryer place 100 yards from old bivouac. The Commander-in-Chief Sir Douglas Haig inspected the Batn. Men fallen in by Sections outside their bivouacs for same	[illegible]

Instructions regarding War Diaries and Intelligence Summaries are contained in F. S. Regs., Part II. and the Staff Manual respectively. Title pages will be prepared in manuscript.

WAR DIARY
or
~~INTELLIGENCE SUMMARY~~.
(*Erase heading not required.*)

October 1916

Army Form C. 2118.

2nd Royal Marines

Place	Date	Hour	Summary of Events and Information	Remarks and references to Appendices
	Oct			
ENGLEBELMER	29th		Working Parties	[initials]
	30th		Working Parties. Temp. Lieut C.L. Andrews (Act. Adjt) to Field Ambulance	[initials]
HEDAUVILLE	31st		Battn moved back into shelters at HEDAUVILLE	[initials]

A. R. H. Hutchison
Lieut Colonel
Commanding 2nd Royal Marines.

T2134. Wt. W708–776. 500000. 4/15. Sir J. C. & S.

SECRET

Appendix I to Volume V of War Diary 2nd Royal Marines

ISSUED AT 4-50 p.m. COPY NO. ?.....

OPERATIONS ORDERS NO. 50

BY LIEUT., COLONEL A.R.H. HUTCHISON C.M.G. R.M.L.I.

COMMANDING 2ND., ROYAL MARINES.

Battalion Headquarters,

3rd., October 1916.

1..The 188th., Brigade will move by rail to a new area to-morrow. Accomodation will consist mainly of shelters and tents.

2..The 2nd., Royal Marines will parade in Marching Order at 11-40 a.m. and be formed up in Column of Route in the following order "D" "A" "B" "C" on the road ~~.........~~. C. 31 c.8. d., the head of the column resting on the cross roads W.31. c. facing west by 11-50 a.m. Battalion will march to the entraining point at LIGNY ST. FLOCHEL (W. 33 d.)

3..Dinners will be at 11-0 a.m. unexpired portion of days ration to be carried on the men.

4..The Battalion Quartermaster Sergeant and 10 Men from "A" Co., will parade at 11-15 a.m. and proceed to entraining station arriving there by 12-30 p.m. This party will take over the following days rations from the S.O. and load the same on to the train.

5..A lorry to carry blankets to station will call at Co., Headquarters in the following order "C" "B" "A" "D" commencing at 9-0 a.m. Blankets to be tightly rolled in bundles of 10 and distinctly labelled. "A" Co., will detail One N.C.O. to accompany the blankets to the station and remain in charge of them until Battalion arrives. On arrival of the Battalion at the station blankets will be distributed to individuals; as there will be no transport for them at the other end, they will be carried on banderole round the pack

6..The Mess Cart will call at Officers Messes in the same order as the Motor Lorry commencing at 11-0 a.m. Mess Gear ONLY is to be put in to the cart.

7..The transport remaining with the Battalion will parade at 4-30 p.m. and march to cross roads at ORLENCOURT where they will join the Brigade Column and march to entraining station.

8..One Officer and one N.C.O. per Co., as advanced Billeting Party will report to the Staff Captain at 9-30 p.m. to-night at LIGNY ST. FLOCHEL station. PARADE AT ORDERLY ROOM at 8-0 p.m.

C.G. Farquharson
Captain and Adjutant,
2nd., Royal Marines.

Copies to :-
No., 1 Retained. No., 5 O.C. "D" Co.,
No., 2 O.C. "A" Co., No., 6 Quartermaster.
No., 3 O.C. "B" Co., No., 7 War Diary.
No., 4 O.C. "C" Co.,

Appendix II to
Volume V. of War Diary
2nd Royal Marines

9-45 a.m.
ISSUED AT........ SECRET COPY NO. 7......

OPERATION ORDERS NO...71

BY MAJOR C.E.C. EAGLES R.M.L.I.

COMMANDING 2ND., ROYAL MARINES.

"-"-" -"-"-" -"-"-"-"-"-"- 2"

Battalion Headquarters,
9th., October 1916

1.....The 63rd., (R.N.) Division will releive the 2nd. , Division in the REDAN SECTION to-day.

2.....The 2nd., Royal Marines will move to ~~XXXXX~~ HEDAUVILLE and go into Billets.

3.....Starting point will be at the cross roads Q. 35. a. 5.7. Order of march "A" "B" "C" "D" Cos., Lewis Guns, Transport.

4....Cos. , will parade on Alarm Posts in marching order at 12-45 p.m.

5....Blankets tightly rolled in Bundles of 10 are to be dumped by Co's., by NOON.

6....Transport Officer will arrange to have horses for Cookers and Water Carts, and ~~Maltese~~ G.S. limbers and Mess Cart and Medical Cart at ENGLEBELMER by NOON.

7....Mess Cart will collect Officers Mess Gear starting at "C" and "D" Co., Mess at 12-15 p.m.

8....Officers Valises to be at Co., Dumps by NOON.
Co., Stores to be taken to Quartermasters Stores by 11-30 a.m.

9....Headquarters will close at ENGLEBELMER at 12-30 p.m. and re-open at HEDAUVILLE on arrival (place ~~xxx~~ will be notified later)

"- "- "-"-"- "-"-"-"-

Copies to :-

No., 1 Bata ined.
No., 2 O.C. "A" Co.,
No., 3 O.C. "B" Co.,
No., 4 O.C. "C" Co.,
No., 5 O.C. "D" Co.,
No., 6 Transport Officer.
No., 7 War Diary.

C G Farquharson
Captain and Adjutant,
2nd., Royal Marines .

"CONFIDENTIAL"

Headquarters,

2nd., Royal Marines,

6th., June 1916.

188/63.

VOLUME 6.

WAR DIARY

OF

2 ND., ROYAL MARINES.

FROM

1ST., NOVEMBER 1916.

TO

30th., NOVEMBER 1916.

C.C. Ragle

Major R.M.L.I. for

Officer Commanding 2nd., Royal Marines

TO:- The A.G's Office,

3rd., Echelon.

9260

Instructions regarding War Diaries and Intelligence Summaries are contained in F. S. Regs., Part II. and the Staff Manual respectively. Title pages will be prepared in manuscript.

WAR DIARY
or
~~INTELLIGENCE~~ SUMMARY. November 1916

(Erase heading not required.)

Army Form C. 2118.

2nd Royal Marines

Place	Date	Hour	Summary of Events and Information	Remarks and references to Appendices
Hedauville	1 Nov		Working parties – 2nd Lieut Yeldham from duty to sick list	CCL
–"–	2 "		Working parties – Battalion bathed at ACHEUX –	CCL
–"–	3 "		Working parties at MESNIL	CCL
–"–	4 –		Working parties at MESNIL – Casualties two O.R. killed & five O.R. wounded –	CCL
–"–	5 –		Battalion proceeded to PUCHEVILLERS by march route & billetted there –	CCL
PUCHEVILLERS	6 –		Battalion preparing for inspection by Div^l Commander.	CCL
PUCHEVILLERS	7 –		Battalion returned to billets at HEDAUVILLE by march route – Very wet.	CCL
HEDAUVILLE	8 –		Working parties at KNIGHTSBRIDGE –	CCL
–"–	9 –		do — do –	CCL
–"–	10 –		do do.	CCL
–"–	11 –		Battalion proceeded to ENGLEBELMER & bivouacked:	CCL
ENGLEBELMER	12 –		Served out extra days ration, ammunition, flares, bombs, sandbags etc in preparation for attack – O.C. Companies instructed companies in their duties for attack –	CCL
		2 pm.	Battalion left bivouac & took up battle stations	CCL

T2134. Wt. W708–776. 500000. 4/15. Sir J. C. & S.

Instructions regarding War Diaries and Intelligence Summaries are contained in F. S. Regs., Part II. and the Staff Manual respectively. Title pages will be prepared in manuscript.

WAR DIARY
or
~~INTELLIGENCE SUMMARY.~~
(Erase heading not required.)

Army Form C. 2118.

2nd Royal Marines

Place	Date	Hour	Summary of Events and Information	Remarks and references to Appendices
	Nov. 13 } 14th }		Battalion attacked according to attached orders. 2nd Lieuts. Stokes, Welman + Dewar killed. Capt + Adjt C. G. Farquharson, Capt Edwards, Capt Staughton, Capt. Goldring, Capt. Bisset Lieuts. Thorold, Thomas 2nd Lieuts. Holloway, Grayson, Wrangham + Garnett wounded. Surg. J. MacB. ROSS R.N. wounded, remained at duty.	Appendix II CCL
	15th	12 noon	Battalion relieved in Station Road by 37th Div. Marched to HEDAUVILLE via ENGELBELMER and went into huts.	
HEDAUVILLE	16th		Battalion moved by motor lorries to PUCHEVILLERS and billetted.	CCL
PUCHEVILLERS	17th		Marched to GEZAINCOURT + billetted.	CCL
GEZAINCOURT	18th		Marched to BERNAVILLE + billetted.	CCL
BERNAVILLE	19th		Cleaning up wagons, kit, etc. 14 Lewis gunners + 80 O.R. joined.	CCL
—"—	20th		G.O.C. 63rd Div. addressed Brigade on recent operations.	CCL
—"—	21st		Marched to CRAMONT + billetted. Col. Hutchison went on leave. Major L. W. Miller assumed command.	CCL
CRAMONT	22nd		Marched to BRAILLY. Sub Lt. Ritson (Howe Bn.) + Sub Lt Marshall (ANSON Bn.) attached for duty.	CCL
BRAILLY	23rd		Marched to Forest L'Abbaye and billetted.	CCL
Forest L'Abbaye	24th		Marched to ROMAINE + billetted.	CCL

T2134. Wt. W708—776. 500000. 4/15. Sir J. C. & S.

Instructions regarding War Diaries and Intelligence Summaries are contained in F. S. Regs., Part II. and the Staff Manual respectively. Title pages will be prepared in manuscript.

WAR DIARY
or
~~INTELLIGENCE~~ SUMMARY.
(Erase heading not required.)

Army Form C. 2118.

2nd Royal Marines

Place	Date	Hour	Summary of Events and Information	Remarks and references to Appendices
ROMAINE	25th		Mustered kit – one Coy. armourers inspection. 233 O.R.s joined –	C.A.E.
—"—	26th		Divine Service – Medical inspection	C.A.E.
—"—	27th		Commenced training on Batn training area. 72 O.R.s joined –	C.A.E.
	28th		Training and armourers inspection	C.A.E.
	29th		Route march to Le Crotoy.	C.A.E.
	30th		Training – Sub Lieut Ritson (lent from HOWE Bn) left – armourers inspection	C.A.E.

[signature]
Major R.M.L.I.
Comdg 2nd R.M.

Appendix I

S E C R E T. COPY NO...1......

MEDICAL ARRANGEMENTS 2ND., ROYAL MARINES.

Battalion Stretcher Bearers will lie out in the open behind their respective Co's.,

When the Cos., advance they will ~~xxxxxx~~ evacuate any wounded there may be to the Aid Post at Battalion Headquarters. (St., James St.,)

As soon as these are dealt with the Battalion Aid Post will be transferred to that evacuated by the 1st., Royal Marines in our original front line.

The Battalion Stretcher Bearers will then under the direction of the Battalion Medical Officer evacuate wounded from 'No mans land', handing them over to the Field Ambulance Bearers who will have a relay post in the original front line. There will be numerous Field Ambulance Men to assist in the clearing of "No mans land"

When Battalion Headquarters move to the new position in the green line, the Aid Post will again move and take up a position near the new Bn., H.Q. its exact position will be indicated by a small Red Cross Flag. The collection of the wounded will then commence.

Should cases owing to heavy shelling or other causes be unable to be evacuated to the Field Ambulance Bearers, they will be collected in dug-outs which will be marked by a wooden peg, bearing a red Cross with the Battalion Distinguishing Mark underneath,

thus :- 

As each successive objective is gained, a suitable site, near Bn., Headquarters and marked with a red Cross Flag, will be chosen as a temporary Aid Post.

Officers are particularly reminded of the following:-

(a) That every man must be in possession of a ~~xxxxxxxx~~ serviceable Field Dressin
Only very small supplies can be carried by the Medical Personnel

continued.

continued.

Hence the dressing for a man's wound will depend almost entirely on his being in possession of a field dressing.

(b) Many Officers have private supplies of morphia. This should on no account be used unless there is no chance whatever of seeing a Medical Officer within an hour. Morphia taken by the mouth will have no analgesic effect for at least an hour. If given hypodermically it acts in a few minutes. As the risk of a poisonous dose would be great if some has already been taken by the mouth, an additional dose, hypodermically can not be given with any safety.

<u>WATER</u>. No water found in the German Trenches must be drunk until pronounced by a medical Officer to be free from poison.

J. N. McB. Ross.

Temp., Surgeon, R.N.
Medical Officer, 2nd., Royal Marines.

Copies to :-

No., 1 Retained.

No., 2 O.C. 2/R.M.

No., 3 A.D.M.S. 63rd., (R.N.) Division.

No., 4 O.C. "A" Co.,

No., 5 O. C. "B" Co.,

No., 6 O.C. "C" Co.,

No., 7 O.C. "D" Co.,

No., 8 Surgeon Sparrow.

No., 9 War Diary.

Appendix II

ISSUED AT. 3.30. . . . S E C R E T. COPY NO. . .1. . . . .

OPERATION ORDERS NO. 32
BY LIEUT., COLONEL A.R.H. HUTCHISON C.M.G. R.M.L.I.

COMMANDING 2ND., ROYAL MARINES.

"-"-"-"-"-"-"-"-"-"-"-"- "-"-"-"-"-"

Reference:- Attached Maps.

Bn., Headquarters,
23rd., OCTOBER 1916.

1.....(a) The 188th., Infantry Brigade will take part in an attack on the enemy to be carried out on both sides of the River ANCRE.

(b) The 189th., Infantry Brigade will be on the ri ght, and 51st., Division will be on the left of the Brigade.

(c) Date of attack, to be referred to as "Z" day, and the hour of zero will be notified later.

2.........The objectives allotted to the MMMMM., Battalions of the 188th., Brigade ame shown on the attached Map.

3.........GREEN, YELLOW and BLUE lines will be captured by the 188th., Brigade.

4.........The Brigade wi ll assault with two Battalions in Front Line and two Battalions in Support. Each Battalion will have four Cos., in line in column of Platoons, the Platoons forming, First, Second, Third and 4th., waves respectively. Platoons will be in single rank with 10 Yards distance between 1st., and 2nd., waves and 50 yards distance between the remainder.

5.........The attack wi ll be carried out in accordance with the table of barrages already issued. It must be clearly understood however that the times are published merely as a guide to the Infantry and are not orders for the exact time of assault.
It is of paramount mmmmmmmmm and vital importance that the Infantry keeps close up to the Artillery Barrage, and advances whenever it lifts.

6.........The assembly trenches of the Battalion aee as follows:-
First and Second waves in REGENT STREET.
Third and Fourth " in BUCKINGHAM PALACE RD., and ST., JAMES STREET.
"A" Co., will be on the right with its Right flank resting on GABION AVENUE, "B" "C" and "D" Cos., will be prolonged to the left. The frontage of each Co., will be 75 yards.
The Dividing Line between "B" and "C" Co., will be LONG ACRE.

7.........The jumping off place of the Øos., will be in adwance of these trenches, in the open. The position of the front wave will be marked by a tape, the succeeding waves forming up in rear parallel to this wave and at the prescribed distances.
These jumping off places will be occupied by 4-45 a.m. on "Z" day, by which time, every Officer, N.C.O. and man will be in position.

continued.

continued.

No movement of any sort whatever must take place after this time until Zero as the position can be overlooked from the THIEPVAL RIDGE.
Bayonets wi ll be fixed before daylight.

8........At Zero hour all four waves will rise up and advance, the leading wave being 150 yards behind the fourth wave of the 1st., Royal Marines.

9.........The 1st., Royal Marines and "Howe" Battalions will be responsible for the capture of the first objective i.e. Dotted GREEN LINE.

10.........The 2nd., Royal Marines with the "Anson" Bn., on their right will pass through this objective and capture the GREEN LINE. T he First and second waves will advance straight through to this line and consolidate it. The 3rd., wave will clean up dug-outs in STATION ROAD. The Fourth wave will clean up dotted BLUE LINE a nd the many dug-outs on the reverse slope of the Hill.
Bombers from "A" Co., will block STATION ALLEY.

11.........The 1st., Royal Marines will pass through this objective and capture the YELLOW LINE. As soon as they have passed through Cos., will be reformed in their four waves and follow the 1st., Royal Ma rines.

12.........The advance against the dotted YELLOW LINE will be carried out by the 2nd., Royal Marines. All Four waves gaining this objective.

13.........The 1st., Royal Marines will again pass through and capture the dotted BROWN LINE.

14....... Immediately the dotted BROWN LINE is captured the whole of the Brigade will advance to and consolidate the BLUE LINE. Battle Patrols will be sent forward from this line along the entire front especially torwards ARTILLERY ALLEY, which will be blocked by Bombers.

15.........The 190th., Infantry Brigade will pass through and capture the BROWN LINE.

16.........During our advance strong points will be formed by "D" Co., at Q. 11. d. 4.5. on the dotted BLUE LINE and at Q. 6.d.8.4. on the dotted YELLOW LINE. Half a section of No., 2 Company Divisional Engineers will assist. If these points are not completed when the line again advances, men are NOT to be left behind for this purpose.

17.........Two Stokes Mortars will accompany the Battalion. Thes e will be used on the Left Flank and also against any Strong Points met with.

18.........Contact aeroplanes will be employed to fix the positions gained by the Infantry in accordance with the principles lately practised.
Flares will be lighted :-

(a) On attaining each objective.
(b) Whenever hung up.
(c) When an aeroplane sounds its Klaxon Horn.
(d) Just before dark and in the early morning if an

continued.

continued.

an aeroplane is above.

As the supply of these is limited, they must be used sparingly.

19............The 63rd., Division attack will be assisted by Six Tanks. These have been ordered to keep as close to the barrage as possible. Infantry must however be specially warned <u>NOT</u> to wait for the Tanks.

20............Watches will be synchronised at 9-0 p.m. on "Y" Day and at one hour before Zero.

21............All Troops will be in Battle Order; Great Coats and Waterproof Sheet will be carried on the back in place of the pack. Each Man will carry four sandbags (passed through the belt, two each side); One day' ration, one Iron Ration.

22............Platoon Bombers will be organised into parties and will each carry a bucket with 15 Bombs.
Each Man of Lewis Gun Teams will carry two bombs.

23...... . .50% of the Troops will carry Tools. These will be carried by the 2nd., 3rd., and 4th., Waves and will be carried slung across the back. Spun Yarn is available for this purpose.

24............Men carrying wire cutters will wear a Yellow Armlet.

25............Runners will wear a Blue Armlet with a white stripe.They will be lightly equipped and will not carry rifles.

26............No Papers likely to be of value to the enemy will be taken over the parapet.

27............It must be impressed on all concerned that they are on no account to halt because Units on their Flanks aee held up. The best way of assisting their neighbours on such occasions will be to continued their own advance.

28............O.C. Cos., will ensure that water bottles are filled before marching off from Bivouac. Two petrol tins of water per platoon will be carried up to the assembly trenches for use on "Y" night, thus enabling men to start the attack with full waterbottles.

29............Prisoners taken will be sent down in batches to Bn., H.Q. Escorts for prisoners must be reduced to a minimum and walking wounded cases utilised for this duty as far as possible.

30............All reports are to be sent in duplicate at a few minutes interval.

31............Battalion Headquarters will be established in the first place in ST., JAMES STREET near its junction with LONG ACRE. As each objective is captured Bn., H.Q. will be advanced to that objective.

continued.

continue d.

32.......Battalion Aid Post will be near Battalion Headquarters.

C.G. Ingharson

Captain and Adjutant,

2nd., Royal Marines.

Copies t o:-

No., 1 War Diary.
No., 2 Briga de Headquarters. (188th.,Bde.,)
No ., 3 O.C. "A" Co.,
No., 4 O.C. "B" Co.,
No., 5 O.C. "C" Co.,
No., 6 O.C. "D" Co.,
No., 7 O.C. 188th., T.M. Battery.

Appendix III

ISSUED AT. 3:30 pm . . . . . S E C R E T. COPY NO. . . . 7 . . .

OPERATION ORDERS NO..33

BY LIEUT., COLONEL A.R.H. HUTCHISON C.M.G. R.M.L.I.

COMMANDING 2ND., ROYAL MARINES.

"-"-"-"-"-"-"-" -" -"-"-"-" -" -" -"-" -" -"

Bn., Headquarters,

2nd., Royal Marines.

23rd., October 1916.

1..........The 2nd., Royal Marines will take up it's Battle position to-morrow.

2..........The Battalion will parade at 4-0 p.m. and move off by Platoons at 2 00 yards distance in the following order :- "D" "C" "B" and "A" Co., via GABION AVENUE.

3..........Blankets will be rolled in bundles of 10 and labelled and will be ready by 9-0 a.m. to-gether with all packs for conveyance to Q.M. Stores.
Officers Baggage will be ready at the same time.

4..........During the forenoon, rations for the following day will be served out to individuals, also sandbags, ammunition, flares and Bombs as in O.O. No., 32.

5..........On arrival in the Trenches, all Company runners are to report at Battalion Headquarters.

6..........Co., Cooks will proceed with their Cos., to the trenches and will take all available dixies. Further orders will be given them by the Sergeant Cook.

7..........Battalion Headquarters will be in ST. JAMES. STREET near its junction with LONG ACRE.

C.G. Farquharson

Captain and Adjutant,
2nd., Royal Marines.

Copies to:-
No., 1 Retained.
No., 2 O.C. "A" Co.,
No., 3 O.C. "B" Co.,
No., 4 O.C. "C" Co.,
No., 5 O.C. "D" Co.,
No., 6 Q.M. and T.O.
No., 7 War Diary.

C O N F I D E N T I A L.

Headquarters,

2nd., Royal Marines.

31st., December 1916m

VOLUME 6

W A R D I A R Y

O F

2ND., ROYAL MARINES.

F R O M

1st., December 1916

T O

31st., December 1916.

T O /

The A.G's Office.

3rd., Echelon.

A. R. H. Hutchison

Lieut., Colonel R.M.L.I.

Commdg., 2 nd., Royal Marines.

Instructions regarding War Diaries and Intelligence Summaries are contained in F. S. Regs., Part II. and the Staff Manual respectively. Title pages will be prepared in manuscript.

WAR DIARY
or
~~INTELLIGENCE SUMMARY~~.
(Erase heading not required.)

December 1916.

2nd Royal Marines.

Army Form C. 2118.

Place	Date	Hour	Summary of Events and Information	Remarks and references to Appendices
ROMAINE	1st		Battalion training. Fatigue party of 1 Off. + 110 O.R. unloading RE stores at ROMAINE station. Fifty four reinforcements received.	ACL
— " —	2		Battalion training. 30 yards range completed.	ACL
— " —	3rd		Divine Service at PONTHOILE. Lieut. Col. ARH Hutchison returned from leave.	ACL
— " —	4th		Battalion training. Sub Lt Marshall RNVR rejoined ANSON Bn	ACL
— " —	5th		Lieut. Col ARH. Hutchison command 188th Inf Bde temporarily. Batn route march to LE CROTOY. One hundred & three reinforcements joined.	ACL
— " —	6th		Battalion digging Brigade practice trenches. 2nd Lt. A.B. WOODHALL officially reported wounded.	ACL
— " —	7th		Battalion training.	ACL
— " —	8th		Battalion training. Cross country run. One hundred and three reinforcements joined	ACL
— " —	9th		Capt. Mathew RAMC relieved T/Surg. J McB. Ross who proceeded on leave	ACL
— " —	10th		Battalion Training	ACL
— " —	11th		Battalion Training. Issued operation order	ACL
— " —	12th		Battalion moved by march route to RUE area & billeted in RUE + LANNOY	ACL Appendix I

T2134. Wt. W708—776. 500000. 4/15. Sir J. C. & S.

Instructions regarding War Diaries and Intelligence Summaries are contained in F. S. Regs., Part II. and the Staff Manual respectively. Title pages will be prepared in manuscript.

WAR DIARY
or
~~INTELLIGENCE SUMMARY~~.
(*Erase heading not required.*)

December 1916.

Army Form C. 2118.

Place	Date	Hour	Summary of Events and Information	Remarks and references to Appendices
RUE.	13th		Battalion training. P.m. Cross country running	ACL
	14th		Battalion training. Prepared 30 yards range & bayonet fighting ground	ACL
	~~15th~~		Brigade cross country running & bombing competitions. Capt. H.B INMAN R.M.L.I. and T/2nd Lts. F.H WRENN, W.A. LAKE, R.H. VANCE, E.A.N. PALMER, E.S. MAXWELL, R WELLS, C.C. PALMER, G.A NEWLING, R. BRAGG, W.E GREENLAND, R.J. WILLIAMS, A.E HUGHES, J. FITZGERALD, J SWALE with twenty five O.R. joined. T/Lieut. H.N PEARCE rejoined from base.	ACL
	15th		Battalion training. T/Lieut C.O. MITCHELL rejoined from 188th L.T.M. Baty	ACL
	16th		Battalion training. Bn. H.Q. moved from LANNOY to RUE.	ACL
	17th		Divine Service. Issued operation order. Three O.R. joined	ACL
	18th		Battalion moved by march route to VRON & billeted.	ACL Appendix II
VRON	19th		Battalion training.	
	20th		Battalion training. Capt. MATHEW RAMC relieved by T/Surg J McB Ross & returned to 1st F.A.	ACL
	21st		Battalion training. Lieut. A.E. MARSHALL to 63rd Div school at NOUVION	ACL

T2134. Wt. W708—776. 500000. 4/15. Sir J. C. & S.

Army Form C. 2118.

Instructions regarding War Diaries and Intelligence Summaries are contained in F. S. Regs., Part II. and the Staff Manual respectively. Title pages will be prepared in manuscript.

WAR DIARY
or
~~INTELLIGENCE~~ SUMMARY. December 1916

(*Erase heading not required.*)

Place	Date	Hour	Summary of Events and Information	Remarks and references to Appendices
VRON	22nd		Battalion training.	ARH
"	23rd		Battalion training. Army Commander visited Bde. area & inspected	ARH
"			billets and the Bn whilst at training.	ARH
"	24th		Divine Service	ARH
"	25th		Divine Service. Battalion Sports.	ARH
"	26th		Battalion training. Lieut H.N. PEARCE to Lewis gun Course at Le TOUQUET.	ARH
"	27th		Battalion training	ARH
"	28th		Battalion training	ARH
"	29th		Battalion training	ARH
"	30th		Battalion training.	ARH
"	31st		Divine Service.	ARH

A.R.H. Hutchison
Lieut. Colonel R.M.L.I.
Comdg 2nd Royal Marines

T2134. Wt. W708–776. 500000. 4/15. Sir J. C. & S.

APPENDIX I

SECRET.

COPY NO...6.....

OPERATION ORDERS NO.....34

BY MAJOR L.W. MILLER R.M.L.I. COMMDG.,

2ND., ROYAL MARINES.

Bn., Headquarters,

11th., December 1916.

1.........The 2nd., Royal Marines will move by march route to RUE AREA to-morrow and go into billets.

2.........Cos., will parade at 9-0 a.m. and form up at the Quartermaster's Stores by 9-30 a.m. in the following order ~~"[illegible]"~~ ., "H.Q" "B " "A" "C" and "D" Co.,
Head of the column to be 200 yards N.E. of the Q.M. Stores.

3.........Blankets tightly rolled in Bundles of 10 ~~with~~ and clearly marked are to be ready for loading by 7-30 a.m.
These Blankets will be collected by Platoons and Cos., are to make arrangements to have them loaded. Water-proof sheets are NOT to rolled up with the blankets, but are to be carried under the flap of the pack.

4.........."B" Co., will detail a loading party to be at Q.M. Stores at 8-0 a.m. Strength:- 1 N.C.O. and 10 Men. This party will if necessary remain behind until all stores are loaded.
"A" Co., will detail a party of one N.C.O. and 6 Men for loading straw and tools at Orderly Room at 8-0 a.m.

5.........Each Co., and Headquarters will detail a party of 1 N.C.O. and 8 Men to clear up Billets and to fill in latrines. These parties will assemble at Q.M. Stores at 10-30 a.m and follow in rear of Bn., Sergt. Holman will be in charge of this party.

6.........Transport Officer will arrange to collect Officers Valises commencing with "C" Co., at 8-0 a.m. The Mess Cart will ~~be~~ collect Officers Mess Traps at 8-30 a.m. commencing with Q.M. Billet.
Medical Cart will be at the Medical Inspection Room at 8-0 a.m.

7.........Transport will form up ~~immediately~~ and proceed immediately in rear of Battalion

8.........Special attention is to be paid to the cleanliness of Billets. Platoon Sergeants and N.C.O's i/c of Platoons will be held responsible that all Tins are collected into a central spot and that arrangements are made for the disposal of same.
Billets will be inspected by Acting Adjutant and

P.T.O.

continued.

and Medical Officer after the departure of Cos., from their billets. Any neglect will be the subject of disciplinary action.

9..........Lewis Gun Carts will be drawn by their teams, and will march in rear of their respective Cos., The Headquarters guns will proceed in rear of the Battalion and will be drawn by ~~xxxxxx~~ Pack animals.

"-"-"-"-"-"-"-"-"-"-"-"

Major R.M.L.I.

Act. Adjutant, 2nd., Royal Marines.

Copies to :-

No., 1 Officer Commanding,

No., 2 Retained.

No., 3 O.C. "A" and "B" Co.,

No., 4 O.C. "C" Co.,

No., 5 O.C. "D" Co.,

No., 6 War Diary.

Issued at..10.0 p.m   Copy No., 8.

APPENDIX 2

OPERATION ORDERS NO. 35

BY MAJOR L.W. MILLER R.M.L.I.

COMMDG., 2ND., ROYAL MARINES.

"-"-"-"-"-"-"-"-"-"-"-"-"-"-"-"-"-"

Bn., Headquarters,

17th., December 1916.

1..........The Battalion will move by march route to-morrow to VRON, and go into Billets.

2..........Starting point :- CHATEAU at CANTERENE. Head of the column will pass the starting point at 9-30 a.m. Order of March "A" "B" Band "C" "D" and Transport.

3..........Lewis Guns will march with their Co's., Handcarts will be drawn by Co., Pack Animals. Headquarter Guns will march in rear of "D" Co., handcarts being drawn by hand.

4..........Two G.S. Wagons will be available for each Co's Blankets. Guides for these wagons are to be at the Q.M. Stores by 8-0 a.m. The Blankets of Headquarter Details will be collected by a Limber G.S. Wagon at 8-0 a.m.
All Blankets are to be collected in a Central Area in the Co., Billets and loaded under Co., arrangements.
These wagons are to join the Transport in rear of the Column by 9-15 a.m.
Blankets will be clearly marked and rolled in Bundles of 10 before loading.

5..........Billets. Every care is to be taken that the billets are left clean in every respect and O.C.Co's., will report personally to the Officer Commanding before the Column moves off that they have inspected all Billets occupied by their Cos., and found them in a satisfactory condition

6..........O.C. "A" "C" and "D" Co., will send a Guide to Bn., Headqrs., to guide a Limber G.S. Wagon for Officers Valises and Mess Traps at 8-0 a.m.
A Limber wagon will report at "B" Co., H.Q. at 8-30 a.m. for Valises and Mess Traps.
ALL OFFICERS VALISES WILL BE READY BY 8-30 a.m. and Co's., will make their own arrangements for loading.

7..........Attention is called to the necessity of maintaining correct dressing in fours, and that Platoon Commanders keep in the ranks whilst on the march, and maintain the correct intervals.

8..........The Mess Tins and Mugs are to be carried in the pack. The Steel Helmet will be carried on the back of the pack, inside the supporting straps. Waterproof Sheets will be carried folded under the flap of the pack. GREATCOATS ARE NOT TO BE WORN.

continued. P.T.O.

continued.

9............**STRAGGLERS.** No man is to fall out on the line of march without a chit signed by an Officer. O.C."D" Co., will arrange for a rear party of One Officer, 1 N.C.O. and 4 Men to march in rear of the Transport and collect stragglers.

10...........**FATIGUE PARTY.** O.C. "C" Co., will detail a Fatigue Party of One N.C.O. and 12 Men to parade in Marching Order at the Q.M. Stores at 7-50 a.m. for Loading Stores.
O.C. "A" Co., will detail a party of One N.C.O. and 6 Men to load up Straw. A G.S. Wagon collecting the same from "A" Co., Billets. This Party will if necessary remain behind until this task is completed.
O.C. "A" Co., will also detail a Party of One N.C.O. and 6 Men to dismantle the Rifle Range at 7-30 a.m.
All Planks, Timber and Sandbags are to be removed.
Transport will be arranged for these stores at 8-15 a.m. This party will then proceed with the wagon to the Transport Lines and load Bayonet Fighting Straw on it.
This party will proceed to the Rifle Range in FULL Marching Order.

11...........**BREAKFAST.** O.C. Co's., will take steps to ensure that breakfast is over in sufficient time for the above orders to be carried out.

"-"-"-"-"-"-"-"-"-"-"-"-"-"

12............**GUARD.** The Guard at present mounted will march with Headquarter Details.
"C" Co., will provide a Guard of one N.C.O. and Six Privates to mount two hours after the arrival of the Battalion in Billets.

"-"-"-"-"-"-"-"-"-"-"-"-"-"

C.E. Eagles
Major R.M.L.I.
Act., Adjutant, 2nd., Royal Marines.

Copies to :-
No., 1 Officer Commanding.
No., 2 Retained.
No., 3 O.C. "A" Co.,
No., 4 O.C. "B" Co.,
No., 5 O.C. "C" Co.,
No., 6 O.C. "D" Co.,
No., 8 War Diary.

8

C O N F I D E N T I A L.

""""""""""""""""""""""""""""

Headquarters,

2nd., Royal Marines.

1st., February 1917.

VOLUME 8

WAR DIARY OF

2ND., ROYAL MARINES.

FROM

1st., January 1917

TO

31st., January 1917

TO:- A.G's Office.

3rd., Echelon.

A.R.H. Hutchison

Lieut., Colonel R.M.L.I.

Commanding 2nd., Royal Marines.

January 1917

Instructions regarding War Diaries and Intelligence Summaries are contained in F. S. Regs., Part II. and the Staff Manual respectively. Title pages will be prepared in manuscript.

WAR DIARY
or
~~INTELLIGENCE SUMMARY.~~
(Erase heading not required.)

Army Form C. 2118.

2nd Royal Marine Battalion

Place	Date	Hour	Summary of Events and Information	Remarks and references to Appendices
VRON	1st		Battalion Training.	[illegible]
"	2nd		Battalion Training.	[illegible]
"	3rd		Battalion Training.	[illegible]
"	4th		Battalion Training.	[illegible]
"	5th		Battalion Training.	[illegible]
"	6th		Battalion Training.	[illegible]
"	7th		Battalion attended Divine service.	[illegible]
"	8th		Battalion Training.	[illegible]
"	9th		Battalion Training.	[illegible]
"	10th		Dismantling training grounds. Corps commander inspected transport.	[illegible]
"	11th		Battalion filled in training trench system at VERCOURT.	[illegible]
"	12th		Issued Operation order No 36.	[illegible] Appendix I
"	13th		moved by march route to LE TITRE and billetted there. Operation order No 37 issued.	[illegible] Appendix II
LE TITRE.	14th		moved by march route to FONTAINE and billetted there. Operation order No 38 issued.	[illegible] Appendix III
FONTAINE	15th		moved by march route to AUTHEUX and billetted there.	[illegible]
AUTHEUX.	16th		Resting and inspection of feet. Lieut Bennie joined. Issued operation order No 39.	[illegible] Appendix IV

T2134. Wt. W708—776. 500000. 4/15. Sir J. C. & S.

January 1917

Instructions regarding War Diaries and Intelligence Summaries are contained in F. S. Regs., Part II. and the Staff Manual respectively. Title pages will be prepared in manuscript.

WAR DIARY
or
~~INTELLIGENCE~~ SUMMARY.
(*Erase heading not required.*)

Army Form C. 2118.

2nd Royal Marine Battalion

Place	Date	Hour	Summary of Events and Information	Remarks and references to Appendices
AUTHEUX	17th		Continued march to RAINCHEVAL and went into billets there. Transport in difficulties owing to ice and snow. Capt BURTON-FANNING R.M. and 2nd Lieut ANDREWS joined from entrenching Battalion. Operation order No 40 issued.	[illegible] Appendix V
RAINCHEVAL	18th		Resumed march and went into billets at ENGLEBELMER. Issued operation order No 41	[illegible] Appendix VI
ENGLEBELMER	19th		Battalion relieved 9th Bn Sherwood Foresters in St PIERRE DIVION Sector.	[illegible]
St PIERRE DIVION	20th		Issued operation order No 42. Very cold with sharp frost.	[illegible] Appendix VII
"	21st		Carried out internal relief. B Coy relieved D & A Coy relieved C Coy.	[illegible]
"	22nd		Lieut. SPINNEY Intelligence Corps and two Battalion Scouts captured enemy's outpost of seven men about noon.	[illegible]
"	23rd		Carried out internal relief. C Coy relieved B Coy and D Coy relieved A. Issued Operations orders Nos 43 + 44	[illegible] Appendices VIII + IX
"	24th		Very cold with more frost.	[illegible]
"	25th		Relieved by 1st Battalion Royal Marines and went into billets at ENGLEBELMER.	[illegible]
ENGLEBELMER	26th		Working parties and baths.	[illegible]
"	27th		Working parties.	[illegible]
"	28th		Working parties. Issued Operation order No 45.	[illegible] Appendix X
"	29th		Working parties. Issued Operation order No 46.	[illegible]
	30th		Working parties.	[illegible]

T2134. Wt. W708-776. 500000. 4/15. Sir J. C. & S.

2nd January

Instructions regarding War Diaries and Intelligence Summaries are contained in F. S. Regs., Part II. and the Staff Manual respectively. Title pages will be prepared in manuscript.

Army Form C. 2118.

WAR DIARY
or
~~INTELLIGENCE SUMMARY~~.
(Erase heading not required.)

2nd Royal Marine Battalion.

Place	Date	Hour	Summary of Events and Information	Remarks and references to Appendices
ENGLEBELMER	31st		Relieved 1st Battalion Royal Marines in St PIERRE DIVION.	[illegible]

A. R. H. Hutchison
Lieut.-Colonel
Commanding 2nd Royal Marines

T2134. Wt. W708—776. 500000. 4/15. Sir J. C. & S.

~~Secret~~ Secret

Appendix I

Operation Order No 36.

By Lt Colonel A R H Hutchison C M G D S O R M L I
Commanding 2nd Royal Marines.

Ref Map ABBEVILLE 14 $\frac{1}{100,000}$

In the Field
11th January 1917

(1) The Battalion will move by march route to LE TITRE on 13th inst.

(2) Companies will move in the following order:-
Hd Qrs "C" "D" "B" "A" & will march at interval of 200 yds between the head of each Company; 50 yds between the Hd Qrs & "C" Company

(3) The Transport will follow at an interval of 200 yds
Pack Horses will march with their Companies

(4) There will be an interval of 500 yds between the Head of the Battalion & the unit in front.

(5) The Battalion will be formed ready to move at 9.25 A.M.
Hd Qrs & "C" Coy on the RUE NATIONALE N of the Cross Roads at the S. end of VRON. "D" "B" "A" Coys & Transport on the side road just N & E of the Cross Roads.

(6) The first halt will take place at 10.50 AM & at every ten minutes to the Clock hour afterwards.
The march will be resumed at each Clock hour

(7) Watches will be synchronised at 9.0 AM.

(8) Lewis Guns will be packed in 3 L.G.S. Wagons by 5.0 P.M. on the 12th. These wagons will march at the head of the Transport. Lewis Gun Teams will march in rear of their Coys

(9) Blankets of "A" Coy will be rolled & dumped at their Westernmost billet by 8.0 AM. The Blankets of the remainder of the Battalion will be dumped at the Q.M. Store at the same hour. Particular care is to be taken with the rolling of Blankets. They are to be tightly rolled in Bundles of 10 only & labelled. Each Coy will provide a loading party of 1 NCO & 4 men who will be required to re-roll Blankets if necessary.

Contd P.T.O.

(10) Officers baggage will be dumped at Q M Stores by 8.30 AM

(11) Officers Mess Cart will call at Coy Hd Qrs Messes in the order "A" "D" "B" "HQ" & "C" commencing at 8.15 A.M. It will not remain more than 5 minutes at any Mess

(12) O.C Coys will report personally by 8.45 AM that all billets are left in a clean & satisfactory state

(13) A billetting party of 1 NCO per Coy under 2nd Lt Vance will leave at 9.0 AM on bicycles & report to Bde Staff Officer at Church LETITRE at 11.0 A.M. They will parade at Orderly Room at 8.45 A.M.

O.C "A" Coy
" "B" "
" "C" "
" "D" "
War Diary File

J Campbell 2nd Lt
A/Adjt 2/RM

Secret

Appendix II

Operation Order No 37.

By Lt Colonel A. R. H. Hutchison C M G D.S.O R.M.L.I.
Commanding 2nd Royal Marines

In the Field
13-1-17.

Ref. map. ABBEVILLE 14

(1) The battalion will resume it's march tomorrow and go into billets at FONTAINE

(2) Coys will march in the following order, maintaining the same intervals as today.
Hd Qrs. "B" "A" "D" "C"

(3) Coys will parade at 9.15 A.M. and be ready to move at 9.25 A.M.

(4) Blankets will be at Q.M. Store at 8.0 A.M. Loading parties of 1 NCO + 4 men per Coy to attend at that time

(5) Billetting party of 1 N.C.O. per Coy. 1 for H.Q + 1 for Transport will parade at the Orderly Room at 9.0 A.M. + proceed by bicycle to FONTAINE. 2nd Lieut VANCE will be in charge, + report to Town Major if there is one, otherwise to the Mayor.

(6) "C" Coy will provide Rear party of 1 Officer, 1 NCO + 4 men to collect + bring on stragglers.

(7) Transport arrangements will be as for today's march.

(8) Officers baggage will be collected at Q.M. Stores at 8.30 A.M.

(9) O.C. Coys will report personally by 8.45 A.M. that all billets are left in a clean & satisfactory state

Contd P.T.O.

(10). Officers Mess Cart will call at Coy H.Q Messes in the order "A" "B" "D" "C" H.Q. commencing at 8.15 AM.
It will not remain more than 5 minutes at any Mess.

J. Campbell.
2nd Lieut. R. M.
Act Adj. 2nd R/M.

War Diary

Appendix III

Secret

Operation Order. No 38.

By Lt Colonel. A. R. H. Hutchison C.M.G. D.S.O. R.M.L.I
Commanding 2nd Royal Marines

Ref. Map - ABBEVILLE 14 — In the Field
LENS 11 — 14-1-17.

(1) The battalion will resume its march tomorrow and go into billets at AUTHEUX.

(2) Coys will march in the order. H.Qrs. "A" "D" "C" "B" The same intervals will be maintained untill 12 noon, when the battalion will close to normal interval.

(3) A haversack ration will be carried

(4) Coys will be ready to move at 8.30 A.M.

(5) Billetting party under 2nd Lt Jewling will parade at Orderly Room at 8.15 A.M. and will report to Staff Officer at Church at AUTHEUX at 11.0 A.M.

(6) Blankets will be at Q.M. Store by 7.0 A.M. Officers baggage by 7.30 A.M. Loading parties as for today

(7) Transport Officer will make same arrangements as for today, but one hour earlier

(8) O.C Coys will report billets correct at 8.0 A.M.

J. Campbell

2nd Lieut R.M.
Act. Adj. 2nd R/M.

Secret.

Appendix IV

Operation Order No 39.

By Lt Colonel A. R. H. Hutchison C.M.G. D.S.O. R.M.L.I.

Commanding 2nd Royal Marines

In the Field

Ref Map - Lens 11.

16-1-17.

(1) The battalion will resume its march tomorrow and go into billets at RAINCHEVAL.

(2) Coys. will march in the following order. H. Qrs. "D" "C" "B" "A"

(3) The Battalion will assemble at the N.E. exit of the village and move off at 11. A.M.

(4) Transport will march at 10.0 A.M. and move via MACFER to the ~~FEIN~~ FIEN VILLERS - HEM Road where it will wait for the Battalion

(5) Blankets will be at Q.M. Stores by 9.0 A.M. O.C. Coy will provide the usual loading parties.
Officers baggage will be at Q M Store at same time

(6) A haversack ration will be carried. Dinners will be served on arrival at ~~at~~ RAINCHEVAL about 4. P.M.

(7) Billetting party under 2nd Lieut A. J. Palmer will parade at the Orderly Room at 10.45. A.M. They will report to Bde. Staff Officer at Mairie RAINCHEVAL at 1. P.M.

(8) O.C. Coys will report billets clean & correct at 10.0 A.M.

C Campbell Lieut RM
Adjt 2 R.M.

Secret

Appendix V

Operation Order No. 40

By Lt Colonel A R H Hutchison C M G D S O R M L I
Commanding 2nd Royal Marine

Ref Map Lens 11

In the Field
17-1-17

(1) The Battalion will resume its march tomorrow & go into Billets at ENGLEBELMER

(2) Coys will parade at 9 45 AM Starting point 400 yds E of Church on the ARQUEVES Road at 10 0 AM Order of March H Qrs 'C' 'B' 'A' 'D' Transport & the same interval will be kept as for today

(3) A Haversack ration will be carried Dinner will be served on arrival at ENGLEBELMER

(4) Billetting party as for today & will report to Town Major ENGLEBELMER by noon Parade at Orderly Room at 9 0 AM

(5) Officer Commanding will see O C Coy at 9 0 AM.

(6) Blankets will be at Q M Store at 8 30 AM O C Coy will provide the usual Loading parties.
Officers baggage will be at Q M Store at 9 0 AM

A C Hayes

Major R M L I
Act Adjt 2nd R/M L I

Secret

Operation Order No 41. Appendix VI

By Lt Colonel A. R. H. Hutchison C M G. D.S.O. R M L I
Commanding 2nd Royal Marines

In the Field
18-1-17

Ref Map Lens 11.

(1) The 2nd R M will relieve the 9th Sherwood Foresters in the Line immediately S of the ANCRE tomorrow

(2) "C" Coy will hold CANAL & FERDAN Trench
"D" Coy will occupy HANSA Trench "A" & "B" Coys will be in Reserve at ST PIERRE DIVION.

(3) Coy will move from ENGLEBELMER as follows
C Coy at 10 AM "D" Coy at 10.15 AM "A" Coy at 10.30 AM
"B" Coy at 2.30 P.M.

(4) Coys will move as far as MESNIL by Companies after which they will move by Platoons at 250 yds Distance

(5) Cookers & Limbers with Lewis Guns will march with Companies maintaining the same interval as Platoons.

(6) The route will be MARTINSART – MESNIL – Cross Roads E of AVELUY Wood where guides will meet them – HAMEL MILL ROAD – ST PIERRE DIVION.

(7) Packs will be left at Q.M. Stores. "A" & "B" Coys will take one Blanket per man.
Officers Kits must be returned to Q.M. Stores tomorrow morning before marching off.

(8) Coys will report as as soon as relief is complete
Code word for Relief Complete – BAGS.

Copy 5 War Diary

C. C. Eagles
Major R M L I
Act Adjt 2nd R/M.

WAR DIARY

No 8

Secret

Appendix VII

Operation Order No 42.

By Lt Colonel A. R. H. Hutchison C.M.G. D.S.O. R.M.L.I.
Commanding 2nd Royal Marines

Bn. H.Q.
20-1-17.

(1) The Battalion will carry out an interval relief as under tomorrow 21st Inst.

(2) "B" Coy will relieve "D" Coy in HANSA, commencing at 1.30 P.M. Platoon guides from "D" Coy will report to O.C. "B" Coy at E entrance to tunnel at that time. Platoons will move at intervals of 10 minutes. On relief "D" Coy will move into E end of tunnel.

(3) "A" Coy will relieve "C" Coy in FERDAN and CANAL commencing at 5.0 P.M. Guides from "C" Coy to report to O.C. "A" Coy at W. end of tunnel at that time. Platoons will move at intervals of 5 minutes. On relief "C" Coy will go into W. end of tunnel.

(4) "A" Coy will have tea before going up + "C" Coy will have dinner + tea when it comes down.

(5) O.C. Coys will report when relief is complete. Code word BABY.

C.C. Eagles Major
RMLI
A/adjt

O.C. A Coy
" B "
" C "
" D "

B.S.M.
Cook Sergt
War Diary
File

Operation Order No 45

by

Lieut Col. [illegible] Cmdg [illegible]

[illegible]

1. The Bn will stay out in [illegible] today.

2. [illegible] Coy will relieve B in HAWSH[illegible] commencing at 1.30 p.m. Platoon guides from B Coy will report to [illegible] Coy at that time. Platoons will move at [illegible] intervals. [illegible] Coy will move [illegible] the [illegible] to the [illegible].

3. [illegible] Coy will relieve A Coy in FERDAN(?) and [illegible] guides [illegible] at 5 p.m. [illegible] from A Coy will report [illegible] at that time. Platoons will move at five minutes interval. [illegible] A Coy will occupy the E end of [illegible]. All Lewis guns will be left in position and taken over by the in-going Coy. A Coy will take over the guns in the [illegible].

4. [illegible] Coy will have tea before going up [illegible] A Coy will have their tea [illegible] after [illegible].

5. [illegible] Coy will [illegible] blankets [illegible] ready to be taken over by [illegible] Coy.

1. [illegible]

2. B [illegible]

C [illegible]

[illegible]
Major [illegible]

23.1.17 [illegible]

Copy No. 1 to OC A Coy
No. 2 to OC B Coy
No. 3 to OC C Coy
No. 4 to OC D Coy
No. 5 to War Diary

Appendix VIII

Secret

1.9
Appendix IX

Operation Order No. 44.

Lieut. Colonel H. F. H. Hutchison C.M.G. D.S.O. R.M.L.I.
Commanding 2nd Royal Marines

Bn. H.Q.
23.1.17.

1. The 1/R.M. will relieve 2/R.M. in the sector on 25th. On relief the battalion will go into billets in ENGLEBELMER.
2. Route – HAMEL – AVELUY WOOD – MARTINSART – ENGLEBELMER. MESNIL may be entered after dark.
An interval of 250 yds will be maintained between platoons until AVELUY WOOD (or MESNIL) is reached, after which 500 yds. between companies. Strict march discipline is to be maintained.
4. All company trench stores will be handed over and duplicate receipts obtained from O.C. incoming company.
5. "A" "B" & "C" Coys. will have dinner at 11.30 A.M. and tea on arrival at billets. Soup will be prepared for D Coy. and will be given out as they pass the tunnel. They will have tea & dinner on arrival in billets.
6. The Field cookers will be handed over to 1/R.M. and theirs will be taken over at ENGLEBELMER.
7. "A" & "B" Coys. will be ready to move at 12.30 P.M. and will move out of the E. end of Tunnel as the companies of 1/R.M. move in at the W. end.
8. "A" Coy will send 4 guides & "B" Coy. 8 guides to the S. end of HAMEL to conduct the first three Coys. of 1/R.M. to the tunnel. B Coy. will detail an officer to be in charge of these guides.
9. "C" Coy will send platoon guides to report to Bn. Sergt. Major at E. end of Tunnel at 1.30 P.M. to conduct HANSA Coy. to its position.
10. "D" Coy. will send platoon guides to report to Bn. Sergt. Major at E. end of Tunnel at 4.45 P.M. to conduct the front line Coy.
11. Four Bn. H.Q. runners will be detailed to be at the S. entrance to HAMEL at 2.30 P.M. to conduct the remaining 1/R.M. Coy. to the Tunnel.

13. O.C. Coys will ensure that all Gum boots are returned to the Drying room [illegible]

14. Head Quarter Coy will be ready to march off at [illegible] p.m.

15. [illegible] will be responsible that all Lewis Guns and [illegible] are brought down and [illegible] [illegible] for guns with A & B Coys. One for guns with C Coy and one for guns with D Coy. The Lewis Guns will be [illegible] near the [illegible]

16. As soon as C & D Coys have had their dinners the Coys will march to billets under [illegible] [illegible] orders [illegible]

16. O.C. Coys will report relief complete as follows:

A & B Coys by Runner

C & D Coys personally

17. O.C. Coys will ensure that [illegible] and the tunnel are left perfectly clean.

18. Billeting party consisting of [illegible] Coy Q.M. Sergeants will report to TOWN MAJOR ENGLEBELMER on forenoon of 25th to take over billets. The Q.M. Sergts will meet their Coys on arrival and conduct them direct to their billets.

19. O.C. Coys will report when their Coys are settled in their billets.

20. [illegible] will close here on completion of relief and reopen at ENGLEBELMER.

Copies to:
No. 1 [illegible]
2 O.C. 1st R.M.
3 O.C. A Co.
4 O.C. B Co.
5 O.C. C Co.
6 O.C. D Co.
7 Q.M. & T.O.
8 Bn. S.M.
9 War Diary

[illegible signature]

Major R.M.L.I.
Comdg 1st R. Marines

Continued.

10............DRESS for BATTALION - Fighting Order- Greatcoats folded inside Waterproof Sheet carried on the back.

11............O.C. Co's., will report when relief is complete. Code word for Relief Complete- T W I N S.

Major R.M.L.I.

Act., Adjt., 2nd., Royal Marines.

2[illegible]-1-17

Copies to :-

No., 1 Retained.

2 O.C. 1st., R.M.

3 O.C. "A" Co.,

4 O.C. "B" Co.,

5 O.C. "C" Co.,

6 O.C. "D" Co.,

7. Quartermaster and Transport Officer.

8. Medical Officer.

9. Bn., S.M. and Cook Sergt.,

10. War Diary.

Appendix X

ISSUED AT...NOON... COPY No. ....5......

OPERATION ORDERS No. ...[illegible]

BY LIEUT., COLONEL A.R.H. HUTCHISON C.M.G. D.S.O. R.M.L.I.

COMMANDING 2ND., ROYAL MARINES.

Reference Map ...[illegible]
57D.S.E. 1/10,000

Bn., Headquarters,

26-1-17.

1...........“C” Co., will move to-morrow [illegible] inst., from ENGLEBELMER to dugouts in [illegible] ROAD just behind Brigade Headquarters.

2...........The Co., will parade ready to march off at 11-30 a.m.

3...........A Guide from the First Field Co., R.E. will meet the Co., at Bde., Headquarters at 3-30 p.m.

4...........The Co., Field Cooker will accompany the Co.,

5...........ROUTE - MARTINSART - Cross Roads West of AVELUY - AVELUY Wood Road - PASSERELLE DE MAGENTA.

6...........A Battalion Runner will be detailed as GUIDE as far as Brigade Headquarters.

7...........Blankets will be rolled in BUNDLES and stacked ready for loading in limbers. The place where they are stacked to be communicated to the Transport Officer. They will be sent up at the same time as the rations.

8...........Route for rations - MARTINSART - MESNIL - [illegible].

9...........All Trench Stores such as periscopes, Verys Pistols etc., will be taken.

10...........DRESS...Marching Order, Trench [illegible] will be worn.

[signature]
Major R.M.L.I.
Act., Adjt., 2nd., Royal Marines.

Copies to :-
No., 1 Retained.
2 O.C. “C” Co.,
3 Q.M. and T.O.
4 Bde., H.Q.
5 War Diary.

Appendix XI

ISSUED AT 4.0 p.m. S E C R E T. COPY NO. 10

OPERATION ORDERS NO......46

BY LIEUT., COLONEL A.R.H. HUTCHISON C.M.G.D.S.O.R.M.L.I.

COMMANDING 2ND., ROYAL MARINES.

Bn., Headquarters,

Ref:- Map- LENS 11
57D. S.E.

29-1-17.

1..........The 2nd., Royal Marines will relieve the 1st., Royal Marines in the Trenches on Wednesday 31st., inst.,

2..........."B" Co., will occupy CANAL and SERDAN Trenches. "A" Co., will occupy LAMSA Trench. "C" and "D" Co., will be in Reserve in the TUNNEL.

3..........."A" Co., will move at 10-0 a.m. Headquarters will move at 10-15 a.m. "B" Co., will move at 10-30 a.m. "C" Co., will move at 1-0 p.m. and "D" Co., at 3-15 p.m.

4...........Route for "A" "B" and "D" Co., and Headquarters - MARTINSART Cross Roads W. of AVELUY [illegible].
Companies will move as such as far as the Cross Roads on MESNIL- AUTHUILLE ROAD, after which they will move by platoons at 200 yards interval.

5..........."A" and "B" Cos., will go in at the W. end of TUNNEL and move along to the E. end as soon as there is room. "A" Co., will commence relief of LAMSA at 1-30 p.m. "B" Co., will then move to the E. end of TUNNEL and "C" Co., will enter at W. end. "B" Co., will commence relief of Front Line at 3-0 p.m. When clear "D" Co., will enter at E. end.

6...........Co., Cooks of "A" and "B" Cos., will leave ENGLEBELMER under the Cook Sergt., at 8-30 a.m. and take over the Cookers.
Dinner for "A" Co., must be ready by NOON.
Transport Officer will detail a wagon to go with the Cooks to carry the rations.

7...........Lewis Guns will be packed in the limbers by 5-0 p.m. on the 30th., inst., "D" Co., will hand over their guns to "B" Co., The Guns of these two Cos., will be packed in the same limber which will accompany "B" Co.,

8...........Transport Officer will convey the blankets of "C" Co., to the TUNNEL for use of the two Reserve Cos., "C" Co., will leave a small guard on the Blankets if they are not removed before marching off.

9...........Packs and Blankets of "A" "B" and "D" Cos., will be taken to the Q.M. Stores by 9-0 a.m. Transport Officer will collect the Packs of "C" Co., and take them to the Q.M. Store on the forenoon of the 31st., inst.,

continued.

C O N F I D E N T I A L.

Headquarters,

2nd., Royal Marines.

2nd., March 1917.

VOLUME 9

WAR DIARY OF

2ND., ROYAL MARINES

FROM

1st., Feb., 1917

TO

28th., Feb., 1917

[signature]

TO:- A.G's Office.

3rd., Echelon.

Major R.M.L.I.

Commdg., 2nd., Royal Marines.

9 of 9

Instructions regarding War Diaries and Intelligence Summaries are contained in F. S. Regs., Part II. and the Staff Manual respectively. Title pages will be prepared in manuscript.

WAR DIARY
or
~~INTELLIGENCE SUMMARY.~~
(Erase heading not required.)

Army Form C. 2118.

2nd Battn Royal Marines -

Place	Date	Hour	Summary of Events and Information	Remarks and references to Appendices
February				
St PIERRE - DIVION	1st		Operation order No 47 issued - Intense frost	CCL Appendix I
"	2nd		Internal relief carried out by companies - Intense frost	CCL
	3rd		Operation order No 48 issued. Intense frost	CCL Appendix II
	4th		Operation orders No 49 issued. Intense frost - carried out internal relief.	CCL
	5th		Lieut H.E. BENNIE RM. and 2nd Lieut C.C. PALMER RM. wounded in FERDAN TRENCH.	CCL
	6th		Major L.W. MILLER assumed command during the temporary absence of Col. Hutchison on duty. During the night we occupied GRANDCOURT without serious opposition.	CCL
	7th		Consolidated position just east of Grandcourt with ~~by~~ 'B' Coy under Capt. H B INMAN R.M.L.I. supported by 'C' Coy under Capt. G.E. CUTCHER RM.	CCL
	8th		Issued operation orders Nos 50 and 51.	CCL Appendix III & IV
	9th	a.m.	'B' & 'C' Coys relieved by two companies 1st Royal Marines and moved into reserve	CCL
		p.m.	A & D Coys relieved by two companies 1st Royal Marines and moved into reserve.	CCL

T2134. Wt. W708-776. 500000. 4/15. Sir J. C. & S.

Instructions regarding War Diaries and Intelligence Summaries are contained in F. S. Regs., Part II. and the Staff Manual respectively. Title pages will be prepared in manuscript.

WAR DIARY
or
~~INTELLIGENCE~~ SUMMARY.
(Erase heading not required.)

Army Form C. 2118.

2nd Batt: Royal Marines

Place	Date	Hour	Summary of Events and Information	Remarks and references to Appendices
St PIERRE DIVION	10th		Operation order No 52 issued and Battalion moved by march route to MACKENZIE huts. MARTINSART.	Appendix V
MARTINSART	11th		Working parties	
—"—	12th		Lieut. Col A R H Hutchison resumed Command of Battalion. Working parties	
—"—	13th		Working parties. Capt H.B. INMAN RMLI wounded.	
—"—	14th		Battalion relieved 4th Bedfords in left divisional sector North of the river ANCRE.	
	15th		Long spell of frost breaks. 2nd Lieut PER HARDY RM wounded and remained at duty.	
BEAUCOURT				
—"—	16th		2nd Lieut R.J. WILLIAMS and 2nd Lieut J. SWALE wounded whilst out wiring in front of posts.	
—"—	17		T/Capt. H.W PEARCE wounded. Battalion started to consolidate a line of shell holes on northern front of the advance of 1st Royal Marines.	
—"—	18th		Continuation of consolidation. Much inconvenience from hostile snipers and M.G.s.	

Instructions regarding War Diaries and Intelligence Summaries are contained in F. S. Regs., Part II. and the Staff Manual respectively. Title pages will be prepared in manuscript.

WAR DIARY
or
INTELLIGENCE SUMMARY.
(Erase heading not required.)

Army Form C. 2118.

Place	Date	Hour	Summary of Events and Information	Remarks and references to Appendices
	February			
BEAUCOURT	19th		Relieved 1st Royal Marines in their new position in SUNKEN Road, with R3 a 2.5	Ref. ANCRE VALLEY map.
— " —			'C' Coy. 'D' Coy moved into PUISIEUX Rd Trench. R2 Central.	AEL
— " —	20th		Occupied and consolidated series of shell holes at R2 b06 - R2 b9.9	AEL
— " —	21st		Relief commenced by 7th Royal Fusiliers.	AEL
ENGELBELMER	22nd	AM	Relief completed by 7th Royal Fusiliers, and Battalion moved to billets in ENGELBELMER.	AEL
— " —				
	23rd		Battalion resting and cleaning up.	AEL
— " —	24th		Lieut E.L ANDREWS, 2nd Lieuts J C. LEE. A.A. RICE, E.G. VAGG, E.A. Godfrey and 90 O.R. joined –	AEL
— " —	25th		Major L.W MILLER assumed command during the temporary absence of Lieut. Col. A.R.H. Hutchison CMG DSO RMLI on leave. Working parties	AEL
— " —	26th		2nd Lieut A.A. RICE proceeded to ENGLAND on transfer to R.E.	AEL
			2nd Lieut C.H KEARNEY and 17 O.R joined from base and 54 O.R from 8th Entrenching battalion.	AEL
— " —	27th		Working parties	AEL
— " —	28th	PM	Moved from ENGELBELMER and went into billets at BOUZINCOURT 'C' Coy moved to PUCHEVILLERS –	AEL

L W Miller
Major RMLI
Commanding 2nd Royal Marines

T2134. Wt. W708–776. 500000. 4/15. Sir J. C. & S.

APPENDIX No I

ISSUED AT..7-0 pm.   COPY No....6...

OPERATION ORDER No...47

BY

LIEUT., COLONEL [illegible] C.M.G.D.S.O. R.M.L.I.

COMMANDING 2ND., ROYAL MARINES.

"."

Bn., Headquarters,
1-3-17.

1......The usual internal relief will be carried out tomorrow the 2nd., inst.,

2......"D" Co., will relieve "A" Co., in [illegible], commencing at 7-[illegible] p.m. On relief "A" Co., will move into E. end of Tunnel.

3......"C" Co., will relieve "B" Co., in [illegible], commencing 8-15 p.m. On relief "B" Co., will move into W. end of Tunnel.

4......"A" Co., will provide Guard for Bn., H.Q. one hour after relief is complete.

5......All Lewis Guns will be left in position and taken over by the incoming company.

6......Code word for relief complete – A D A M.

[illegible signature]
Major R.M.L.I.,
Act., Adjt., 2nd., R.M.

COPIES to :-
No. 1 Retained,
No. 2,3,4,5 [illegible],
L.G. "A" "B" "C" & "D" Co.,
No., 6 War Diary.

APPENDIX No 2 4

ISSUED AT 12.45pm. S E C R E T. C O P Y No. 7...

OPERATION ORDER NO....48

BY LIEUT., COLONEL A.R.H. HUTCHISON C.M.G. D.S.O. R.M.L.I.

COMMANDING 2ND., ROYAL MARINES.

"-"-"-"-"-"-"-"-"-"-"-"-"-"-"-"-"-"

Bn., Headquarters.

3rd., February 1917

1.......The 189th., Infy., Brigade on our left will attack PUISIEUX and RIVER TRENCH To-night.

2.......Zero Time will be notified later under the code Word "COOT" i.e. COOT 10-0 p.m. etc.,

3.......The 2nd., Royal Marines will co-operate by Lewis Gun Fire against the enemy trenches S. of GRANDCOURT immediately to our front.

4.......O.C. "C" Co., will therefore arrange for Lewis Gun Fire from the Posts in CANAL.

5.......All Troops will be in a state of readiness. as retaliation may possibly ensue on the Battalion Sector, as many troops as possible will be kept under cover, but ready to "Stand to".

6.......O.C. "C" and "D" Co., will keep Battalion Headquarters informed of Progress of Events at least every quarter of an hour and oftener if necessary.

The following code will be used :-

CRAB = Heavy Shelling on our front.
SALMON = Moderate Shelling on our Front.
SOLE = Quiet on our Front.
LOBSTER = Enemy counter attacking.
COD = Our attack progressing.
SHARK = Our attack held up.

7.......Wiring parties for to-night are cancelled.

Copies to :-
No., 1 Retained.
No., 2 O.C. "A" Co.,
No., 3 O.C. "B" Co.,
No., 4 O.C. "C" Co.,
No., 5 O.C. "D" Co.,
No., 6 Lewis Gun Officer.
No., 7 War Diary.

C.C. Chagles
Major R.M.L.I.
Acting Adjt., 2nd., Royal Marines.

APPENDIX 3

ISSUED AT 11.0 AM SECRET. COPY NO. 6...

""""""""""""""""""""

OPERATION ORDER NO...49

BY LIEUT., COLONEL A.R.H. HUTCHISON C.M.G.D.S.O.

R.M.L.I.

COMMANDING 2ND., ROYAL MARINES.

1... Bn., H.Q. 4-2-17.

1......"A" Co., will relieve "C" Co., in Front line to-day, commencing at 5-30 p.m.

2......"B" Co., will relieve "D" Co., in LANSA to-morrow, commencing at 12-30 p.m.
"B" Co., will have dinner BEFORE, and "D" Co., AFTER relief.

3......"B" Co., will relieve the Guard of "A" Co., on Battalion Headquarters at 1-30 p.m. TO-DAY.
"C" Co., will relieve "B" Co., Guard at 10-0 a.m. TO-MORROW.

4......Code Word for relief of trenches complete - EVE.

C.E.Eagles

Major R.M.L.I.
Act., Adjt., 2nd., Royal Marines.

Copy. No. 1 Retained.
No., 2,3,4, and 5 O.C. "A"B"C" & "D" Co.,
No., 6 War Diary.

APPENDIX 3

ISSUED AT....4-30 p.m. S E C R E T. COPY NO......

OPERATION ORDER NO.........50

BY MAJOR I.W. MILLER R.M.L.I. COMMANDING

2ND., ROYAL MARINES.

"-"-"-"-"-"-"-"-"-"-"-"-"-"-"-"-"-"

Reference. Map 1/20,000. Bn., Headquarters.

8th., February 1917.

1.........."B" and "C" Cos., will be relieved to-night by Two Cos., of the 1st., Royal Marines.

2..........On relief "B" Co., will move into the Tunnel and "C" Co., into the Dug-outs at GORDON CASTLE.

3..........After relief is complete, "A" and "D" Cos., will come under the orders of the Officer Commanding, 1st., Royal Marines.

4..........O.C. "B" and "C" Cos., will if possible, send back a small billetting party to take over Billets.

5..........All information, re situation, will be carefully handed over to the relieving Cos., also all tools and stores.

6..........O.C. Cos., will report personally at Battalion Headquarters on relief.

Major R.M.L.I.

Act., Adjt., 2nd., Royal Marines.

Copies to :-

No., 1 Retained.
No., 2 O.C. "A" Co.,
No., 3 O.C. "B" Co.,
No., 4 O.C. "C" Co.,
No., 5 O.C. "D" Co.,

APPENDIX H.

ISSUED AT...11.50 pm... S E C R E T. COPY NO...8...

OPERATION ORDERS NO......51

BY MAJOR L.W. MILLER R.M.L.I. COMMDG.,

2ND., ROYAL MARINES.

"-"-"-"-"-"-"-"-"-"-"-"-"-"-"-"-"-"-"-"

Bn., Headquarters,

8th., February 1917.

1.........."A" and "D" Cos., will be relieved to-morrow by 2 Cos., of the 1st., Royal Marines.
"D" Co., will be relieved at 9-30 a.m. and on relief will occupy the Dug-outs at MILL ROAD BANK.
"A" Co., on relief will occupy the W. end of the TUNNEL, sending one Platoon to the 1st., Field Ambulance.

2..........O.C. "A" Co., will arrange for Platoon Guides to be at the junction of COCKSHYE and FERDAN at 10-0 a.m. for the relief of O.G. 1.

3..........O.C. "A" Co., will arrange to collect all Trench Stores in CANAL TRENCH and FERDAN into a central Dump off COCKSHYE AVENUE. He will also arrange for the new Dump at R.14.b.5.0. to be tabulated and handed over, receipts being obtained. O.C. "D" Co., will hand over Trench Stores in their present position, obtaining receipt for same.

4..........The Transport Officer will arrange for the Cookers of "C" and "D" Cos., to be moved to their new positions by 3-0 a.m. to-morrow.

5.........."B" Co., having taken over 554 Blankets from the 1st., Royal Marines, the Quartermaster will arrange to hand over a similar number forthwith.
He will arrange for the Blankets of "A" Co., less One Platoon to be sent to ST., PIERRE DIVION TUNNEL and those of "D" Co., to PAISLEY DUMP. The packs of Cos., will be sent up as convenient.

6..........After relief, the disposition of Cos., will be :-

"A" Co., (less One Platoon at First Field Ambulance) ST., PIERRE DIVION.

"B" Co.,.......ST., PIERRE DIVION.

"C" Co., at THIEPVAL.

"D" Co., in Dug-outs at MILL ~~BANK~~ ROAD BANK.

7..........The Scouts and Dug-out Platoon will rejoin their Cos., after dinner.

8.........."A" and "D" Cos., will dine after relief. Ordinal

continued.

9............O.C. "D" Co., will send an Advance Party of 1 N.C.O. and 4 Men to take over Dug-outs at 6-0 a.m.

10.........O.C. Cos., will report personnaly on relief.

11.........Battalion Headquarters will remain as at present.

C.E.Eagles

Major R.M.L.I.

Act., Adjt., 2nd., Royal Marines.

6-3-17.

Copies to :-

No., 1 Retained.

No., 2 O.C. 1st., Royal Marines.

No., 3 O.C. "A" Co.,

No., 4 O.C. "B" Co.,

No., 5 O.C. "C" Co.,

No., 6 O.C. "D" Co.,

No., 7 Quartermaster and Transport Officer.

No., 8 War Diary.

APPENDIX 5

Issued at 12-45 a.m. S E C R E T. COPY NO...7.....

OPERATION ORDER NO........52

BY MAJOR [illegible] MILLER R.M.L.I. COMMANDING

2ND., ROYAL MARINES.

"-"-"-"-"-"-"-"-"-"-"-"-"-"-"-"-"

Reference :- 1/20,000. Bn., Headquarters,

Sheet 57D, S.E. 10th., February 1917.

1.........The 2nd., Royal Marines will be relieved to-day by a Battalion of the West Kent Regiment, and will go into huts at W.30.c.3.[illegible] The relieving Battalion will take over the present Co., Billets

2.........Advanced Party of One N.C.O. per Platoon under Lieut., Campbell will assemble at PASSEROLLE de MAGENTA, Q. 2[illegible].d.4.4. by [illegible]-15 a.m. and proceed to take over Billets by 11-0 a.m.

3.........ROUTE :- MILL ROAD BRIDGE, LANCASHIRE DUMP, Q. 35.d.1.8. and AVELUY ROAD.

Cos., will march at five minutes interval with 100 yards between platoons until the First Field Ambulance is passed, when platoons will close up.

ORDER OF MARCH...."B" "A" "D" H.Q. and "C" Co.,

The head of "B" Co., will pass the cross roads at Q.24.b.[illegible] at 12 NOON.

"C" Co., will join the march at PASSEROLLE de MAGENTA.

4.........Guides, One per Co., and One for H.Q. will meet the incoming Companies of the relieving Battalion at PASSEROLLE de MAGENTA at [illegible]-[illegible] a.m.

continued.

continued.

5..........One Blanket per man will be carried on banderole, the remaining Blankets are to be tightly rolled in Bundles of 10 and dumped at Co., Headquarters by 9-30 a.m. Transport Officer will arrange to collect these blankets at that time, making two trips if necessary.
He will also arrange for Transport of Medical Stores and Orderly Room Gear.

6..........Cookers will accompany their Cos.,

7..........Quartermaster Stores and Transport Lines will remain in their present position.

8..........O.C. Cos'., will ensure that their Billets are handed over clean, and that all Co., Stores are taken back.

9..........ACKNOWLEDGE.

Major R.M.L.I.

Act., Adjt., 2nd., Royal Marines.

Copies to :-
No., 1 Retained.
No., 2 O.C. "A" Co.,
No., 3 O.C. "B" Co.,
No., 4 O.C. "C" Co.,
No., 5 O.C. "D" Co.,
No., 6 Q.M. and T.O.
No., 7 War Diary.

C O N F I D E N T I A L.

Headquarters,

2nd., Royal Marines.

~~31st., March 1917~~.

1st., April 1917.

Vol 10

VOLUME 10

W A R D I A R Y.

OF

2ND., ROYAL MARINES.

FROM

1st., March 1917 to

31st., March 1917.

A.C. Eagles

Major R.M.L.I.

Commanding 2nd., Royal Marines.

TO/ The A.G's Office.

3rd., Echelon.

1917

Instructions regarding War Diaries and Intelligence Summaries are contained in F. S. Regs., Part II. and the Staff Manual respectively. Title pages will be prepared in manuscript.

WAR DIARY
or
~~INTELLIGENCE SUMMARY.~~
(Erase heading not required.)

VOL X

Army Form C. 2118.

2nd Battn. R.M.L.I.

Place	Date	Hour	Summary of Events and Information	Remarks and references to Appendices
	MARCH			
BOUZINCOURT	1st		Working parties repairing roads under French authorities –	CEE
— " —	2nd		do. do	CEE
— " —	3rd		do do Nineteen reinforcements joined	CEE
— " —	4th		Working parties on roads and ammunition dump. A & D Coys moved to CANDAS by train and went into billets there.	CEE
— " —	5th		working parties – Heavy snow.	CEE
— " —	6th		working parties	CEE
— " —	7th		working parties	CEE
— " —	8th		working parties.	CEE
— " —	9th		working parties.	CEE
— " —	10th		working parties	CEE
— " —	11th		working parties. Major C E C EAGLES assumed command temporarily Lieut Col. A R H HUTCHISON CMG DSO assumed command of 188th Inf Bde.	CEE
— " —	12th		working parties	CEE
— " —	13th		'B' proceeded by march route to PUCHEVILLERS and relieved 'C' Coy. which returned to BOUZINCOURT	CEE

T2134. Wt. W708–776. 500000. 4/15. Sir J. C. & S.

Instructions regarding War Diaries and Intelligence Summaries are contained in F. S. Regs., Part II. and the Staff Manual respectively. Title pages will be prepared in manuscript.

WAR DIARY
or
~~INTELLIGENCE SUMMARY.~~
(Erase heading not required.)

Army Form C. 2118.

2nd Battn R.M.L.I

Place	Date	Hour	Summary of Events and Information	Remarks and references to Appendices
	MARCH			
BOUZINCOURT	14th		Working parties	CEE
—"—	15th		Working parties	CEE
—"—	16th		Working parties. G.O.C. 63rd (RN) Divn inspected 1st Line Transport.	CEE
			Lieut. Col. A.R.H. HUTCHISON resumed command of the Bn	CEE
—"—	17th		Working parties	
—"—	18th		Working parties. Lieut. Col A.R.H. HUTCHISON assumed command of 188th Inf. Bde	
			MAJOR C.E.C. EAGLES assumed command of the Bn temporarily. Issued operation	
			orders No 53. 54. 55.	CEE Appendices 1A. 1B. 1C.
—"—	19th		Battalion moved by march route to RUBEMPRÉ and went into billets. O.O. No 56 issued	CEE Appendix 2.
RUBEMPRE	20th		Battalion moved by march route to GÉZAINCOURT. A.B.&D. Coys rejoined. O.O. No 56 issued	CEE App. 3.
GEZAINCOURT	21st		Battalion moved by march route to RÉBREUVE. Ten reinforcements arrived. O.O. No 57 issued	CEE App. 4.
REBREUVE	22		Battalion moved by march route and billeted three Coys in BEAUVOIS and one in SIRACOURT	CEE
SIRACOURT	23rd		Battalion rested. Cleaning equipment. O.O. No 58 issued. Seventeen reinforcements joined	CEE App. 5.
—"—	24th		Battalion moved by march route to CAUCHY À LA TOUR. O.O. No 59 issued. Thirteen reinforcements	CEE App. 6.
CAUCHY	25th		Battalion moved by march route to St HILAIRE. O.O. No 60 issued.	CEE App. 7
St HILAIRE	26th		Battalion moved by march route to CALONNE SUR LA LYS. Much rain. O.O. No 61 issued	CEE App. 8

T2134. Wt. W708—776. 500000. 4/15. Sir J. C. & S.

Instructions regarding War Diaries and Intelligence Summaries are contained in F. S. Regs., Part II. and the Staff Manual respectively. Title pages will be prepared in manuscript.

WAR DIARY
or
~~INTELLIGENCE SUMMARY.~~
(Erase heading not required.)

Army Form C. 2118.

2nd Battalion R.M.L.I.

Place	Date	Hour	Summary of Events and Information	Remarks and references to Appendices
	MARCH			
CALONNE	27th		Battalion moved by march route to FOUQUIÈRES les BETHUNE.	CCE
FOUQUIÈRES	28th		Cleaning up equipment and transport. Three reinforcements arrived. O.O.s 62 + 63 issued	CCE App. 9.10
FOUQUIÈRES	29th		Battalion moved by march route to SAILLY LABOURSE and billeted.	CCE
SAILLY LABOURSE	30th		Battalion training. Thirty six reinforcements joined.	CCE
— " —	31st		Battalion training.	CCE

C.R. Cragles
Major RMLI
1.4.17 Comdg 2nd Battn R.M.L.I.

ISSUED AT 7.50 p.m. S E C R E T. COPY NO. 5

APPENDIX: I/A

-(-(-(-(-(-(-(-(-(-(-(-

OPERATION ORDERS NO. 58

BY MAJOR C.E.C. EAGLES D.S.O. R.M.L.I.

COMMANDING 2ND., ROYAL MARINES

-"-"-"-"-"-"-"-"-"-

Bn., Headquarters,
18th., March 1917.

1.........The Battalion less three Cos'., will proceed by march route to-morrow, and billet at RUBEMPRE preceded by 188th., Infy., Bde., Headquarters.

2.........Battalion will pass the starting point, Cross Roads BOUZINCOURT and ALBERT-HEDAUVILLE main road at 9-5 a.m.

3.........Advanced Billeting Party of 1 N.C.O., per Co., and H.Q. will proceed on bicycles under 2nd., Lieut., Rewling and report to Staff Officer of the 188th., Infy., Bde., at the Town Major's Office RUBEMPRE at 11-0 a.m.
Party to leave at 8-0 a.m.

4.........Order of march :- Bn., H.Q. "C" Co., & Details. Transport.
Interval of three hundred yards between Units and one hundred yards between Cos., and Cos., and Transport.

5.........Fall in at 8-30 a.m. in Full Marching Order. W.P. Sheets will be carried under the flap of the pack, and steel helmets will be carried between the supporting straps of the pack.
Leather Jerkins will be worn.
Rifle Covers will not be carried on the Rifles.

6.........Billets and latrines are to be ready for inspection by the Officer Commanding at 8-30 a.m. Every effort is to be made to see that they are left tidy.

7.........Officers Valises and Mess Gear are to be at the Q.M. Stores by 8-0 a.m.
Blankets are to be tightly rolled in bundles of TEN and stowed at the Q.M. Stores by 7-0 a.m.
Platoon Sergts., will take care that the bundles do not contain anything but blankets.

8........."C" Co., will provide a loading party of 1 N.C.O. and 12 Men to be at the Q.M. Stores at 7-0 a.m.
This party is to take their equipment, and be ready to march when the stores are loaded.

9.........A crew of Six men and 1 N.C.O. per Lewis Gun Cart is to be detailed from "C" Co., to march with the Six L.G. Cs.
They will march immediately in rear of "C" Co.,

J Campbell
Lieut., R.M.
Act., Adjt., 2nd., ROYAL MARIN

APPENDIX I3

Issued at....8.15 p.m.

OPERATION ORDERS NO...54.

BY MAJOR C.E.C. EAGLES D.S.O. R.M.L.I.

COMMANDING 2ND., ROYAL MARINES.

-C-C-C-C-C-C-C-C-C-C-C-C-C-C-C-C-C-

Bn., Headquarters,

18th., March 1917.

1.........On the night of the 19/20th., the Battalion will billet in RUBEMPRE, proceeding on the 20th., inst., to billets in GEZAINCOURT.

2........."B" Co., will join the Battalion at the latter place, and will march as follows :-

Starting Point, Road Junction 200 yards E. of N in Val - de MAISON. Time of passing starting point 9-0 a.m.

Route :- via Fms du RESEL - CANDAS.

3.........Every effort is to be made to ensure that Billets and Latrines are left tidy.

4... ...Rifle Covers will not be carried on the Rifles. Leather Jerkinsx will be worn.

5.........~~One G.S. Wagon will report to you for the carriage of all Stores, Blankets etc.,~~ Transport arrangements for Blankets etc. will be notified later.

6.........You will send one N.C.O. to report to the Brigade Staff Officer at the Town Major's Office at GEZAINCOURT at 11-0 a.m. for Billets.

7....... Rations for the 21st., onwards will be issued by the Battalion Quartermaster.
Your Cooker will accompany you.

NOTE :-

The 14th., Worcester Regt., and the 247th., Field Co., R.E's. will be marching ahead of you to the same destination.
An interval of 300 yards between Units will be maintained.

Coyp to :-
No., 1 Retained.
No., 2 O.C. "B" Co.,
No., 3 Q.M.
No., 4 War Diary.

J. Campbell

Lieut., R.M.

Act., Adjt., 2nd., Royal Marines

APPENDIX IX To

ISSUED AT....... 8.15 pm

OPERATION ORDER NO......55

BY MAJOR C.E.C. EAGLES D.S.O. R.M.L.I.

COMMDG., 2ND., ROYAL MARINES.

Bn., Headquarters,
18th., March 1917.

1.......On the night of the 19/20th., the Battalion less three Cos., will billet at RUBEMPRE, proceeding on the 20th., inst., to Billets in GEZAINCOURT, when the detachment at CANDAS will rejoin.

2.......You will arrange to march independently to GEZAINCOURT clearing CANDAS by 11-0 a.m.

3.......Rifle covers will not be carried on the Rifles. Leather jerkins will be worn.

4.......Every effort is to be made to ensure that Billets and Latrines are left in a tidy and sanitary condition.

5.......Advance Billeting Party of 1 N.C.O. per Co., and one Officer in Charge will report to Staff Officer of 188th., Infy., Bde., at Town Major's Office, GEZAINCOURT at 11-0 a.m.

6.......You will maintain an interval of 100 yards between Cos., when on the march.

7.......Rations for consumption on the 21st., will be drawn from the Battalion Quartermaster on arrival.
Cookers and G.S. Limber Wagon will accompany Cos.,

8.......Acknowledge by bearer.

9.......The G.S. Wagon which was sent you yesterday, will be utilized for Transport of Stores and Blankets.

Lieut., R.M.

Act., Adjt., 2nd., Royal Marines.

Copies to :-
No., 1 Retained.
No., 2 O.C. Detachment CANDAS.
No., 3 Q.M.
No., 4 War Diary.

APPENDIX 2/

Issued at...........

SECRET.

OPERATION ORDERS NO.......56.

BY MAJOR C.E.C.EAGLES D.S.O. R.M.L.I. COMMANDING

2ND., ROYAL MARINES.

Bn., Headquarters,
19th., March 1917.

1.........The Battalion will resume its march to-morrow at 8-45 a.m. and will billet in GEZAINCOURT.

2.........ROUTE :- via TALMAS, VERT GALAND - CANDAS.

3.........An advance Billeting Party of One N.C.O. per Co., H.Q. and Transport will report to a Staff Officer of the 188th., Bde., at the Town Major's Office GEZAINCOURT at 11-0 a.m. leaving RUBEMPRE at 8-45 a.m. on bicycles.

4.........Blankets will be rolled in Bundles of 10, and deposited at Q.M. Stores by 7-0 a.m. Section Commanders are responsible that NOTHING else is included in these bundles.
O.C. "C" Co., will detail a loading party of One N.C.O. and 12 Men for loading stores at 7-0 a.m.
This party will remain until all stores are loaded.

5.........Starting Point :- Cross Roads 200 yards N.E. of last E in SEPTONVILLE.

6.........Order of march as for to-day.
3 Lewis Gun Carts will be drawn by Pack animals.
The following intervals will be maintained :- 300 Yards between Units, and 100 Yards between Companies and Transport.

7.........Billets are to be ready for inspection by 8-15 a.m.

8.........If it is raining at 7-0 a.m. Waterproof Sheets will be worn.

Lieut., R.M.

A ct., Adjt., 2nd., Royal Marines.

ISSUED AT 5-55 p.m. S E C R E T. COPY NO...5..

APPENDIX 3.

OPERATION ORDERS NO...56

BY MAJOR C.E.C. EAGLES D.S.O. R.M.L.I.

COMMANDING 2ND., ROYAL MARINES.

Bn., Headquarters,
20th., March 1917.

1........Battalion will resume its march to-morrow at 9-45 a.m. and will go into billets at REBREUVE., preceded by 188th., Infy., Bde., Headquarters.

2........Battalion will pass the starting point Cross Roads 200 yds., E. of Station GEZAINCOURT at 9-30 a.m.

3.......Advance Billeting Party of One N.C.O. per Co., H.Q. and Transport will proceed on bicycles under Command of 2nd., Lieut., Purdy and report to Staff Officer of the 188th., Infy., Bde., at the Town Major's Office at REBREUVE at 11-30 a.m. leaving here at 9-15 a.m.

4.......Order of march:- H.Q. "A" "B" "C" and "D" Co.,
The following distances will be maintained :-
100 yards between Cos., and 500 yards between Units.

NOTE :-

After passing DOULLENS Cos, will close to normal distance, i.e. 30 yards.

5.......Battalion will fall in at 8-10 a.m. by which time all Billets will be ready for inspection.
If it is raining at 7-30 a.m. Waterproof Sheets will be worn, and Officers will wear Waterproofs.
Leather Jerkins will be worn.
Rifle Covers will NOT be carried on the rifles.

6.......Blankets tightly rolled in Bundles of 10 will be deposited at the Q.M. Stores by 7-30 a.m. Section Commdrs., are responsible that the bundles do not contain anything but blankets.
Officers Valises and Mess Gear to be at the Q.M. Stores at 8-30 a.m.

7.......\"D\" Co., will detail a Loading Party of One N.C.O. and 12 men to be at the Q.M. Stores at 7-30 a.m. This party will take their equipment and be ready to march when the stores are loaded.

8.......Lewis Guns will march with their Cos., and O.C. Co's., will detail the necessary teams for drawing the Lewis Gun Handcarts.

9.......O.C. Co's., will be mounted.
Attention is called to the necessity of maintaining strict March discipline.

continued.

10.........Sergeant Trevett and a Party of 15 Other Ranks will report to the Orderly Room at 8-30 a.m. for Sanitary Work.
The 15 Other Ranks will be detailed as follows from men who are least fitted to march:-

"A" Co.,......3
"B" Co........4
"C" Co........5
"D" Co........3

11.........O.C. "D" Co., will detail a rear party to march in rear of Transport.
Strength of Party.......1 N.C.O. and 4 Men.

In the event of any man falling out he must halt by the roadside until the arrival of the rear party.

This order is to be made known to all Ranks before marching off.

12.........Steps will be taken to ensure that all steel helmets are properly cleaned.

-0-0-0-0-0-0-0-0-0-0-0-0-

J. Campbell

Lieut., R.M.

Act., Adjt., 2nd., Royal Marines.

20-3-17.

APPENDIX H.

ISSUED AT 6.30 P.M.

OPERATION ORDERS NO...57

BY MAJOR C.E.C. EAGLES R.M.L.I. COMMDG.,

COMMANDING 2ND., ROYAL MARINES.

-0-0-0-0-0-0-0-0-0-0-0-

Bn., Headquarters,

21st., March 1917.

1.........Battalion will resume its march to-morrow at 9-40 a.m. and go into Billets at BEAUVOIS and SIRACOURT.

2.........The Battalion will pass the starting point Road Junction half mile north of E. in LE CONTURE at 9-40 a.m.

3.........Headquarters, Transport and "C" Co., will be billeted in SIRACOURT, the remainder of the Battalion in BEAUVOIS.

4.........Advance Billeting Party of One N.C.O. per Co., H.Q. and Transport will proceed on bicycles under command of 2nd., Lieut., Vance. Report at the Orderly Room (No., 15 Billet) at 8-15 a.m.

5.........Order of march :- H.Q. "B" "C" "D" and "A" Co.,
"A" Co., will provide a rear party of One N.C.O. and 4 Privates to march in rear of Transport and pick up stragglers.

6.........Blankets tightly rolled in Bundles of 10 will be deposited at the Q.M. Stores at 7-30 a.m. Section Commanders are held responsible that the Bundles contain nothing but Blankets.
Officers Valises and Mess Gear will be dumped at the Q.M. Stores by 8-30 a.m.

7.........Battalion will fall in at 9-10 a.m. by which time all Billets will be ready for inspection. If it is raining at 7-30 a.m. W.P. Sheets will be worn, and Officers will wear Waterproofs.

8.........."B" Co., will provide a Loading Party of One N.C.O. and 12 Men to report at Q.M. Stores at 7-30 a.m. Party will take equipment and be ready to march off on completion of duty.

9.........Lewis Guns will march as to-day.

10........Attention of O.C. Co.'s is again drawn to necessity of ensuring that all Steel Helmets are properly cleaned.

11.........Sergt., Trevett and a party of 15 will report at the Orderly Room at 8-45 a.m. for Sanitary Work. This party will be detailed after the Sick Parade to-morrow morning.

SICK PARADE WILL BE ~~AT 6.30 a.m.~~

J. Campbell

Lieut. R.M. ~~ASSIST. ADJT.~~, Act Adjt.

APPENDIX 5

Issued at..4-0..p.m. S E C R E T.

OPERATION ORDERS No...58

BY MAJOR [illegible] D.S.O. R.M.L.I.

COMMANDING 2ND., ROYAL MARINES.

Bn., Headquarters,

23rd, March 1917.

1..........The Battalion will resume its march to-morrow and go into Billets at CAUCHY-a-la- TOUR.

2..........Battalion starting Point Road Junction 400 yards E. of the U in BEAUVOIS.

3..........."C" Co., H.Q. and Transport will parade at [illegible] a.m. and the remainder of the Battalion at 6-15 a.m. by which time, all billets will be ready for inspection.
"H.Q." "C" Co., and Transport will move at [illegible] a.m. and the remainder of Bn., in time to reach the starting point at [illegible] a.m.

4..........Order of March :- H.Q. "C" "D" "A" and "B" Co.,

5..........The Battalion will pass the point - Road Junction just N.E. of the A in [illegible] at [illegible] at 10-27 a.m.

6..........ROUTE :- [illegible] - [illegible] - TANGRY - PERNES - [illegible] - PERNES.

7..........Advance Billeting Party of one N.C.O. per Co., H.Q. and Transport under the Command of Lieut., Mitchell will report to a Staff Officer of the [illegible] Infy., Bde., at the Church at CAUCHY-a-la-TOUR at [illegible] a.m.
This party will leave BEAUVOIS at [illegible]-45 a.m. H.Q. Trans. and "C" Co., N.C.O's., will leave [illegible] at [illegible] a.m.

8..........Blankets tightly rolled in BUNDLES OF 10 will be dumped at the Q.M. Stores at [illegible], and opposite the Church at BEAUVOIS at 7-0 a.m. Officers Valises and Mess Gear, at the same places at 8-0 a.m.
Attention is called to the attached memo RE BLANKETS.

9..........."C" Co., will provide a loading party of 1 N.C.O. and 4 Men to report to the Q.M. Stores at 7-0 a.m. and "[illegible]" Co. 1 N.C.O. and [illegible] Men to load stores at the CHURCH at BEAUVOIS.

10..........Lewis Gun handcarts will be drawn as for yesterday's march.

11..........If it is raining at 7-30 a.m. W.P. Sheets will be worn.

[illegible]

Lieut., R.M.

Adjutant 2nd. Royal Marines.

APPENDIX 6.

Issued at..5.15.P.M.

OPERATION ORDERS

NO........59

BY MAJOR C.E.C. EAGLES D.S.O. R.M.L.I.

COMMANDING 2ND., ROYAL MARINES.

-0-0-0-0-0-0-0-0-0-0-

Ref., Hazebrouck 5A 1/100,000.

Bn., Headquarters,

24th., March 1917.

1.........The Battalion will resume its march to-morrow and go into Billets at ST., HILAIRE.

2.........Battalion will fall in at 10-15 a.m. by which time all Billets will be ready for inspection .

3.........Battalion Starting Point - Cross Roads 300 Yards N. of the Y in CAUCHY-a-la-TOUR. The Battalion will pass this point at 10-45 a.m.

4.........ROUTE- FERFAY - LIERES.

5.........Blankets tightly rolled in Bundles of 10 will be deposited at the Q.M. Stores by 8-15 a.m. Officers Valises and Mess Gear by 9-0 a.m.

6.........Order of march as for to-day.

7.........Advance Billeting Party of 1 N.C.O. per Co., H.Q. and Transport under the Command of Lieut., Mitchell will assemble at the Orderly Room at 9-45 a.m. This party will meet a Staff Officer of the 188th., Bde., at the Town Major's Office ST., HILAIRE at 11-0 a.m.
In the event of their being no Town Major at this place they will report at the MAIRE.

8.........."B" Co., will detail a Loading Party of 1 N.C.O. and 10 Men to report at the Q.M. Stores at 8-15 a.m.

9.........If it is raining at 9-0 a.m. W.P. Sheets will be worn.

10.........."A" Co., will detail a rear Party of One N.C.O. and 4 Men to march in rear of Transport. N.C.O. will report at Bn., Orderly Room on arrival of Bn., at ST., HILAIRE.

J. Campbell.

Lieut., R.M.

Act., Adjt., 2nd., Royal Marines.

APPENDIX 1.

Issued at..10 pm...... SECRET.

OPERATION ORDERS NO. 60

BY MAJOR C.E.C. EAGLES D.S.O. R.M.L.I. COMMDG.,

2ND., ROYAL MARINES.

-@-@-@-@-@-@-@-@-@-@-@-@-@-@-@-@-@-

Bn., Headquarters,
25th., March 1917.

1........The Battalion will resume its march to-morrow and go into billets at LABEUVRIERE.

2........Battalion will fall in at 8-15 a.m. by which time all Billets will be ready for inspection.

3........Battalion Starting Point :- ~~Cross Roads S.W.~~ Road Junction S.W. of the Church St., HILAIRE, this point will be passed at 8-35 a.m.

4........ROUTE :- LILLERS. CHOCQUES.

5........Order of March :- "H.Q." "D" "A" "B" "C" Co., Lewis Guns with their Cos.,

6........Blankets tightly rolled in Bundles of 10 will be deposited at the Q.M. Stores by 7-0 a.m. Officers Valises and Mess Gear by 8-0 a.m.

7m.......Advance Billeting Party of One N.C.O. per Co., H.Q. and Transport under the Command of Lieut., Mitchell will assemble at the Orderly Room at 7-30 a.m. This party will meet a Staff Officer of the 188th., Infy., Bde., at the Church at LABEUVRIERE at 11-0 a.m.

8........"A" Co., will detail a Loading Party of One N.C.O. and 10 Men to report at the Q.M. Stores at 7-0 a.m.

9........If it is raining at 7-0 a.m. W.P. Sheets will be worn.

10.......“C" Co., will detail a rear party of One N.C.O. and 4 Men to march in Rear of the transport. N.C.O. will report on arrival at destination at the Bn., Orderly Room.

11.......The Division now forms party of G.H.Q. Reserve while in this area, and all Units of the 188th., Bde., Group will be held in readiness to move at 24 Hours notice.

12........Summer Time will be adopted at eleven p.m. to-day. At that moment clocks will be advanced one hour and eleven p.m. will become midnight.

J Campbell

Lieut., R.M.
Act., Adjt., 2nd., Royal Marines.

APPENDIX 8

Issued at 9.50pm   SECRET.   COPY NO. 1

@@@@@@@@@@@@@@@@@@

OPERATION ORDERS NO. 60

BY MAJOR C.E.C. EAGLES D.S.O. R.M.L.I.

COMMANDING 2ND., ROYAL MARINES.

-@-@-@-@-@-@-@-@-@-@-@-@--

Bn., Headquarters,

26th., March 1917.

1.........The Battalion will resume its march to-morrow and go into Billets at FOUQUIERES-LEZ-BETHUNE.

2.........Starting Point :- Road Junction 200 Yards due E. of 2nd., E. in CLARENCE. The Battalion will pass this point at 9-47 a.m.

3.........Headquarter Co., will fall in at the Orderly Room at 9-30 a.m. "B" Co., will commence its march at 9-15 a.m. The remainder in time to pass the starting point at the required time.

4.........ROUTE :- LE CORNET MARLO - HINGES - BETHUNE.

5.........Order of march :- H.Q. "B" "A" "C" "D" Co., Lewis Guns with their Cos.,

6.........Blankets tightly rolled in Bundles of 10 will be deposited as follows :- "A" "C" and "D" Cos., at the Road Junction 200 yards S.E. of the Starting Point at 8-0 a.m.
"B" Co., at a convenient ~~spot~~ place in Co., Area at 8-0 a.m.
"B" Co., will provide a guide for lorry reporting at Q.M. Stores at 7-30 a.m. and will also provide their own loading party.
"A" Co., will provide a loading party of One N.C.O. and 6 Men to be at "A" "C" and "D" Dumping Ground at 8-0 a.m.

7.........A G.S. Wagon will collect Officers Mess Gear, and Valises, also Orderly Room Gear commencing at "B" Co., H.Q. at 8-0 a.m. thenceto Orderly Room "A" "D" and "C" Co.,

8.........Advance Billeting Party as for to-day will report to Lieut., Mitchell at the Battalion Starting Point at 8-30 a.m.

9.........."D" Co., will detail the usual rear party.

10........On arrival in the new area to-morrow the 188th., Infy., Bde., will be at the disposal of 1st., Corps, and all Units of the Bde., will be held ready to move at 6 Hours notice.

J. Campbell

Lieut., R.M.

ACT., ADJT., 2ND., ROYAL MARINES.

APPENDIX 9.

Issued at 6.30PM   SECRET.   COPY NO 1.

OPERATION ORDERS NO....62

BY MAJOR C.E.C. EAGLES D.S.O. R.M.L.I. COMMDG.,

2ND., ROYAL MARINES.

-0-0-0-0-0-0-0-0-0-0-0-0-0-

Reference Hazebrouck 5A and
LENS 11

Bn., Headquarters,

28th., March 1917.

1..........The Battalion will move to SAILLY-LABOURSE and go into Billets there.

2..........ROUTE :- VERQUIN - VERQUIGNEUL - LABOURSE.

3..........Battalion will fall in at 9-30 a.m. Starting point :- Road Junction 400 yards N. of the "F" in FOUQUIERES, Bn., will pass this point at 10-0 a.m.

4..........Order of march :- H.Q. "B" "C" "D" "A" Co., Lewis Guns with their Cos.,

5..........Advance Billeting party of One N.C.O. per Co., H.Q. and Transport will report at the Orderly Room at 8-45 a.m. Lieut., Mitchell will be in command of this party.

6..........Blankets tightly rolled in Bundles of 10 will be deposited at the Q.M. Stores at 8-0 a.m.

7..........Loading Party of One N.C.O. and 10 Men will be found by "C" Co., report at Q.M. Stores at 8-0 a.m.

8..........A G.S. Wagon will collect Orderly Room Gear, Officers Valises and Mess Gear commencing at the Orderly Room at 8-30 a.m. thence to "A" "D" "C" "B" Co., H.Q.

9.........."A" Co., will detail the usual rear party.

10..........Length of march - 5½ Miles.

J Campbell
Lieut., R.M.

Act., Adjt., 2nd., Royal Marines.

28-3-17.

APPENDIX 10

Issued at......6:50pm SECRET. Copy No.1......

OPERATION ORDERS NO....63

BY MAJOR C.E.C. EAGLES D.S.O. R.M.L.I.

Commanding 2nd., Royal Marines.

-@-@-@-@-@-@-@-@-@-

Bn., Headquarters,

28th., March 1917.

1.........Two Officers and Two N.C.O's per Co., will report at the Orderly Room at 7-15 a.m. to-morrow. They will proceed by march route to NOYELLES where they will be met at the point L.11.d.O.I.(Map to be issued later) by a guide from the South Irish Horse. They will reconnoitre the MAESTRE LINE. at 9-30 a.m.

DRESS :- Steel Helmets, Light March Order and Both Gas Helmets.

Packs of N.C.O's will be dumped with Blankets.

This party will rejoin the Bn., at SAILLY LABOURSE.

-@-@-@-@-@-@-@-@-@-@

J. Campbell

Lieut., R.M.

Act., Adjt., 2nd., Royal Marines.

D/53/17

"CONFIDENTIAL". Headquarters,

2nd., Bn., Royal Marine Light Infantry.

3rd., May 1917.

VOLUME 11

W A R D I A R Y

OF

2nd., Bn., Royal Marine Light Infantry.

FROM

1st., APRIL 1917

TO

30th., APRIL 1917.

A. R. H. Hutchison

Lieut., Colonel R.M.L.I.
Commanding 2nd., Bn., Royal Marine Light Infy.,

TO:- A.G's Office.

3rd., Echelon.

Instructions regarding War Diaries and Intelligence Summaries are contained in F. S. Regs., Part II. and the Staff Manual respectively. Title pages will be prepared in manuscript.

1

WAR DIARY
or
~~INTELLIGENCE SUMMARY.~~
(*Erase heading not required.*)

April 1917

Army Form C. 2118.

2nd Battn Royal Marine Lt Infy

Vol XI

Place	Date	Hour	Summary of Events and Information	Remarks and references to Appendices
April				
SAILLY-LABOURSE (I.1)	1st		Battalion Training	Reference:- Map LENS 11 1/100,000
"	2nd		Battalion Training	
"	3rd		Battalion Training. Nineteen reinforcements joined from Base Depot	
"	4th		Battalion Training	
"	5th		Battalion Training. Lt Col. Hutchison resumed command and Major [illegible] duties of 2nd in Command	
"	6th		Battalion Training	
"	7th		Battalion Training. Sixteen reinforcements recd from Base Depot	
"	8th		Kit & Billet inspection. Church Parade. Lt Andrews and 6 OR's left for [illegible]	
"	9th		Battalion Training. Lt A.B. MARHAM & 2nd Lt A FARMER joined. Capt C.G. FARQUHARSON RMLI rejoined from England. 18 OR's joined from BASE DEPOT	
"	10th		Battalion Training. Capt C.G. Farquharson resumed duties of Adjutant. Major C.E.C. EAGLES RMLI to command 'B' Company	
OURTON	11th		Battalion moved by March Route to OURTON (F.1) and went into Billets	
"	12th		Battalion resting and cleaning up equipment etc	
"	13th		Battalion training during forenoon. Operation Order No 61 issued	Appendix I

T2134. Wt. W708—776. 500000. 4/15. Sir J. C. & S.

Instructions regarding War Diaries and Intelligence Summaries are contained in F. S. Regs., Part II. and the Staff Manual respectively. Title pages will be prepared in manuscript.

2

WAR DIARY
or
~~INTELLIGENCE SUMMARY.~~
(Erase heading not required.)

April 1917

Army Form C. 2118.

2nd Bn Royal Marine Lt Infy

Place	Date	Hour	Summary of Events and Information	Remarks and references to Appendices
	April			
OURTON to ECOIVRES	14th		Battalion moved by March Route to ECOIVRES and went into X Hutments there	
ECOIVRES	15th		Working parties	
"	16th		Working parties	
"	17th		Working parties. Tempy Surg. J. N. McB Ross R.N rejoined	
"	18th		Working parties. Capt M.A. POWER RAMC rejoined 1st Field Ambulance	
"	19th		Working parties	
"	20th		Working parties	
"	21st		Working parties. 'C' Coy proceeded to ANZIN and went into Billets there	
Trenches	22nd		Battalion moved up to original Enemy Support line North of the ARRAS – BAILLEUL Road. 188th Infy Bde formed the	
"			Bde in Div. Reserve for the taking of GAVRELLE	
"	23rd		GAVRELLE taken by 189th & 190th Inf Bdes of 63rd (R.N) Divn. Battn at 2 hours notice.	
"	24th		Moved up from Reserve trenches at 9 o'pm and relieved 1st HAC & 4th BEDFORDS in the trenches and posts	
			NORTH of GAVRELLE. Prisoner of 84th Prussian Guard Regt captured immediately after taking over posts occupied by BEDFORDS	
"	25th		Heavy hostile shelling during the forenoon. Air duel in afternoon – one of our planes forced to land. S.O.S sent up in the	
			evening on account of enemy counter attacking. Enemy dispersed by our Barrage. Casualties ~~[illegible]~~	
			Killed other ranks 3 wounded other ranks 8.	

Instructions regarding War Diaries and Intelligence Summaries are contained in F. S. Regs., Part II. and the Staff Manual respectively. Title pages will be prepared in manuscript.

3

WAR DIARY

or

~~INTELLIGENCE SUMMARY~~. April 1917

(Erase heading not required.)

Army Form C. 2118.

2nd Bn Royal Marine Light Infy

Place	Date	Hour	Summary of Events and Information	Remarks and references to Appendices
	April			
GAVRELLE Trenches	26th		Village heavily shelled all day. Aircraft active on both sides. One of our balloons set fire to. Wire cutting in the afternoon. Casualties Missing Temp. Lieut MARKHAM. Killed other ranks 3 wounded other ranks 30	
	27th		Hostile artillery more than usually active during early morning. At about 8 am one of our aeroplanes was brought down South of OPPY WOOD by hostile AA gun. Bn proceeded to Assembly positions ready for attack. Casualties Killed other ranks 8. wounded other ranks 14 missing other ranks 4.	
	28th	4.25am	Battn attacked in 4 waves the enemy trenches N.E of GAVRELLE with one platoon under 2nd Lt NEWLING detailed to take the windmill. The windmill on the left of the Bn front was reached and held, but as 1st Battn Rmt on our left and 2nd Divn on their left were hung up apparently by wire, owing to a large number of machine guns, casualties were very heavy. Only two Officers besides the Officer Comd & Adjt who took part in the operations came out alive. Casualties Killed Officers 1 other ranks 25 wounded other ranks 72. Missing Officers 8 other ranks 387.	
	29th		Situation unchanged. Enemy made several violent counter attacks. Casualties wounded ORs 16	
	30th	2.30am	Bn relieved by 15th & 18th West Yorks. Marched back to St CATHERINES	

A. R. H. Hutchison
Lieut Colonel Rmt
Commanding 2nd Bn Royal Marine Lt Infy

T2134. Wt. W708–776. 500000. 4/15. Sir J. C. & S.

Appendix I to War Diary (April 1917)

Issued at.....7-30. p.m. Copy No..6........

OPERATION ORDER NO...61

BY LIEUT., COLONEL A.R.H. HUTCHISON C.M.G. D.S.O. R.M.L.I.

COMMANDING 2ND., BN., ROYAL MARINE LIGHT INFTY.,

-"-"-"-"-"-"-"-"-"-"-"-"-"-"-

Bn., Headquarters,

18th., April 1917.

1....The Battalion will move with its transport at about 8-30 a.m. to-morrow.

2....Blankets neatly rolled in bundles of 10 will be dumped at the Quartermaster's Stores by 7-30 a.m.

3....Officers Valises are to be stowed in the G.S. Wagon outside the Q.M. Stores by 7-30 a.m.

4....Caps will be worn.
Attention is called to Battalion Routine Order No., 300 Para 4 "Steel helmets if NOT worn will be carried under the supporting straps at the back of the PACK, and Waterproof sheets folded under the flap of the pack".

5....Order of march H.Q. "A" "B" "C" "D" Coys.,

6.... Usual Billeting Parties to be held in readiness to proceed when ordered.

7....Hour of starting and further details will be notified later.

Copy No., 1 Retained.
" " 2 O.C. "A" Co.,
" " 3 O.C. "B" Co.,
" " 4 O.C. "C" Co.,
" " 5 O.C. "D" Co.,
" " 6 War Diary.

C.G. Farquharson
Captain and Adjutant,
2nd., Bn., R.M.L.I.

CONFIDENTIAL. I

Headquarters,
2nd Bn. Royal Marine Light Infantry.

1917 .

WAR DIARY

of

2nd Battalion

ROYAL MARINE LIGHT INFANTRY.

from

1st May

to

31st May

Volume 12.

To,

THE A. G's OFFICE,

3rd ECHELON.

L W Miller

Major. R.M.L.I.

Commanding 2nd Bn. Royal Marine Light Infy.

W 12

Army Form C. 2118.

Instructions regarding War Diaries and Intelligence Summaries are contained in F. S. Regs., Part II. and the Staff Manual respectively. Title pages will be prepared in manuscript.

1.

WAR DIARY or ~~INTELLIGENCE SUMMARY~~. MAY 1917

(Erase heading not required.)

2nd Battn. Royal Marine Light Infantry
Volume XII

Place	Date	Hour	Summary of Events and Information	Remarks and references to Appendices
	MAY			
ECOIVRES to FREVILLERS	1st		Battalion moved by march route from ECOIVRES to FREVILLERS and went into billets. Eighty-eight reinforcements received from 11th Entrenching Battn.	Reference Map LENS 11 1/100,000
— " —	2nd		Battalion resting and cleaning up equipment &c. Formed up at 6 pm. and were addressed by G.O.C. 188th Bde, who congratulated the battn. on the gallantry shown during the recent operations. Sixty-one reinforcements received from FLORINGHEM. Lt. ANDREWS, 2nd Lt. VANCE + 2nd Lt. LEE rejoined.	
— " —	3rd		Battalion training. Lt. B.G. ANDREWS to command 'D' Coy.	
— " —	4th		Battalion training.	
— " —	5th		Battalion training. 2nd Lt. WELLS took command of 'A' Co. Lt. MITCHELL and 2nd Lt. VANCE evacuated 'sick'.	
— " —	6th		Parade Service.	
— " —	7th		Battalion training. Operation Orders No. 62 issued.	Appendix I
ECOIVRES	8th		Battalion moved by march route to "X" Hutments, ECOIVRES. Operation Order No. 63 issued.	— " — II
A26 b.6.1	9th		Battalion resumed march route and went into tents at A26 b.6.1	Reference Map [illegible] 1/20,000
— " —	10th		Battalion training. 7 reinforcements arrived from Base. Lt. E.K. ANDREWS evacuated 'sick'. 2nd Lt. Newling to command 'C' Coy commencing this day.	

T2134. Wt. W708–776. 500000. 4/15. Sir J. C. & S.

Instructions regarding War Diaries and Intelligence Summaries are contained in F. S. Regs., Part II. and the Staff Manual respectively. Title pages will be prepared in manuscript.

WAR DIARY
or
~~INTELLIGENCE SUMMARY~~. MAY 1917

(Erase heading not required.)

2.

Army Form C. 2118.

2nd Battn. Royal Marine Lt. Infantry

Place	Date	Hour	Summary of Events and Information	Remarks and references to Appendices
	MAY			Reference map 51 B. N.W. 1/20000
A28 a 96	11th		Battn. training forenoon. Battn. resumed march route in afternoon and went into huts and bivouacs at A28 a 9.6. Bn. relieved by 23rd Royal Fusiliers.	[initials]
— " —	12th		Working parties (night) on Green Line of defence at B13.	[initials]
— " —	13th		Working parties (night). Church parades. 5 O.Rs reinforcements.	[initials]
— " —	14th		Working parties (night) about B27. RC. Chaplain T.J. BRADLEY left Bn	[initials]
— " —	15th		Working parties (night) RC. Chaplain J.R. DAVEY joined Battn.	
— " —	16th		Battn. training in afternoon. 2nd LT. P.S. WATTS joined Battn. 8 O.Rs Reinforcements joined from Base.	[initials]
— " —	17th		Battn. training forenoon. LT. P. LIGERTWOOD joined Battn. from 1/RMLI.	[initials]
— " —	18th		Battn. training forenoon.	[initials]
H3. b 3.9	19th		Battn. moved at 8 p.m. into trenches at H3.C. relieving 18 West Yorks. B.H.Q. H3 b 3.9. 5 O.Rs joined Battn. from Base.	[initials]
— " —	20th		Battn. rested and improved trenches in occupation.	[initials]
— " —	21st		In trenches. Working parties (night) on communication trench about H5.	[initials]
— " —	22nd		In trenches. Working parties (night)	[initials]
— " —	25th		In trenches. Working parties (night). 2nd LT. GREENLAND rejoined and to command "B" Coy. LT. P. LIGERTWOOD to command "C" Coy.	[initials]

T2134. Wt. W708—776. 500000. 4/15. Sir J. C. & S.

Instructions regarding War Diaries and Intelligence Summaries are contained in F. S. Regs., Part II. and the Staff Manual respectively. Title pages will be prepared in manuscript.

WAR DIARY ~~or~~ ~~INTELLIGENCE SUMMARY.~~

(*Erase heading not required.*)

Army Form C. 2118.

MAY. 1917

2nd Bn. Royal Marine Light Infantry

Place	Date	Hour	Summary of Events and Information	Remarks and references to Appendices
H.3.d.3.9	24th		In trenches. Working parties (night). 12 ORS. reinforcements arrived from Bse.	REF. MAP: 51 B N.W.
—"—	25th		In trenches. Working parties (night). 2nd Lt. GREENLAND evacuated WOUNDED	
—"—	26th		In trenches. Working parties (night). Lieut CALLIFORD joined Bn., and to command "B" Coy.	
—"—	27th		In trenches. Working parties (night). Lieut CALLIFORD transferred to 1st Bn. RMLI. 2nd Lt. NEWLING assumed command of "B" Coy.	
—"—	28th		In trenches. Working parties (night). Temp. Lt. W.M. GOLDIE. RM. joined Bn. Lt. Col. A.R.H. HUTCHISON C.M.G., D.S.O., RMLI leave to England. Major L.W. MILLER. RMLI assumed command. Operation Order No 64 issued.	APPENDIX 3
—"—	29	10-15 pm	Proceeded to Close Support trenches, W. of GAVRELLE (old German front line) and took over from 1st Bn, RMLI. Relief completed, 12-30 a.m.	
B.30.a.6.2. H.6.a.	30	12-30 am	Worked in the trenches occupied (deepening) until daylight. Thunderstorm and deluge of rain during afternoon. All dug-outs & trenches flooded.	
—"—	31st		Working on trenches during the day, baling out dug outs and cleaning up trenches. Issued Operation Order No 65.	APPENDIX. 4.

L.W. Miller
Major RMLI
Commanding 2nd Battn. Royal Marine Light Infantry.

Appendix I to War Diary Vol XII of 2nd Bn RMLI

COPY NO. 6....

Issued at....8-0 p.m.

SECRET.

OPERATION ORDER NO...62

BY LIEUT., COLONEL A.R.H. HUTCHISON C.M.G. D.S.O. R.M.L.I.

COMMANDING 2ND., BN., ROYAL MARINE LIGHT INFANTRY.

-.-.-.-.-.-.-.-.-.-.-.-.-.-.-.-

Reference Maps :-
Lens 11 Ed., 2-1/100,000.
51B. N.W. Ed., 6A. 1/20,000

Bn., Headquarters,

7th., May 1917.

1........The Battalion will proceed by march Route to-morrow May 8th., to "X" Hutments, ECOIVRES.

2........Parade on Co., Parades and form up in the order H.Q. "B" "C" "D" and "A" Coys., Transport by 9-15 a.m. Head of Column to be at Bn., Headquarter Mess.

3........Coys., will move off at 200 yards distance, which distance will be maintained throughout the march.

4........O.C. Coys., will ensure that billets vacated by them are left in a clean and sanitary condition, reporting same before moving off.

5........Dress - Marching Order, Caps will be worn, attention is called to Battalion Routine Order No., [illegible] Para 4 " Steel Helmets if NOT worn will be carried under the Supporting Straps at the back of the PACK, and W.P. Sheets folded under the flap of the pack".

6........Lewis Gun limbers are to be packed to-night.

7........Blankets tightly rolled in bundles of 10 are to be dumped at Q.M.Stores by 7-0 a.m.
Officers Valises by 8-30 a.m.

8........Advanced Billeting Party of 1 N.C.O. per Co., H.Q. and Transport will report to the Assistant Adjutant at the Orderly Room at 8-30 a.m.

9........Dinners on arrival.

10........The march will be resumed the following day May 9th., and the Battalion will relieve 7th., Royal Fusiliers at A. 28. b.6.1. Details will be issued later.

C.G. [illegible]

Captain and Adjutant,
2nd., Bn., Royal Marine Light Infantry.

Copies to :-

No., 1 Retained.
No., 2 O.C. "A" Co.,
No., 3 O.C. "B" Co.,
No., 4 O.C. "C" Co.,
No., 5 O.C. "D" Co.,
No., 6 War Diary.

Appendix II to War Diary Vol XII of 2nd Bn R.M.L.I.

SECRET. Copy No......6.....

Issued at.....7-40 p.m.....

OPERATION ORDER NO.....83.

BY LIEUT. COLONEL A.R.H. HUTCHISON C.M.G. D.S.O. R.M.L.I.

COMMANDING 2ND BN., ROYAL MARINE LIGHT INFANTRY.

Reference Maps:-
51c., 1:40,000
51b N.W. 1:20,000.

Bn., Headquarters,
8th May 1917.

1.............. The Battalion will resume its march tomorrow May 9th to 125 destination A. 26b 6.1 . Route ANZIN ST AUBIN-MADAGASCAR.

2..............The Battalion will parade at 2 p.m. and will be on the road facing N.E. ready to move off at 2-10 p.m. in the order "H.Q." "C", "D", "A", "B" Co.,s and Transport. Head of column to be at Light Railway crossing.

3.............Co.,s will move off at 200 yds distance, which will be maintained throughout the march.

4.............O.C. Co.,s will ensure that lines vacated by them are left clean clean, reporting same before moving off.

5.............Dress... Marching Order. Caps will be worn.

6.............Officers valises to be dumped at Guard Room at 12 noon.

7.............Advanced Billeting Party of 1 N.C.O. per Co., H.Q. and Transport will parade at the Orderly Room at 10 a.m. and under the 2nd in Command will proceed to take over accommodation and work in hand from the 7th Royal Fusiliers.

[illegible signature]
2nd Lieut.
Asst. Adjt. 2nd Bn., Royal Marine Light Infantry.

Copies to :-

No., 1 Retained
No., 2 O.C. "A" Co.,
No., 3 O.C. "B" Co.,
No., 4 O.C. "C" Co.,
No., 5 O.C. "D" Co.,
No., 6 War Diary.

Appendix III 6
War Diary Vol XII
of 2nd Bn R.M.L.I.

SECRET.

Copy. No. 7....

OPERATION ORDERS NO....64.

BY LIEUT. COLONEL A.R.H. HUTCHISON C.M.G. D.S.O. R.M.L.I.

COMMANDING 2ND BN., ROYAL MARINE LIGHT INFANTRY.

Reference Map :- Sheet 51B. N.W.
1/20,000.

Bn., Headquarters,
28th May 1917.

1........ The 2nd Bn., R.M.L.I. will relieve the 1st Bn., R.M.L.I. in the Close Support line on the night 29/30th May.

2........ The following Company representatives from 2nd Bn., R.M.L.I. will proceed into the line tonight 28th May :-

1 Officer per Double Co.,
1 N.C.O. per platoon.
1 Lewis gunner " "
1 Observer " "
2 H.Q. Signallers.

3....... The Bn., will move in the following order :- H.Q. "A", "B", "C" "D" Co.,s. One hundred yards distance will be maintained between platoons and ten minutes interval between Co.,s. H.Q. will start at 10-0 p.m.

4....... Bombs will be detonated and carried by Bombing sections, 8 by throwers and 10 by remainder.

5...... Box respirators will be worn in the "ALERT" position during the relief.

6....... Trench stores will be handed over to Co., representatives of 1st Bn., R.M.L.I. and receipts in duplicate obtained, both receipts to be forwarded to Orderly Room after relief. Co., representatives from 2nd Bn., R.M.L.I. will take over Trench stores from 1st Bn., R.M.L.I.

7....... Packs will be dumped(after dark)tonight by 10-0 p.m. at the ration dump. They will be taken back by ration limbers.

8....... Blankets will be dumped in Co., dumps by noon tomorrow and numbers reported to the Orderly Room. They will be handed over to the relieving Bn.,

---

C.G. Farquharson
Captn and Adjt.
2nd Bn., Royal Marine Light Infantry

Copies to :-
No.,1 Retained.
2 O.C. 1st Bn.R.M.L.I.
3 O.C.,"A" Co.,2nd Bn., R.M.L.I.
4 " "B" "
5 " "C" "
6 " "D" "
7 War Diary.

Issued at ... 12-30 p.m.

Appendix IV

SECRET. O.O. No 65

By Major F.W. Weller R.M.L.I.
Commanding 2nd Bn. Royal Marine L. Infy.

REF. MAP:-
GLOSTER WOOD 1/20,000.

1. It is believed that the enemy is likely to withdraw before very long to the DROCOURT-QUEANT LINE.

2. Constant & careful watch must be maintained by day & night, so that the enemy may not be allowed to withdraw unmolested.

Touch must on no account be lost with the enemy & any trenches he evacuates must be at once occupied.

3 In the event of an advance taking place it will be carried out in accordance with the following instructions.

(1) The advance will be by bounds, the object of each bound being securely held & consolidated before the advance is ~~[illegible]~~ continued to the next.

(2) The advance will be carried out by Battns in close support (at present this Bn) on the left.

Contd

(These places will be filled up by Reserve & Support Bns, respectively).

(a) SOUTHERN boundary:
Main GAVRELLE-FRESNES road (inclusive)
NORTHERN boundary:
GAVRELLE-IZEL road through square C.19.d. C.20. Central C.21.a, to cross roads in C.15.d. thence to MAUVRILLE FARM (inclusive)

FRONTAGE. One Coy (Y Coy) in line of section column at 100 yds interval protected by a screen of scouts 150 yds to 200 yds in advance.

Other Coy in support in Artillery formation 500 yds from Front line Coy.

Greatest care & careful arrangements should be made to ensure the maintenance of touch laterally & from front to rear.

4 (a) The first bound will be to the RED line, SQUARE WOOD, HOLLOW COPSE, C.20. Central.

(b) The second bound will be the FRESNES-ROUVROY line until we are firmly established there, nor will the Battn move forward from the RED LINE to the BLUE LINE, until the Support & Reserve Bns.

Cont'd

have occupied the former.

Communication must be maintained with Bn. H.Q. (which will be with rear Co. near GAVRELLE-FRESNES Rd) & it is again impressed on Coy and Junior Commanders the value of negative reports. Reports therefore will be sent back to H.Q every ½ hour. Every effort will be made to run out telephones – but visual signalling ought to play a very large part in the scheme of communications.

Brigade H.Q will move to dugouts in old German line about B.30.c.

Attention is drawn to the traps, mines etc which have invariably been laid by the retiring enemy. Attractive looking dugouts & souvenirs generally should be ~~[illegible]~~ avoided – wires should be treated very gingerly & should usually not be touched by anyone except sappers.

Water Arrangements for this will be notified in due course. No water should be taken from wells before it has been tested by a Medical Officer. Should water

"be discovered to be polluted, a sentry should be posted over it at once, as should any suspicious dug-out be marked plainly as "Unsafe".
RATIONS. Guide from "X" Coy will be sent to dump when the rations are due, to guide convoy to the advanced dump. He should make certain where the advanced dump will be, before setting out.
TOOLS. As many as possible will be taken by "Y" Coy, "X" Coy clearing the trenches & dump before moving off & taking the remainder.
Pioneers will take theirs with them. Bombs & flares will be carried as ordered, "X" Coy drawing flares at RE Dump near WIDOW, "Y" at present Bn. HQ

Copies to:-
1 – Retained
2 – OC "X" Co
3 – OC "Y" Co
4 – War Diary

Capt & Adjt.
2nd Bn, RMLI.

VOLUME 13.

Vol 13

CONFIDENTIAL.

Headquarters,

2nd Bn. ROYAL MARINE LIGHT INFANTRY.

3rd JULY 1917.

W A R   D I A R Y

O F

2nd B n. R O Y A L   M A R I N E   L I G H T
I N F A N T R Y ,

from

1st JUNE 1917

to

30th JUNE 1917.

To :-

The A. G.s. Office,

3rd Echelon.

[signature]

Major. R.M.L.I.
Commanding 2nd Bn. Royal Marine Light Infy.

Army Form C. 2118.

Instructions regarding War Diaries and Intelligence Summaries are contained in F. S. Regs., Part II. and the Staff Manual respectively. Title pages will be prepared in manuscript.

WAR DIARY JUNE 1917
~~or~~ ~~INTELLIGENCE SUMMARY.~~

(*Erase heading not required.*)

2nd Bn. Royal Marine Light Infantry

Place	Date	Hour	Summary of Events and Information	Remarks and references to Appendices
June				
In the trenches	1st		Working and burial parties (night)	[initials]
(Close Support)	2nd		Working and burial parties (night)	[initials]
"	3rd		Working and burial parties (night)	[initials]
"	4th		Working and burial parties (night). 31 O.R. reinforcements joined from Base.	[initials]
"	5th		Working parties (night). Lt. Col. A.R.H. Hutchinson appointed to command 190th Inf. Bde and to be Brigadier General.	[initials]
"	6th		Working parties (night)	[initials]
"	7th		Working parties (night). Lt. Wrangham, Lt. Wrenn, 2/Lt. Lewis and 2/Lt. White joined battn.	[initials]
"	8th		Working parties (night). Lt. Weeks M.C. rejoined battn. Operation Order No. 66 issued	[initials] Appendix
"	9th		Battn. relieved by 16th West Yorks Regt.	[initials]
Roclincourt	10th		Battn. moved by march route and went into billets at MAROEUIL	[initials]
Maroeuil	11th		Battn. cleaning of equipment &c. All ranks had baths.	[initials]
"	12th		Battn. training and reorganisation	[initials]

T2134. Wt. W708—776. 500000. 4/15. Sir J. C. & S.

2.

Instructions regarding War Diaries and Intelligence Summaries are contained in F. S. Regs., Part II. and the Staff Manual respectively. Title pages will be prepared in manuscript.

WAR DIARY
or
~~INTELLIGENCE SUMMARY~~.
(Erase heading not required.)

Army Form C. 2118.

2nd Bn. Royal Marine Light Infantry

Place	Date	Hour	Summary of Events and Information	Remarks and references to Appendices
June				
MAROEUIL	13th		Battn. training	[initials]
"	14th		Battn. training. 2nd Lt. SLAUGHTER joined battn.	[initials]
"	15th		Battn. training. 32 O.R. reinforcements joined from Base.	[initials]
"	16th		Battn. training. 4 O R reinforcements joined battn. from XIII Corps D.T.D.	[initials]
"	17th		Church Parade. Divisional Sports.	[initials]
"	18th		Battn. training. Inspection by Divisional Commander and Admiral Lord Charles Beresford postponed.	[initials]
"	19th		Battn. training. Battn. inspected by Divisional Commander and Admiral Lord Charles Beresford. 5 O.R. reinforcements from XIII Corps D.T.D.	[initials]
"	20th		Battn. training. Temp. Brig. Gen. A.R.H. Hutchison C.M.G., D.S.O., R.M.L.I. assumed command of 190th Infy. Bde. and 63rd (R.N.) Div. (temporarily)	[initials]
"	21st		Battn. training. Operation order No. 67 issued. 2nd Lt. G.A. NEWLING resumed duties of Asst. Adjt.	[initials] Appendix I.
"	22nd		Battn. moved by march route to A 30 C 5.5 (Map 51 B NW. 1/20000) and relieved DRAKE Battn. 2nd Lt. J.C. LEE to F.A.	[initials]
A 30 C 5.5	23rd		Working parties (night) 3 Cos. Major J.C. WAINWRIGHT R.M.L.I., Lt. R.	

T2134. Wt. W708–776. 500000. 4/15. Sir J. C. & S.

3

Army Form C. 2118.

Instructions regarding War Diaries and Intelligence Summaries are contained in F. S. Regs., Part II. and the Staff Manual respectively. Title pages will be prepared in manuscript.

WAR DIARY
or
~~INTELLIGENCE~~ SUMMARY.
(*Erase heading not required.*)

2nd Bn. Royal Marine Light Infy

Place	Date	Hour	Summary of Events and Information	Remarks and references to Appendices
	June			
A30 C5.5	23rd		BURTON R.M.L.I., A/Lt G.N.W. DENMAN-DEAN R.M.L.I. joined from Base. Major G.C. WAINWRIGHT appointed 2nd in Command.	[initials]
"	24th		Working parties (night) - 3 Cos.	[initials]
"	25th		Working parties (night) - 3 Cos.	[initials]
"	26th		Working parties (night) - 3 Cos.	[initials]
"	27th		Working parties (night) - 3 Cos.	[initials]
"	28th		Working parties (night) - 3 Cos. 7 O.R. reinforcements joined from Base. Div. Routine Order dated 28th inst. announces the award of the Victoria Cross to L/Cpl. WALTER RICHARD PARKER R.M.L.I. Po. 259 S. (R.N.) Div.	[initials]
"	29th		Working parties (day) - 3 Cos.	
"	30th		Church Service. 7 O.R. reinforcements arrived from Base	[initials]

[signature] Miller
Major
Comdg 2nd Bn RMLI

T2134. Wt. W708–776. 500000. 4/15. Sir J. C. & S.

SECRET Copy No. 6

OPERATION ORDER No. 66

By Major [illegible] R.M.L.I.
Commanding 2nd Bn Royal Marine Light Infantry

REFERENCE MAP Bn. Headquarters
51B, NW 1/20,000 8th June 1917.

1. .... The 188th Inf. Bde will be relieved by the 93rd Inf. Bde on the night 9th/10th June. The 2nd Bn. R.M.L.I. will be relieved by the 18th West Yorks.

2. .... The provisions of Part 1 of 63rd (R.N.) Div. Trench Standing Orders will be strictly adhered to.

3. .... Receipts for Stores & Ammunition handed over will be forwarded in Duplicate to Bn. HQ by noon 10th June.

4. .... Bombers will hand over their bombs on relief.

5. .... Advance party of 1 N.C.O per Coy (A.B.C.&D) & HQ under 2nd Lt. Watts will meet guides from 18th West Yorks at junction of BAILLEUL-ARRAS Rd with the ROCLINCOURT Rd (G.6.c.9.1) at 9.0 a.m. tomorrow (9th June) to take over trench accomodation.

[illegible]

5. ..... S.T. March Discipline is to be maintained on the march.

C. G. [illegible]
Capt & Adjt
2nd Bn. R.I.R.I.

Copies to:-
All recipients of O.O. 66
(except O.C. 12th West Yorks)

Issued at 5.15 a.m.

5 continued]

They will meet Coys at the bridge over railway at BOIS de la MAISON BLANCHE on the night of the 9th/10th and guide them to their trenches

6. ... Route to be taken on relief is left to the discretion of O.C Coys but at least 200 Yards distance will be maintained between platoons EAST of the bridge at BOIS de la MAISON BLANCHE

7. ... The 188th Inf Bde will move to MONT. ST. ELOY area on the evening of the 10th June

8. ... Relief complete to be reported by runner & telephone to Battn Headquarters by each double Coy.

9. ... Code word for relief — BULL.
" " " complete BUSH.

Copies to
(1) Retained
(2) O.C 18th West Yorks
(3) O.C "X" Coy
(4) O.C "Y" Coy
(5) Q.M & T.O
(6) War Diary.

A G Farquharson
Capt & Adjt
2nd Bn R.M.L.I.

Issued at 10-26pm

SECRET

Copy No. 5

Addendum to O.O. No. 66 of June 8th 1917.

Bn. Headquarters
June 9th 1917.

1. . . . The Transport Officer will arrange to send Packs to trenches G 6 & 4 2 by 10.0 a.m. on June 10th 1917.

2. . . . Water carts & cookers to be sent up at the same time.

3. . . . O.C. Coys will ensure that all men are shaved and clean in their equipment & clothing before the march is commenced.

4. . . . Attention is called to previous orders on the subject of uniformity of Dress on the march. "Mess tins will be carried in packs"
"Steel Helmets if not worn will be carried on the back of the pack under the Supporting Straps"
Waterproof sheets under the flap of the pack.

Issued at 8.40pm   SECRET.   Copy No. 6

OPERATION ORDER No. 67.

BY MAJOR L. W. MILLER, R.M.L.I.

COMMANDING 2nd Bn. ROYAL MARINE LIGHT INFANTRY.

Reference Map.
51.B. N.W. 1/20,000.

Bn. Headquarters,
21st JUNE 1917.

1. The 188th Inf. Bde. will relieve the 189th Inf. Bde. tomorrow morning, 22nd inst.
The 2nd Bn. R.M.L.I. will relieve the Drake Bn. at A.30.c.5.5. and will take over the tasks now being carried out by them.

2. The Bn. will move in the following order, :- H.Q. "D" "C" "B" "A" Coy. One hundred and fifty yards distance will be maintained between Cos. on the march.

3. Cos. will form up facing ARRAS by "D" Co's Alarm Post, on the ANZIN ROAD, in time to move off by 8.15. a.m.

4. O/C. Cos. will inspect Billets and report same clean and tidy before moving off.

5. Baggage Wagon will call for Officers' Mess gear and Valises, starting at "A" and "B" Cos. Mess at 7.30. a.m.

6. Advance Billeting Party of one N.C.O. per Co. H.Q. and Transport will parade at Orderly Room at 7.30. a.m.

7. DRESS : Full Marching Order, Steel helmets strapped round back of the Pack, Waterproof Sheets under the Flap.

8. Lewis Gun Limbers to be loaded by 7.30. a.m.

G.A. Newling 2/Lt
for Capt. & Adjutant,
2nd Bn. Royal Marine Light Infantry.

COPIES to :-
No. 1. Retained.
2. O/C. "A" Co.
3. O/C. "B" Co.
4. O/C. "C" Co.
5. O/C. "D" Co.
6. War Diary.

"CONFIDENTIAL"

Headquarters,

2nd Bn. ROYAL MARINE LIGHT INFANTRY.

1st AUGUST 1917.

WAR DIARY

(Vol. XIV)

of

2nd Battn. ROYAL MARINE LIGHT INFANTRY.

from

1st JULY 1917
- to -
31st JULY 1917.

To,

The A.G's Office,

3rd. Echelon.

Lieut. Colonel. R.M.L.I.
Commanding 2nd Bn. Royal Marine Light Infy.

Instructions regarding War Diaries and Intelligence Summaries are contained in F. S. Regs., Part II. and the Staff Manual respectively. Title pages will be prepared in manuscript.

WAR DIARY

or

~~INTELLIGENCE SUMMARY.~~

(Erase heading not required.)

Army Form C. 2118.

2nd Bn Royal Marine Light Infantry.

Place	Date	Hour	Summary of Events and Information	Remarks and references to Appendices
July.				
In Camp (Map. 51. B. N.W.) (A. 30. c. 5. 5.)	1st		Church Parade 10.30 A.M. 2/Lt. P. S. Watts to Hospital. 5 O.R reinforcements joined from Base.	
	2nd		Working parties (morning). OP. O. NO. 68 issued.	appendix I
In the trenches	3rd		Battn. relieved 18th Durham L. I. and West Yorks in Close support.	
(Close support)	4th		Working & Burial parties.	
"	5th		" " 1 Casualty a/Capt P. Lightwood to Hospital. 3 O.R. reinforcements	
"			joined from Base.	
"	6th		Working & Burial parties. 4 Casualties.	
"	7th		Operation order. NO. 69 Issued (morning). Relieved 1st Bn R. M. L. I. in front line. 1 Casualty.	appendix II
Front line	8th		T/2/Lieut. H. L. Hardesty and 4 O.R reinforcements joined from Base.	
" "	9th			
"	10th		Major. G. C. Wainwright wounded at duty. T/2/Lt. T. Buckley & T/2/Lt. E. A. Roberts & 47 O.R reinforcements joined from Base 18. Casualties.	
"	11th		Operation order. NO. 70 issued (morning) Relieved by 1st Bn. R. M. L. I. in front line. T/Capt. E. L. Edwards rejoined the Battn from England. 5 Casualties.	appendix III
Close Support	12th		2 O.R transferred from 1st Bn. R. M. L. I. Major. C. W. Miller R. M. L. I. promoted to Lieut. Col. (D. R. O. 2581)	5.6.17
"	13th		Operation Order No. 71. Issued.	appendix IV

2

Army Form C. 2118.

Instructions regarding War Diaries and Intelligence Summaries are contained in F. S. Regs., Part II. and the Staff Manual respectively. Title pages will be prepared in manuscript.

WAR DIARY

~~or~~

~~INTELLIGENCE SUMMARY~~.

(*Erase heading not required.*)

2nd Bn. Royal Marine Light Infantry

Place	Date	Hour	Summary of Events and Information	Remarks and references to Appendices
Close Support 2nd Trenches	14th		Relieved 1st Bn. R.M.L.I. in Front line. T/2nd Lt. J. C. Lee rejoined from base. 3 O.R reinforcements joined from Base. JCH	
Front line	15th		24 O.R reinforcements joined from Base. JCH	
" "	16th		OP. O. No. 72 issued. 9 Casualties. A/Lieut. R.A.R. Neville + Major. G. L. Parry and 2 O.R reinforcements joined from Base. JCH	appendix V
" "	17th		relieved by 1st Bn. R.M.L.I. moved to reserve, previously occupied by Howe Batt. at H.1.C.7.6. 4 Casualties. JCH	
Reserve	18th		Cleaning up. 5 Casualties. Capt. C. G. Farquharson R.M.L.I. promoted T/Major (D.R.O 2622) 5.6.17 JCH	
"	19th		" ", Baths etc. 22 O.R rejoined from Base. JCH	
"	20th		T/2nd Lt. R. St. Q. Downes joined from Base. JCH	
"	21st		JCH	
"	22nd		Church Parade. Op. O. No. 73 issued. JCH	appendix III
"	23rd		Relieved 1st Bn. R.M.L.I. in front line. T/2nd Lt. H. C. Smith joined Bn. 7 O.R. Reinforcements joined Bn. from Base. Major G. C. Wainwright + T/2nd Lt. A. W. Slaughter to Hospital JCH	
Support Front line immediately	24th		Burial + Working Parties. T/Lt. A. P. Cook rejoined Battn. from Base. T/2nd Lts. E. Willis, F. A. Proffitt, E. D. A. Barnard + F. Deaton joined Bn. JCH	

T2134. Wt. W708–776. 500000. 4/15. Sir J. C. & S.

Instructions regarding War Diaries and Intelligence Summaries are contained in F. S. Regs., Part II. and the Staff Manual respectively. Title pages will be prepared in manuscript.

3

WAR DIARY

~~or~~

~~INTELLIGENCE SUMMARY.~~

(*Erase heading not required.*)

Army Form C. 2118.

2nd Bn. Royal Marine Light Infantry

Place	Date	Hour	Summary of Events and Information	Remarks and references to Appendices
In the trenches				
Front line	25th		Working Parties & Burial Parties. 1 casualty. JCh	
"	26th		T/Lt. A. P. Cook Killed 3 Casualties. T/2nd Lts. T. W. Brogan, R. J. Williams, D. R. Reynolds joined the Bn. JCh	
"	27th		Working Parties. JCh	
"	28th		" " 6 Casualties JCh	
"	29th		" " Operation order No. 76 issued. 1 Casualty. T/Lt. S. A. Marshall rejoined from Hospital. JCh	Appendix VII
"	30th		relieved by Hawke Bn. (R.N.) Div. & proceeded to Wakefield Camp. 13 O.R. reinforcements joined Bn from Base. 1 Casualty. Major G. C. Wainwright rejoined from Hospital. JCh	
Wakefield Camp A.28.a	31st		Cleaning up, Baths etc. 8 casualties. JCh	

OPERATION ORDERS No. 62.
BY MAJOR L. W. MILLER R.M.L.I.
COMMANDING 2nd BN. ROYAL MARINE LIGHT INFANTRY.

Bn. Headquarters,
2nd JULY 1917.

~~ME~~ Reference Map. 51B.N.W. 1/20,000.

1\. ... The 188th Inf. Bde. will relieve the 93rd Inf. Bde. and one Bn. of the 92nd Inf. Bde. on the night of the 3rd-4th July.

2\. ... The Bn. will relieve the 18th Durham Light Infantry and 18th West Yorks in the Close Support lines.

3\. ... The Bn. will be formed into two Double Cos. as before. i.e. "A" & "D" Cos. will be known as "X" Co. and "B" and "C" Cos. will be known as "Y"Co.

4\. ... "X" Co. will relieve half Co. of 18th D.L.I. and one Co. of 18th West Yorks South of the ARRAS-GAVRELLE ROAD, and "Y" Co. will relieve one Co. of 18th D.L.I. North of the Road.
Bn. and Co. Headquarters will be in same places as before.

5\. ... Two Officers per double Co. and one N.C.O. per Platoon will proceed into the line tonight, 2nd July, to take over Trench stores, etc, and to make arrangements for the incoming of their particular Units.
Duplicate copies of any Receipts given to be rendered to Bn. H.Q. by Noon 4th July.

6\. ... Small Box Respirators will be worn in the "Alert" position during the relief.

7\. ... Cos. will report Relief complete to Bn. H.Q. by Runner.

8\. ... Cos. will parade at 8.45. p.m. and the Bn. will move off at 9.0. p.m. in the following order. H.Q. "B" "C" "D" "A" Cos. Five mins. interval between Cos. TOMY TRENCH will be used by Cos. going South of the ARRAS-GAVRELLE ROAD.
DRESS. Fighting Order with Steel Helmets. (Caps to be left behind in Packs)

9\. ... Packs will be dumped near "A" Co. Cooker by 7.0. p.m. tomorrow.

10\. ... O.C. Cos. will ensure that Lines vacated by them are clean and tidy, reporting same before moving off.

11\. ... Transport Officer will provide five Pack Horses for carrying Orderly Room and Officers' Mess gear, and Medical Stores.

12\. ... Three Lewis Guns per Co. will be taken and remainder dumped at Q.M. Stores. Two limbers will be available for carrying ammunition as far as B.27.a.0.3. and H.4.c.8.9. respectively, where it will be dumped. Two O.R.s. per L.G.Section will be detailed to accompany Limbers for unloading purposes. Cos. will take over their ammunition as they pass the Dumps.

C.A. Newling
2nd Lieut. R.M.
Assistant Adjutant,
2nd Bn. Royal Marine Light Infantry.

Issued at .. 8.35. p.m.

Copies to / Overleaf.

Copies to :-

No. 1.	Retained.
2.	O.C. 18th Durham Light Infantry.
3.	O.C. 18th West Yorks.
4.	O.C. "A" Co.
5.	O.C. "B" Co.
6.	O.C. "C" Co.
7.	O.C. "D" Co.
8.	War Diary.

Copy No. 8 SECRET

Operation Orders No. 69
by
Major L. W. Miller RMLI
commanding 2 Bn. Royal Marine Light Infy

Ref. Map OPPY 1/10,000

Bn. Headquarters
7th July 1917

1. The 2nd Bn. RMLI will relieve the 1st Bn. RMLI in the Front Line and Immediate Support Line tonight 7/8th July.
The relief will commence at 10.30 pm

2. Coys of the 2 Bn. RMLI will relieve the same Coys of the 1st Bn. RMLI.
One guide per platoon will meet units at 1st RMLI HQrs (B 30 a 8.9) at 10.30 pm.

3. Coys will move at 100 yds interval in the following order B C D ~~HQrs~~
A Coy will move ~~[illegible]~~ off independently

4. O.C. Coys will report relief complete by runner

5. Small Box Respirators will be worn in the ALERT position during relief.

6. List of Trench Stores inter-changed will be sent to Bn HQ by 8 am tomorrow

[illegible]
Capt & a/Adjt
2/R.M.L.I.

Copies to

No 1 Retained
2 O.C. 2/RMLI
3 "A" Co.
4 "B"
5 "C"
6 "D"
7 QM & TO
8 War Diary.

Copy No. ____ SECRET

Operation Orders No. 70
by
Major L. W. Miller R.M.L.I.
Commanding 2nd Bn. Royal Marine Light Infy

Ref. Map COPY 1/10,000

Bn. Headquarters
11th July 1917

1... The 2nd Bn. R.M.L.I. will be relieved by the 1st Bn. R.M.L.I. in the front line on the night 14/15th July.
The relief will commence at dusk.

2... 'A' Co of the 2 Bn. R.M.L.I. will be relieved by 'D' Co of the 1st R.M.L.I., 'B' by 'B', 'C' by 'C' and 'D' by 'A' respectively. No guides will be required.

3... Cos will take over the same areas as previously occupied in the CLOSE SUPPORT LINES and will be formed with Double Cos as before.

4... O.C. Cos will report relief complete by runner to Bn. H.Qs.

5... 'B' Co will again be at the disposal, in an emergency, of O.C. 1st Bn R.M.L.I.

6... Small Box Respirators will be worn in the ALERT position during

Operation Order No. 70 (contd)

Relief

7. Lists of Trench Stores interchanged will be sent to Bn. H.Qs by 9 am 13th inst

[illegible]
Major
[illegible]

Copy No: SECRET

Operation Order No. 71
by
Lieut Colonel L. W. Miller RMLI.
Commanding 2nd Bn Royal Marine Light Infy

Ref. Map. OPPY 1/10,000   Bn. Headquarters 13th July 1917

1... The 2nd Bn. RMLI. will relieve the 1st Bn. RMLI. in the Front Line and Immediate Support Line tomorrow night 14/15th July. The relief will commence at 10·30 pm.

2... Cos. of the 2nd Bn RMLI. will occupy the same sectors as previously, therefore "B" Co 2nd Bn will relieve "B" Co 1st Bn, "C" relieve "C", "A" relieve "D" and "D" relieve "A" respectively.

3... Cos. will move at 100 yds interval between platoons in the following order: "B", "C", "D" & H.Qs "A" Co. will move off independently.

4... OC. Cos. will report relief complete by telephone and confirm by runner.
Code word for Relief Complete for use over phone will be "BUBBLY"

5... Small box respirators will be worn in the ALERT position

Operation Order No. 71 (contd)

during the relief

6\. One officer per Co. and the C.S.M. will proceed to their respective sectors at noon tomorrow to take over Trench Stores and works in hand and in contemplation. Lists of Trench Stores interchanged will be forwarded to Bn. H.Qrs. by 8 pm.

[signature] 2/Lt.

Issued at 10 pm. Act. Adjt. 2 Bn. RMLI.

SECRET — Copy No. 2

Operation Order No 72
by
Lieut. Colonel L. W. Miller RMLI.
Commanding 2nd Bn Royal Marine Light Infy.

Ref. MAP. OPPY and SHEET 51B NW 1/10,000 1/20,000

Bn. Headquarters
16th July, 1917

1.... The 1st Bn. R.M.L.I. will relieve the 2nd Bn. R.M.L.I. in the Front Line and Immediate Support Line tomorrow night 17/18th July.
The relief will commence after the leading platoon of the HOWE Bn. reaches NAVAL TRENCH. (about 11 pm.)

2..... "A" Co. of the 2nd Bn RMLI will be relieved by "A" Co. 1st Bn RMLI, "B" by "D", "C" by "C" and "D" by "B" respectively. No guides will be required.

3.... On relief 2nd Bn. R.M.L.I. will move back into Reserve and take over Camp at present occupied by HOWE Bn. at H.1.c.7.6 (Bois de la Maison Blanche).
One officer per Co. and H.Qrs and one N.C.O. per platoon will parade at Bn. HQrs tomorrow at 12 noon to proceed in advance to take over Camp from HOWE Bn.

Operation Order No. 73 (3)

Co. Q.M.S. will meet these representatives at the Camp at 2 p.m.

4. O.C. Cos. will report relief complete by telephone and confirm by runner to Bn. H.Qrs. Code word for "Relief complete" for use over phone will be "ZIG-ZAG".

5. Small Box Respirators will be worn in the ALERT position during the relief.

6. Lists of Trench Stores handed over to 1st Bn R.M.L.I. will be sent to Bn. H.Qrs. by 9 a.m. 18th inst.
Summary of Intelligence for previous 24 hrs (to be handed over to relieving unit) will be sent to Bn. H.Qrs by 8 p.m. tomorrow.

7. In the event of a hostile attack being made during the relief, platoons will occupy the nearest fire trench immediately reporting their position to Bn. H.Qrs.

8. Transport Officer will arrange for conveyance of Orderly Room gear, Medical Stores and Officers' Mess Gear. This must be at Ration Dump by 10 p.m.
In the event of the Lewis Guns being relieved in advance, Lewis Gun limbers will be at Ration Dump at 10 p.m.,

Operation Order No. 72 (3)

8. When guns and ammunition will be packed under supervision of L.G. Sgt.

9. Cos will move back to the Camp at 100 yds distance between platoons and by the following routes:- "A" Co via CHICO - TOWY ALLEY; H.Q.s, "D", "C" + "B" Cos via MARINE - THAMES EXTENSION - THAMES ALLEY - TOWY ALLEY.

Issued at 7.15 pm.

[signature] 2 Lt

Act Adjt 2nd/RMLI

SECRET. COPY No. ...

OPERATION ORDERS No. 73.
BY
LIEUT. COLONEL I. W. MILLER. R.M.L.I.
COMMANDING 2nd Bn. ROYAL MARINE LIGHT INFANTRY.

Reference Maps.
51.b.N.W. 1/20,000.
OPPY. 1/10,000.

Bn. Headquarters,
22nd JULY 1917.

1. ... The 2nd Bn. R.M.L.I. will relieve the 1st Bn. R.M.L.I. in the Front Line and Immediate Support Line on the night of 23-24th July.
Leading Co. of 2nd Bn. R.M.L.I. will not move East of Brigade Headquarters before 9.45. p.m.

2. ... Cos. of the 2nd Bn. R.M.L.I. will relieve the same Cos. of the 1st Bn. R.M.L.I. No guides will be required.

3. ... An advance party of one Officer per Co. and one N.C.O. per Platoon and Headquarters will proceed into the Line tomorrow morning, to take over Trench Stores etc, and make arrangements for the incoming of their particular Units. Duplicate copies of any receipts given to be rendered to Bn. Headquarters by 9.0. a.m. 24th inst. These details will parade at Orderly Room at 10.0. a.m. tomorrow.

4. ... Small Box Respirators will be worn in the "ALERT" position during the relief, and during the whole time the Bn. is in the Trenches.

5. Cos. will report relief complete by telephone and confirm by Runner to Bn. H.Q. which will be in the same place as before. Code words for "Relief complete" for use over the 'phone will be "HIGH JINKS"

6. Cos. will parade at 9.30. p.m. tomorrow and the Bn. will move off at 9.45. p.m. in the following order. "D" "A" "C" "B" "H.Q". Distance between Platoons - 100 yards.

7. Packs will be dumped near Cookers by 7.30. p.m. tomorrow.

8. O.C. Cos. will ensure that Lines vacated by them are clean and tidy, reporting same before moving off.

9. Transport Officer will arrange for conveyance of Officers' Mess Gear, Medical Stores, and Orderly Room Gear. This must be dumped near Cookers by 8.30. p.m.

10. Four Lewis Guns per Co. will be taken, and Transport Officer will arrange for Limbers to reach Cookers by 8.0. p.m. tomorrow for conveying the Guns and Ammunition to the Ration Dump in THAMES TRENCH. O.C. Cos. will detail one gun's Crew for loading purposes and to accompany Limbers for unloading on arrival at Dump. Cos. will take over their Guns and Ammunition as they pass the Dump.

[signature]
2nd Lieut. R.M.
A/Adjt. 2nd Bn. Royal Marine Light Infantry

Issued at 6.55. p.m.

Copies to - /overleaf.

Copies to :-

No.	
1.	Retained.
2.	O.C. 1st Bn, R.M.L.I.
3.	O.C. "A" Co.
4.	O.C. "B" Co.
5.	O.C. "C" Co.
6.	O.C. "D" Co.
7.	Transport Officer.
8.	War Diary.

SECRET COPY No. 8

Operation Order No. 74
by
Lieut-Colonel A.W. Miller RMLI
Commanding 2nd Bn. Royal Marine Light Infy.

Reference Maps 57 B. N.W. 1/20000 Bn. Headquarters
OPPY. 1/10 000 29th July, 1917

1 The 188th Infy. Bde. will be relieved in the right Sub-sector of the Divisional front on the night of the 30th/31st July by the 189th Infy. Bde.

The 2nd Bn. R.M.L.I. will be relieved by the HAWKE Bn.

Relief will commence about 11 pm

2 Cos of the 2nd Bn. RMLI will be relieved by Cos of the HAWKE Bn as follows: "A" by "A"; "B" by "D"; "C" by "C" and "D" by "B" respectively.

Three guides per Co. will meet platoons of relieving Bn. at commencement of INFANTRY TRACK (immediately E of Canal crossing at H1 d 99) at 9. 30 pm. These guides will report at Bn. H.Qrs at 8 pm. tomorrow.

3 Cos will report "Relief Complete" by telephone and confirm by runner to Bn. H.Qs. Code word for "Relief Complete"

Operation Order No. 74 (2)

for use over the phone will be
CHEER-OH!!

4\. The Bn., on being relieved, will take over WAKEFIELD CAMP, ROCLINCOURT (A28 a) vacated by HAWKE Bn.

Cos. will move from the line by the following route:- MARINE - THAMES EXTENSION - thence by WAGGON TRACK crossing TOWY and leading to BAILLEUL - ARRAS RD via MAISON BLANCHE BRIDGE - CHANTECLER CORNER - ROCLINCOURT RD.

5\. An advance party of 1 officer per Co. and 1 N.C.O. per platoon and H.Qs will proceed to WAKEFIELD CAMP tomorrow afternoon to make arrangements for the incoming of their particular units. These details will parade at Bn. H.Qs. at 1 pm. NCOs will meet their respective platoons at entrance to ROCLINCOURT (about A29 c 75.30)

(1.30) at ■.30 am (31st) to guide them to the camp.

6\. An advance party from HAWKE Bn. will proceed to the line tonight to take over Stores &c. Duplicate receipts of Stores handed over to be rendered to Bn. H.Qs by 5 pm. tomorrow.

7\. Box Respirators will be worn in the "ALERT" position during the relief.

Operation Order No. 74 (3)

8. Lewis Gun ammunition and panniers will be handed over to relieving unit. The Bn. L.G.O. will report to Bn. H.Qrs. by noon tomorrow the number of magazines re. to be handed over.

9. Officers Mess Gear, Medical Stores and Orderly Room Gear must be at the Ration Dump by 10.0 pm, and Transport Officer will provide a limber for conveyance of same. He will also arrange for Officers' chargers to be at the MAISON BLANCHE BRIDGE at 1.30 am, 30th inst.

G.A. Newling
Capt & Adjt.
2 Bn. R.M.L.I.

Issued at 6.30 pm.

Copy No. 1 Retained
2 O.C. HAWKE Bn.
3 O.C. 'A' Co.
4 O.C. 'B' Co.
5 O.C. 'C' Co.
6 O.C. 'D' Co.
7 Quartermaster
8 L.G.O.
9 WAR DIARY

"CONFIDENTIAL"

Headquarters,

2nd Bn. ROYAL MARINE LIGHT INFANTRY.

1st SEPTEMBER 1917.

W A R D I A R Y

(Vol. XV)

---- of ----

2nd Battn. ROYAL MARINE LIGHT INFANTRY.

from

1st AUGUST 1917

to

31st AUGUST 1917.

To :-

The A.G. Officer, Headquarters,

63rd (R.N) Division.

~~3rd Echelon.~~

Majorm R.M.L.I.

Commanding 2nd Bn. Royal Marine Light Infy.

Instructions regarding War Diaries and Intelligence Summaries are contained in F. S. Regs., Part II. and the Staff Manual respectively. Title pages will be prepared in manuscript.

WAR DIARY
or
~~INTELLIGENCE SUMMARY.~~
(Erase heading not required.)

Army Form C. 2118.

2nd Bn Royal Marine Light Infantry.

Place	Date	Hour	Summary of Events and Information	Remarks and references to Appendices
Wakefield Camp (Div Reserve) A28a.	August 1st		Battalion training. Lieut R Burton, R.M.L.I. to F.A. T/Lt M K Goldie RM rejoined from Base. 82 reinforcements (O.R's) joined from Base. RB	
Do -	2nd		Training. T/2nd Lt F W Slaughter. R.M. rejoined from F.A. T/Lieut C.O. Mitchell struck of strength 10-7-17. D.R.O. 2721 RB	
Do.	3rd		Training. RB	
Do	4th.		Training. T/2nd Lieuts C. F. M. Burnside. J. V. Lord, W. C. Whitburn & C. V. Egar joined Bn. T/2nd Lt H. C. Smith to F.A. RB	
Do.	5th.		Church Parades. T/Lt C. W. F. Yeldham to 176th Tunnelling Co. RB	
Do	6th.		Training. RB	
Do	7th.		Training. T/2nd Lt. C. D. A. Barnard to Bde Bombing School. T/2nd Lt H L. Hardisty to XIIIth Corps. D.T. Depot. Operation Order No 75 issued. RB	Appendix I RB
In the trenches	8th.		Relieved Hawke Bn in support. T/2nd Lt H J Wilcox joined Bn from Base RB	

Instructions regarding War Diaries and Intelligence Summaries are contained in F. S. Regs., Part II. and the Staff Manual respectively. Title pages will be prepared in manuscript.

WAR DIARY

or

~~INTELLIGENCE SUMMARY~~.

(Erase heading not required.)

Army Form C. 2118.

2nd Bn Royal Marine Light Infantry

Place	Date	Hour	Summary of Events and Information	Remarks and references to Appendices
	August			
In support	9th		Working parties. Lieut R Burton rejoined from F.A. One casualty. RB	
Do.	10th		Working parties. One casualty. Operation Order No 76 issued. RB	Appendix III a
Front line	11th		Relieved 1st Bn. R.M.L.I. in front line and immediate support. 6 O.R.s reinforcements. RB	
Do.	12th		Working parties. One casualty. RB	
Do	13th		Working parties. Four casualties. RB	
Do	14th		Working parties. Operation Order No 77. issued. RB	Appendix III b
Do / Bde Reserve.	15th		Relieved in front line by 1st Bn. R.M.L.I. proceeded to camp at Maison Blanche. Three casualties. RB	
Reserve.	16th		In reserve. Lt Col L W Miller, R.M.L.I to F.A. Four reinforcements joined Bn from Base. RB	
do.	17th		In reserve. T/Capt T L Edwards to XIIIth Corps D. T. Depôt. RB	
Do	18th		In reserve. T/2nd Lt H. C. Smith rejoined from F.A. Operation Order No 78 issued. RB	Appendix IV RB
Do.	19th		Relieved 1st Bn. R.M.L.I. in front line. Four ~~casualties~~ reinforcements. RB	
Front line	20th		In front line. Burial & Working Parties. One casualty. RB	

T2134. Wt. W708–776. 500000. 4/15. Sir J. C. & S.

Instructions regarding War Diaries and Intelligence Summaries are contained in F. S. Regs., Part II. and the Staff Manual respectively. Title pages will be prepared in manuscript.

WAR DIARY

or

~~INTELLIGENCE SUMMARY.~~

(Erase heading not required.)

Army Form C. 2118.

2nd Bn Royal Marine Light Infantry.

Place	Date	Hour	Summary of Events and Information	Remarks and references to Appendices
	August			
Front line.	21st		Burial & Working Parties. 25 reinforcements O.R's joined Bn from Base. ~~Four~~ Six casualties. RB	
Do.	22nd		Burial & Working Parties. One casualty. RB	
Do	23rd		Burial & Working Parties. Operation Order No 19. issued. Four casualties. RB	Appendix I RB
Do	24th		Relieved in front line by Hawke Bn & proceeded to Wakefield Camp. One casualty. RB	
Wakefield Camp	25th		Baths, clearing up ect. 24 reinforcements joined from base. RB	
Do	26th		Training. RB	
Do	27th		Do — RB	
Do	28th		Do — . Four reinforcements joined Bn from base. RB	
Do	29th		Do — . Eight reinforcements. 2nd Lt C Whitburn to F.A. RB	
Do	30th		Do — . 2nd Lt H. Fielder & 22 O.R's joined Bn from Base. RB	
Do	31st		Do — RB	

[signature] Major R.M.L.I.
Comdg 2nd Bn Royal Marines L.I.

T2134. Wt. W708—776. 500000. 4/15. Sir J. C. & S.

S E C R E T.

Copy No. .

OPERATION ORDER No. 75.
BY LIEUT. COLONEL L. W. MILLER. R.M.L.I.
COMMANDING 2nd Bn. ROYAL MARINE LIGHT INFANTRY.

Reference Maps , :- 51. B. N.W. 1/20,000.
OPPY. 1/10,000.

Bn. Headquarters,
7th Aug. 1917.

---

1. ... The 188th Infantry Brigade will relieve the 189th Infantry Brigade on the nights 7/8th and 8/9th August.
The 2nd Bn. R.M.L.I. will relieve the HOOD Bn. on the night 8/9th Aug. in the Close Support Line. (GAVRELLE).

2. ... "A" and "D" Cos. will occupy NAVAL TRENCH, South of the ARRAS – GAVRELLE ROAD, and "B" and "C" Cos. will occupy MARINE TRENCH, North of the Road.
Bn. Headquarters will be located as before.

3. ... One Officer per Co. and one N.C.O. per Platoon will proceed into the Line tomorrow to take over Trench Stores etc., and make arrangements for the incoming of their particular Units. These details will parade at Orderly Room at 1.0. p.m. tomorrow. Duplicate copies of any receipts given to be rendered to Bn. H.Q. by Noon, 9th August.

4. ... Small Box Respirators will be worn in the ALERT position during the relief and during the whole time the Bn. is in the Trenches.

5. ... Cos. will report "Relief complete" to Bn. H.Q. by Runner.

6. ... Cos. will parade at 8.30. p.m. and the Bn. will move off at 8.45. p.m. in the following order, :- H.Q. "A" "D" "B" "C" Cos. 100 yards distance between Platoons, touch to be maintained by Connecting files. Route ; ROCLINCOURT ROAD – BAILLEUL ROAD – RAILWAY CROSSING – INFANTRY TRACK – RATION DUMP.
DRESS. Fighting Order with Steel Helmets (Caps to be left behind in Packs).

7. ... Packs will be dumped near Co. Cookers by 7.0. p.m. tomorrow.

8. ... O.C. Cos. will ensure that Lines vacated by them are clean and tidy, reporting same before moving off.

9. ... Transport Officer will provide one Limber for conveying Officers' Mess gear, Medical Stores, and Orderly Room gear ; these must be ready for loading at 6.0. p.m.

10. ... Three Limbers will be available for conveying Lewis Guns and Ammunition to the Ration Dump ([illegible] TRENCH). Limbers will be loaded, under the supervision of the Bn. Lewis Gun Sergt, by 7.0. p.m. and one L.G. Crew per Co. will be detailed to accompany Limbers for unloading, on arrival at Dump. Cos. will take over their Guns and Ammunition as they pass the Dump.

[signature]
Capt. & A/Adjutant,
2nd Bn. Royal Marine Light Infantry.

Issued at .. 8.45. p.m.

Copies to (Over)

Copies to :-

No.	1.	Retained.
	2.	C.C. "A" Co.
	3.	C.C. "B" Co.
	4.	C.C. "C" Co.
	5.	C.C. "D" Co.
	6.	War Diary.

SECRET COPY NO. [illegible].

Operation Order No. 76 by Lieut. Colonel L. W. Miller R.M.L.I. Commanding 2nd Bn. Royal Marine Light Infy.

Ref. Maps 51 B.NW. 1/20,000
OPPY: 1/10,000

Bn Headquarters
10th Aug. 1917

1\.... The 2nd Bn. R.M.L.I. will relieve the 1st Bn. R.M.L.I. in the Front Line and Close Support Line on the night 11th/12th Aug.

The relief will commence at 10.0 pm.

2\.... "A" Co. 2nd Bn. R.M.L.I. will relieve "D" Co. 1st R.M.L.I. in CHICO trench; "B" Co. will relieve "A" Co. in CECIL trench; "C" Co. relieve "B" Co. in CHARLES trench and "D" Co. relieve "C" Co. in RAILWAY and MARINE trenches.

No guides will be sent.

3\.... Advance party of 1 officer per Co. and 1 N.C.O. per platoon will proceed into the front line tomorrow afternoon to take over trench Stores and make arrangements for incoming of their particular units. Duplicate copies of any receipts given to be rendered to Bn. H.Qrs. by 9 am. 12th inst.

Operation Order No: 76 (contd)

4.... Small Box Respirators will be worn in the ALERT position during the relief and the whole time the Bn. is in the trenches.

5.... Cos. will report relief complete by telephone and confirm by runner to Bn. H.Qs. which will be in the new dug-out in MARINE trench nearer FOXY ALLEY than the old H.Qs.

Code for "Relief Complete" for use over phone:-

"A" Co:- "A101 received".
"B" Co:- "B101 received"
"C" Co:- "C101 received"
"D" Co:- "D101 received"

6.... Cos. will move off, 100 yds between platoons and 10 mins interval between Cos, in the following order:- "B" "C" "D" "A" H.Qs.

The platoon of "B" Co. at BRILLIANT POST will move off in time to reach junction of THAMES and MARINE trenches at 10.0 pm.

7.... Lewis Gunners will relieve in advance, commencing with "B" Co. at 8.0 pm. and remaining Cos at 10 mins. intervals. Bn. L.G.O. will supervise this relief.

Issued at: 8.15 pm

G.A. Mawling
Capt & a/Adjt
2-R. D.M.L.I

SECRET   Copy No. 2

Operation Order No. 77
by
Lieut Colonel [illegible] Miller RMLI
commanding 2 Bn Royal Marine Light Infy

Ref. Map. 51 B N.W. [illegible]   Bn Headquarters
[illegible]   14 Aug 17

1. The 2 Bn RMLI will be relieved by the 1 Bn RMLI on the night 15/16 Aug in the Front Line and Immediate Support Line.
The relief will commence [illegible] at the junction [illegible] the ANSON Bn [illegible] NAVAL Trench.

2. Cos of the 2 Bn RMLI will be relieved as follows: (by Cos of 1st Bn RMLI) A Co by C Co, B Co by B Co; C Co by A Co; and D Co by D Co.
No guides need be sent.

3. On relief the 2 Bn RMLI will move back into Reserve taking over Camp at MAISON BLANCHE vacated by ANSON Bn.
An advance party of ~~[illegible]~~ ~~[illegible]~~ 1 NCO per platoon & [illegible] will proceed from the Line tomorrow

billet area Camp and arrange for messing of these parties on arrival. These details will report to Bn. HQ. at 12 noon.

4. Small Box Respirators will be worn in the ALERT position during the relief.

5. Coys will report "Relief Complete" by telephone & confirm by runner to Bn. H.Q.

Code for Relief Complete for use over the phone:

A Co. – A 202 received

B Co. – B 202 received

C Co. – C 202 received

D Co. – D 202 received

6. Coys will move out by the following routes:-

C & B Cos. via CHAMBERS – [illegible] – MARINE – THAMES – TOWEY.

A Co. via ELSY – MARINE – THAMES – TOWEY.

and D Co. via MARINE – THAMES – TOWEY.

7. Lewis Guns will be [illegible] and guns and ammunition will be [illegible] and ready for loading on the [illegible] at 10.0 pm. [illegible] will supervise this and detail [illegible] to accompany each limber.

8. All completely [illegible] to [illegible]
[illegible] Camp by 9.0 pm.

9. Summary of Intelligence [illegible]
[illegible]
8.0 pm for [illegible]

10. [illegible]
[illegible]
[illegible]
[illegible]
[illegible]

[illegible]
Capt & Adjt.
[illegible]

Issued at 11.5 pm

Copies to:
[illegible]
2 WD Diary
3 OC A Co
4 OC B Co
5 OC C Co
6 OC D Co

SECRET. 78 COPY No.

OPERATION ORDERS No. [illegible]

BY MAJOR G. C. WAINWRIGHT, R.M.L.I.

COMMANDING 2nd Bn. ROYAL MARINE LIGHT INFANTRY.

Reference Maps.

57.b.N.W. 1/20,000.

OPPY. 1/10,000.

Bn. Headquarters,
18th Augt. 1917.

1. ... The 2nd Bn. R.M.L.I. will relieve the 1st Bn. R.M.L.I. in the Front Line and Immediate Support Lines on the night of the 19-20th Augt. The leading Platoon of 2nd Bn. R.M.L.I. will not move East of Brigade Headquarters before 8.15. p.m.

2. ... Coy. of 2nd Bn. R.M.L.I. will relieve Coy. of 1st Bn. R.M.L.I. as follows :- "A" will relieve "C", "D" will relieve "B", "C" will relieve "A", and "B" will relieve "D" respectively. No guides will be sent.

3. ... An advance party of one Officer per Co. and one N.C.O. per Platoon and Headquarters will proceed into the Line tomorrow afternoon to take over Trench Stores, etc. and make arrangements for the incoming of their particular Units. Duplicate copies of any Receipts given to be rendered to Bn. Headquarters by 9.0 a.m. 20th inst. These details will parade at Orderly Room at 2.0. p.m. tomorrow.

4. ... Small Box Respirators will be worn in the "ALERT" position during the Relief, and during the whole time the Bn. is in the Trenches.

5. ... Coy. will report Relief complete by telephone, and confirm by Runner to Bn. H.Q. which will be in the same place as before.
Code for "Relief complete" for use over 'phone will be
"A" Co. "A.303. received"
"B" Co. "B.303. received"
"C" Co. "C.303. received"
"D" Co. "D.303. received"

6. ... Coy. will parade at 8.0. p.m. and the Bn. will move off at 8.15. p.m. in the following order :- "D" "A" "C" "B" "H.Q.". Distance between Platoons - 100 yards. Route. RAILWAY CROSSING, -- DUCKBOARD TRACK -- [illegible] -- [illegible],

7. ... Packs will be dumped near Cookers by 6.30. p.m. Greatcoats will be carried in Bandoleie.

8. ... O.C. Coy. will ensure that Lines vacated by them are clean and tidy, reporting same before moving off.

9. ... Transport Officer will arrange for conveyance of Officers' Mess Gear, Medical Stores, and Orderly Room Gear. These must be dumped near Cookers by 7.30. p.m.

10. ... Three Limbers will be available for conveyance of Lewis Guns and Ammunition to the Ration Dump in [illegible] TRENCH. Bn. Lewis Gun Officer will arrange for Guns and Ammunition to be dumped near

/ Cookers.

Continued. (2).

[illegible]. ... (continued) Cookers by 7.[illegible] p.m., and Transport Officer will arrange for limbers to be there at that hour.
O.C. Coy. will detail one Lewis Gun Crew for loading purposes and to accompany limbers for unloading on arrival at Dump.
Coy. will take over Guns and Ammunition as they pass the Dump.

[illegible signature]

Capt. & A/Adjutant.
2nd Bn. Royal Marine Light Infantry.

Issued at [illegible] p.m.

Copies to :-

No. 1. Retained.
2. O.C. 1st Bn. R.M.[illegible].I.
3. O.C. "A" Co.
4. O.C. "B" Co.
5. O.C. "C" Co.
6. O.C. "D" Co.
7. War Diary.

SECRET Copy No 9

OPERATION ORDER No 79
by
Major G C Wainwright RMLI

Commanding 2nd Royal Marine Light Infantry.

Ref Maps 51B NW. 1/20,000 Bn Headquarters
SPPY 1/10,000. 23rd Aug 1917

1_____ The 188th Inf Bde will be relieved in the right sector of the Divisional Front, by the 189th Infy Bde on the night of Aug 24th / 25th.

The 2nd Bn RMLI. will be relieved by the "Hood" Bn in the Front Line & Immediate Supports Line Relief will commence about 10.30 pm.

2___ Co's of the 2nd Bn RMLI will be relieved by Co's of the Hood Bn as follows "A" will be relieved by "D". "D" by "B" "C" by "A" & "B" by "C" respectively.

3 Platoon Guides per Co will meet their relieving Co's at the commencement of "TOWER TRACK" (immediately east of level crossing at H.1.6.99.) at 7.45 pm. The guides will report at Bn HQs at 5.0 pm tomorrow.

3____ Representatives from the Hood Bn will proceed into the line tonight to take over Trench Stores Maps etc.

– – – Duplicate copies of receipts to be forwarded to Bn HQs by 2 pm tomorrow.

An advance party of 1 NCO per Platoon & HQs will report to HQs Hood Bn at 3 pm tomorrow to arrange for the incoming of their particular units at WAKEFIELD CAMP ROCLINCOURT. These details will report at Bn HQs in the line at 12 noon.

One Officer per Coy from those at present at the Transport Lines will proceed to take over WAKEFIELD CAMP tomorrow, at 3 pm under the supervision of Capt B. G. Andrews.

4 – – – – – Small Box Respirators will be worn in the ALERT position during the relief.

5 – – – – Coys will forward Summary of Intelligence for the previous 24 hours to Bn HQs, by 8.0 pm tomorrow to be handed over to relieving Bn.

6 – – – – After relief Coys will move back by the following Route:– MARINE – THAMES ALLEY – WAGGON TRACK – TOWEY TRACK – BAILLEUL RD – ROCLINCOURT – RD to WAKEFIELD CAMP.

7 – – – – Co's will report "Relief Complete" by telephone confirm by runner to Bn HQ's.

Code for "Relief Complete" for use over the phone will be:–

"A" Co "A Hour received"
"B" Co "B Hour received"
"C" Co "C Hour received"
"D" Co "D Hour received"

8 – – – – – Transport Officer will provide one limber for Conveyance of Officers Mess Gear, Medical Stores & –

2

Orderly Room Gear & three Limbers for Conveyance of Lewis Guns & Ammunition. O.C. Coys will detail one Lewis Gun Crew for Loading purposes under the Supervision of the Bn Lewis Gun Sergeant. These Limbers will not be required to reach the dump before 11.0. pm.

Transport Officer will arrange also for Officers Chargers to be at level crossing (about H.1.b99) at 2.30. a.m. on the 25th inst:

(sd) G.A. Newling

Capt & a/Adjt.

Issued at 5.30. pm. 2nd Bn R.M.L.I.

Copies to:—

1. Retained
2. O"C" "Hood" Bn
3. O.C. A Coy
4. O.C. B Coy
5. O.C. C Coy
6. O.C. D Coy
7. Transport Officer
8. Capt B.G. Andrews
9. War Diary – 8

"CONFIDENTIAL"

G. 457

Vol 16

Headquarters.

2nd. Bn. Royal Marine Light Infantry

1st. OCTOBER 1917.

WAR DIARY

(Vol. XV.)

2nd Battn. ROYAL MARINE LIGHT INFANTRY.

from

1st. SEPTEMBER 1917.

- to -

30th. SEPTEMBER 1917.

To.

Headquarters.

63rd. (R.N) Division.

[signature]

Lieut Colonel R.M.L.I.

Commanding 2nd Bn. Royal Marine Light Infy.

Army Form C. 2118.

WAR DIARY
or
~~INTELLIGENCE SUMMARY.~~
(Erase heading not required.)

Instructions regarding War Diaries and Intelligence Summaries are contained in F. S. Regs., Part II. and the Staff Manual respectively. Title pages will be prepared in manuscript.

2nd Bn Royal Marine Light Infantry

Place	Date	Hour	Summary of Events and Information	Remarks and references to Appendices
Wakefield Camp. Robecourt. Div Res.	1/9/17		Battalion training. Lieut Col L W Miller RMLI struck off strength. D.R.O 2865. Operation Order No 80 issued.	Appendix 1. R.B.
In the trenches	2/9/17		Relieved Drake Battalion in support trenches. 28 reinforcements joined battalion. Lieuts L Clark & F G Jefferies struck off strength. 63rd (RN) Div memo No 3514/G/a.	R.B.
Ditto	3/9/17		Working and carrying parties. One casualty.	R.B.
"	4/9/17		Ditto	R.B.
"	5/9/17		" " " One casualty, Sec Lt P S Watts & 27 O Rs reinforcements joined battalion. Operation Order No 81 issued. T/Capt G A Newling appointed Adjutant. D.R.O 2893. Lieut P Lightwood struck off strength. D.R.O 2896.	R.B. Appendix 2. R.B.
"	6/9/17		Relieved by Howe Bn & proceeded to Maison Blanche Camp in Bde Reserve.	R.B.

A5834 Wt. W4973/M687 750,000 8/16 D. D. & L. Ltd. Forms/C.2118/13.

Sheet 2

Army Form C. 2118

WAR DIARY
or
INTELLIGENCE SUMMARY
(Erase heading not required.)

2nd Bn Royal Marine Light Infantry

Instructions regarding War Diaries and Intelligence Summaries are contained in F. S. Regs., Part II. and the Staff Manual respectively. Title Pages will be prepared in manuscript.

Place	Date	Hour	Summary of Events and Information	Remarks and references to Appendices
Bde Res.	7/9/17.		Baths & cleaning up. Sec Lt H C. Smith to 63rd (R N) Div Gas School.	RB
Ditto	8/9/17		Baths & cleaning up. 22 reinforcements joined Bn. Operation Order No 82 issued.	appendix 3, RB.
front line	9/9/17		Relieved 1st Bn. R.M.L.I in the front line trenches. T/Sec Lt R. A. R. Roberts to be T/Lieut. D.R.O 2911. Major G C Wainwright. R.M.L.I to be Act. Lieut Colonel and T/Sec Lt R. Wells to be Act Captain. D. R.O. 2915.	RB
"	10/9/17.		Working parties. Two casualties.	RB
"	11/9/17		" " . Two casualties. Lieut P Legertwood and 4 O.R.'s reinforcements joined battalion.	RB
"	12/9/17		Working parties. Operation Order No 83 issued.	appendix 4. RB
"	13/9/17		" " . Inter company relief. Two casualties.	
"	14/9/17		" " . Seven casualties.	RB
"	15/9/17		" " . Two casualties.	RB

1875 Wt. W593/826 1,000,000 4/15 J.B.C. & A. A.D.S.S./Forms/C. 2118.

Instructions regarding War Diaries and Intelligence Summaries are contained in F. S. Regs., Part II. and the Staff Manual respectively. Title Pages will be prepared in manuscript.

WAR DIARY
or
INTELLIGENCE SUMMARY
(Erase heading not required.)

Sheet 3.

Army Form C. 2118

2nd Bn Royal Marine Light Infantry

Place	Date	Hour	Summary of Events and Information	Remarks and references to Appendices
Front line	16/9/17		Working parties. One casualty. Operation Order No 84 issued	Appendix 5. RB
" "	17/9/17		Relieved by Hood Bn. Proceeded by train to St Aubin. Div Res. Lieut Colonel G. L. Wainwright to English leave. Major J. P. Parry assumed command. One casualty.	RB
Div Res	18/9/17		Baths & cleaning up.	RB
" "	19/9/17		Battalion training. Operation Order No 85 issued.	Appendix 6.
" "	20/9/17		Proceeded by route march to Acq & Frevin Capelle. Operation Order No 86 issued.	Appendix 7. RB
Acq.	21/9/17		Proceeded by route march to Frevillers.	RB
Frevillers	22/9/17		Baths & cleaning up. T/Lt C. W. Yeldham rejoined & T/2nd Lt E. D. A. Barnard rejoined.	RB
" "	23/9/17		Church Parades ect.	RB
" "	24/9/17		Battalion in Platoon training. 26 O R's reinforcement joined Bn	RB
" "	25/9/17		" " " " 18 " " "	RB
" "	26/9/17		" " " "	RB
" "	27/9/17		" " " " 38 " " "	
" "	28/9/17		" " " Lt Col G. L. Wainwright rejoined from leave & resumed command of Bn.	RB

1875 Wt. W593/826 1,000,000 4/15 J.B.C. & A. A.D.S.S./Forms/C. 2118.

Army Form C. 2118.

Sheet 4.

Instructions regarding War Diaries and Intelligence Summaries are contained in F. S. Regs., Part II. and the Staff Manual respectively. Title pages will be prepared in manuscript.

WAR DIARY
or
INTELLIGENCE SUMMARY.
(*Erase heading not required.*) 2nd Bn. Royal Marine Light Infantry

Place	Date	Hour	Summary of Events and Information	Remarks and references to Appendices
Frevillers	29/9/17		Battalion in Platoon training.	RB
"	30/9/17		Church Parade ect.	RB

[illegible signature]

Lieut. Colonel R.M.L.I.

Comdg 2nd Bn. Royal Marine Lt Infy

A5834 Wt. W4973 M687 750,000 8/16 D. D. & L. Ltd. Forms/C.2118/13.

S E C R E T.

COPY. No.

OPERATION ORDERS No.80.
BY MAJOR C. C. WAINWRIGHT. R.M.L.I.
COMMANDING 2nd Bn. ROYAL MARINE LIGHT INFANTRY.

Reference Maps. :-
51b.N.W. 1/20,000.
OPPY. 1/10,000.

Bn. Headquarters,
1stSeptember 1917.

1. The 188th Infantry Brigade will relieve the 189th Infantry Brigade on the nights of 1/2nd and 2/3rd Septr.
The 2nd Bn. R.M.L.I. will relieve the DRAKE Battn. on the night of 2/3rd Septr. in the RED LINE and CLOSE SUPPORT LINE (GAVRELLE)

2. "B" and "C" Cos. will occupy MARINE and NAVAL TRENCHES (N.of TOWEY) Half of "D" Co. in NAVAL TRENCH South of TOWEY.
"A" Co. and half "D" Co. (with Co.H.Q) in RED LINE.
Bn. Headquarters will be located as before.

3. "B" Co. 2nd R.M.L.I. will relieve "D" Co. DRAKE Bn. "C" will relieve "B" Co. Half "D" Co (in NAVAL TRENCH) will relieve "A" Co. "A" Co. and half "D" Co. will relieve "C" Co. in RED LINE.

4. One Officer and one N.C.O. per Co. (two N.C.Os. from "D" Co) will proceed into the Line in advance to take over Trench Stores etc and make arrangements for the incoming of their particular Units. These details will parade at Orderly Room at 1.0. p.m. tomorrow.
D uplicate copies of Receipts given to be rendered to Bn.H.Q. by 8.0. p.m. tomorrow.

5. Small Box Respirators will be worn in the "ALERT" position during the relief, and during the whole time the Bn. is in the Trenches.

6. RED LINE Cos. will report "Relief complete" by Code (B.A.B. Ed.3). Close Support Cos. by Runner to Bn. H.Q.

7. Cos. will parade at 6.45. p.m. and the Bn. will move off at 7.0. p.m. in the following order. :- Half "D" Co. (NAVAL TRENCH) "C" Co. "B" Co. "A" Co. and Half "D" Co. (RED LINE). 100 yards distance between Platoons, touch to be maintained by connecting files.
ROUTE. :- ROCLINCOURT ROAD -- BAILLEUL ROAD -- RAILWAY CROSSING - TOWEY TRACK -- WAGON TRACK -- RATION DUMP.
DRESS. :- "Fighting Order" with Steel Helmets, (Caps to be left behind in Packs) Great Coats will be carried in banderole.

8. Packs will be dumped near Cookers by 4.0. p.m.

9. O.C. Cos. will ensure that Lines vacated by them are clean and tidy, reporting same before moving off

10. Transport Officer will provide one Limber for conveying Officers' Mess Gear Medical Stores and Orderly Room gear. These must be ready for loading at 6.30. p.m.

..Continued. (2).

11. Three Limbers will be available for conveying Lewis Guns and Ammunition to the Ration Dump. (TRAMES TRENCH). Limbers will be loaded under the supervision of the Bn. Lewis Gun Sergt. by 4.0. p.m. and one Lewis Gun Crew per Co. will be detailed to accompany Limbers for unloading on arrival at the Dump. Cos. will take over their Guns and Ammunition as they pass the Dump.

[signature]

Capt & A/Adjutant,
2nd Bn. Royal Marine Light Infantry.

Issued at .. 11.15.p.m.

Copies to :-

No. 1. Retained.
2. O.C. "DRAKE" Bn.
3. O.C. "A" Co.
4. O.C. "B" Co.
5. O.C. "C" Co.
6. O.C. "D" Co.
7. War Diary.

Corrigendum to O.O. No 31 attached

Ref para 9. Lewis Gun Ammunition will be handed over to relieving Bn. Lewis Guns will be carried back by the crews.
No limbers will be available for this purpose.

[signature]
Capt & Adjt
2nd Bn RMLI

Sept 5th 1917

SECRET   COPY No 1

Operation Order No 81
by
Major G. C. Wainwright R.M.L.I.

Commanding 2nd Bn Royal Marine Light Infantry

Ref. Maps 51B N.W. 1/20.000   Bn Headquarters
OPPY 1/10.000   Sept 5th 1917

1.----- The 2nd Bn R.M.L.I. will be relieved by the HOWE Bn in the Red Line & Close Support Line tomorrow night 6/7th September.

2.----- Leading Co of the HOWE Bn will not reach the bridge at H.1.d.3.0 before 7.45 p.m.

3.----- On relief the 2nd Bn R.M.L.I. will move into reserve & take over MAISON-BLANCHE camp at present occupied by HOWE Bn.

4.----- Representatives of HOWE Bn will proceed into the line tomorrow at 3 p.m. to take over Trench Stores &c.

Duplicate receipts of Stores handed over to be rendered to Orderly Room by 8.0 p.m.

5.----- Advance parties of 1 N.C.O. per platoon & H.Qs will report to Capt. B.C.V. WEEKS M.C. at H.Qs HOWE Bn at 3. p.m. tomorrow to make arrangements for the incoming of their particular units.

These details will report at Orderly Room

2

at 1.0 p.m. with the exception of Red Line Co's who will proceed direct, O.C. "A" & "D" Coys reporting when these details have moved off.

6. Small Box Respirators will be worn in the "ALERT" position during the relief.

7. Co's will forward Summary of Intelligence for the previous 24 hours to Bn. HQs by 8.0 p.m. tomorrow to be handed over to relieving Bn.

8. After relief Co's will move back to MAISON-BLANCHE Camp by the following routes:-

Red Line Co's VIA WAGGON TRACK - TOWEY TRACK.
"C" Coy VIA WAGGON TRACK - TOWEY TRACK.
"B" Coy & half "D" Coy VIA TOWEY ALLEY - TOWEY TRACK.

Code for "Relief Complete" for use over the phone will be:-

"A" Co	"A 505 received"
"B" Co	"B 505 received"
"C" Co	"C 505 received"
"D" Co	"D 505 received"

9. Transport Officer will provide one limber for conveyance of Officers Mess Gear, Medical Stores & Orderly Room Gear (which must be ready for loading by 9.0 p.m.) & 3 limbers for conveyance of Lewis Guns & Ammunition.

O.C. Coys will detail 1 Lewis Gun Crew for loading purposes under the supervision of the Bn. L.G. Sergt.

3.

These Orders to reach the Ration Dump by 9.30 p.m.

[signature]
Capt & Adjt
2nd Bn RMLI

Issued at 10.15 p.m.

Copies to:-
1 Retained
2 O.C. Howe Bn.
3 O.C. 'A' Coy
4 O.C. 'B' Coy
5 O.C. 'C' Coy
6 O.C. 'D' Coy
7 Quartermaster & Transport Officer
8 Capt. B.C.H. Weeks M.C.
9 War Diary

SECRET.

COPY No. 1

OPERATION ORDERS No. 82.
BY MAJOR G. C. WAINWRIGHT. R.M.L.I.
COMMANDING 2nd Bn. ROYAL MARINE LIGHT INFANTRY.

Reference Maps. :-
51.b.N.W. 1/20,000.
OPPY. 1/10,000.

Bn. Headquarters,
8th Septr. 1917.

1. ... The 2nd Bn. R.M.L.I. will relieve the 1st Bn. R.M.L.I. in the Front Line -- Left Sub-sector -- tomorrow, the 9th inst.
The Relief will be commenced in daylight.

2. ... The 2nd Bn. R.M.L.I. will move forward by half Platoons at 15 mins. interval, (with the exception of "A" Co and H.Qs) via LEVEL CROSSING, (B.1.b.9.9) -- TOWEY TRACK ---XNAVAKX TOWEY --NAVAL --MARINE -- NEW FOXEY -- CECIL SUPPORT, in the following order and at times stated.

"D" Co. 1.45. p.m. to 3.30. p.m.
"B" Co. 3.45. p.m. to 5.30. p.m.
"C" Co. 5.45. p.m. to 7.30. p.m.

"A" Co. and H.Qs. will move off at 7.45. p.m. -- 100 yards distance between Platoons.

Cos. will parade 15. mins. before the first half Platoon moves off

3. ... An Advance Party of one Officer per Co. and one N.C.O. per Platoon and H.Qs. will proceed into the Line tomorrow morning to take over Trench Stores etc, and make arrangements for the incoming of their particular Units. Duplicate copies of any receipts given to be rendered to Bn. H.Qs. by 4.0. p.m. 9th inst.
These details will parade at Orderly Room at 9.0. a.m. tomorrow.

4. ... Small Box Respirators will be worn in the ALERT position during the Relief and during the whole time the Bn. is in the Trenches.

5. ... Cos. will report "Relief complete" by telephone, and confirm by Runner to Bn. H.Qs. which will be located in the same place as before.
Code for "Relief complete" for use over the 'phone will be :-

"A" Co. "A. 606. received"
"B" Co. "B. 606. received"
"C" Co. "C. 606. received"
"D" Co. "D. 606. received"

6. ... Packs will be dumped near Cookers one hour before Cos. parade.
Great Coats will be carried en Banderole.

7. ... O.C. Cos. will ensure that Lines vacated by them are clean and tidy, reporting same, in writing, to Orderly Room before moving off.

8. ... Transport Officer will provide one Limber for conveyance of Officers Mess Gear, Medical Stores, and Orderly Room Gear. These must be dumped near Cookers by 7.0. p.m.

SECRET   Copy No. 4

Operation Order No. [illegible]

Lieut Colonel G C [illegible] RM[illegible]

Reference Map 51 Ed 1   In the Field

12th Sept 1917

1. The following interchange of relief will take place on the afternoon of the 13th inst.
A Co will relieve C Co in the left sub-sector (CLOCK - CHALK - [illegible]) [illegible] Lewis Guns will be relieved one hour earlier under supervision of Bn L G Officer

2. A Co will move up via [illegible]-BEACH CHANNEL at 10 minutes interval between platoons.

3. On relief C Co will move back into Reserve & take over billets at present occupied by A Co.

4. Relief complete will be reported to Bn HQ by telephone in BAB code

5. An advance party from each Co will proceed into the [illegible] tomorrow morning to take over Trench Stores etc, and work in progress [illegible] must be [illegible] handed over [illegible] details of the wiring scheme.
Duplicate copies of lists of Trench Stores exchanged will be rendered to Orderly Room by [illegible]

Copies to
No 1 Retained
2 OC A Co
3 B
4 War Diary

[signature]
Capt & Adjt
2nd Bn RM[illegible]

[illegible]

Continued. (2)

9. ... Lewis Guns and Ammunition will be sent up in advance tonight under arrangements made by the Bn. L.G.O.

Capt. & Adjutant,
2nd Bn. Royal Marine Light Infantry.

Issued at. 5.0. p.m.

Copies to :-

No. 1. Retained.
2. C.C. 1st Bn. R.M.L.I.
3. O.C. "A" Co.
4. O.C. "B" Co.
5. O.C. "C" Co.
6. O.C. "D" Co.
7. War Diary.

SECRET. Copy No. 2

Operation Order No 84
by
Major G. L. Parry R.M.L.I
Commanding 2nd Bn Royal Marine L. Inf

Ref Maps: OPPY 1/10,000
51.B. N.W.

Bn. Headquarters
16th Sept 17

1. The 188th Inf. Bde. will be relieved by the 189th Inf. Bde in the right sector of the Div. Front tomorrow, 17th Sept.
The 2nd Bn R.M.L.I will be relieved by the HOOD Bn in the left sub-sector commencing about 4-30 pm

2. Three guides from each Co. will meet relieving platoons at junction of MARINE & TYNE ALLEY at 4-15 pm
Disposition of "HOOD" Bn. will be as follows:

CHICO & CECIL "A" Co
CECIL & CHARLES "C" Co
CECIL SUPPORT } "B" Co
RAILWAY
MARINE "D" Co.

Co. representatives of relieving Bn. will arrive in the line at 6-0 pm tonight to take over work in hand Trench Stores etc., O.C. Coys will

Contd 2

ensure that ALL details of the wiring scheme are carefully handed over.

Representatives of relieving Bn. will go out with the Wiring parties this evening to ensure continuity of work.

Duplicate copies of receipts for stores, etc to reach Bn. H.Q. by noon tomorrow

3 After relief, 2nd Bn R.M.L.I. will move back in billets at ST AUBIN, via MARINE - TYNE - OUSE - ARRAS BAILLEUL RLY - point 400 yds S.W. of BAILLEUL STN (B.21.c.5.0) where Bn. will entrain for ST AUBIN.

4 An advance party of 1 Officer per Co. & 1 N.C.O. per platoon & H.Q. will report to Lieut R Burton at H.Q. HOOD Bn. ST AUBIN at 2.0 p.m. tomorrow to arrange for the incoming of the Bn. The details will report at Bn. H.Q. at 10-0 a.m.

5 Small Box Respirators will be worn in the ALERT position during the relief.

6. Code for "Relief Complete" for use over the 'phone will be.

"A" Co "A" 404 received
"B" " "B" 404 received
"C" " "C" 404 received
"D" " "D" 404 received

Cont.

3.

7. Transport Officer will arrange for the Mess Cart to be at the first camouflage screen on the ARRAS – – GAVRELLE Rd. at 4.0 p.m for conveyance of Officers Mess Gear – Medical Stores and Orderly Room Gear. These are to be dumped where NAVAL TRENCH crosses the road, by 6-45 p.m.

8. Lewis Gunners will be relieved 2 hours in advance under arrangements made by Bn. L.G.O.

[signature]

Capt. & Adjt.
2nd Bn R.M.L.I

Copies to:
No 1 Retained
2 War Diary.
3 O.C. HOOD Bn.
4 " A Co.
5 "B"
6 "C"
7 "D"
8 Pnl. & T.O.
9 File.

Issued at.

Issued at 5.45 pm SECRET. Copy No., 1

OPERATION ORDERS No., 85.

BY MAJOR G.I. PARRY. R. M. L. I.

COMMANDING 2 ND BN., ROYAL MARINE LIGHT INFANTRY.

Ref. Maps. :- LENS 11. 1/100,000

Bn., Headquarters, 19th September 1917.

1......... The Battalion will move by march route tomorrow 20th Sept., and billet at ACQ for the night.

2......... Battalion will pass the starting point, road junction at "Z" in LOUEZ at 9-0 a.m., and will proceed by the following route MAROEUIL-BRAY-ECOIVRES.

3......... Order of march :- Hd.Qrs., "A","B","C","D" Co.,s and transport -200 yards to be maintained between Co.,s on the march.

4......... Co.,s will parade at 8-30 a.m. and form up facing N.W. in the above order by 8-50 . Head of column to be at Battn., H.Q. Mess.

5......... The instructions contained in Brigade Group Standing March Orders will be stricrly complied with.

6......... The usual halts will be observed, i.e. at 10 minutes to the clock hour, march to be resumed at the hour.

7......... No smoking will be allowed until the first halt, and afterwards pipes only on the march.

8......... Uniformity of Dress must be obtained:- Full Marching Order, waterproof sheets will be carried under the flap of the pack, and Steel helmets between the supporting straps of the pack. Rifle covers will nor be carried on the rifles. Mounted Officers will wear Sam Browne equipment., all other Officers webbing equipment.

9......... A rear party consisting of 1 N.C.O. and 6 men under Lieut R.A.R. Neville will march in the rear of the Battn to collect all stragglers, who will be formed up into a Compact body and will march at the pace of the slowest man. O.C., Co.,s will warn all ranks before moving off that men who fall out without just cause will be punished on arrival at destination.

10......... Advanced billeting party consisting of Bn., Intelligence Off. and 1 N.C.O. per Co., H.Q. and transport will report to the Assistant Adjt. at Orderly Room at 7-30 a.m. tomorrow. They will report to Town Major ACQ at 9-0 a.m.

11......... Lewis Gun limbers will be packed by 7-0 p.m. tonight under arrangements made by Bn., L.G.O.

12......... "A" C ., will provide a loading party of 1 N.C.O. and 8 men to be at Q.M. Stores at 7-0 a.m. This party is to take their equipment and be ready to march when Stores are loaded.

13......... Officers ' Valises to be dumped at Q.M. Store by 8-0 a.m. Mess Cart will call for Officers' Mess gear, commencing with "D" Co., at 7-30 a.m.

14......... O.C. Co.,s will ensure that billets vacated by them are left in a clean and sanitary condition, reporting same before moving off.

15......... Dinners will be had on arrival at ACQ.

16......... The march will be resumed the following day to destination to be notified later.

[signature]

Copies to / overleaf.

Copies to :-

No. 1. Retained
2. O.C."A" Co.
3. "B"
4. "C"
5. "D"
6. WAR DIARY

Issued at 4.30 p.m. SECRET. Copy No. ....

OPERATION ORDERS No., 86.

BY MAJOR G. L. PARRY R. M. L. I.

COMMANDING 2nd BN., ROYAL MARINE LIGHT INFANTRY.

Bn., Headquarters,
20th September 1917.

Ref. Map :- LENS II.
1/100,000.

1....... The 2nd Bn., R.M.L.I. and 2 Companies 14th Worcester Regt will resume their march tomorrow and go into billets at FREVILLERS.

2....... The 2nd Bn., R.M.L.I. will pass the starting point -road junction N. of the "C" in FREVIN-CAPELLE at 8-0 a.m., and will proceed by the following route :- CAPELLE-FERMONT-AUBIGNY STATION-MINGOVAL- BETHONSART to FREVILLERS.

2 Co.,s 14th Worcester Regt. will pass the starting point mentioned above at 9-0 a.m. and will proceed to FREVILLERS independently under the Officer Commanding.

3....... Order of march for 2nd Bn., R.M.L.I. will be H.Q. "B","C", "D" and "A" Co.,s and transport. Normal distance between Co.,s will be maintained, i.e. 10 yards.

4....... Co.,s of 2nd Bn., R.M.L.I. will parade as follows :-

ACQ :- "D" Co., and ½ "C" Co., at 7-30 a.m. and move off at 7-40.

FREVIN CAPELLE :- "A","B" and ½ "C" Co., at 7-40 a.m. and form up facing S.W. at 7-50 a.m. Head of column to be at Bn.,H.Q. Mess at 7-50 a.m.

5....... The instructions contained in Brigade Group Standing March Orders will be strictly complied with.

6....... The usual halts will be observed,i.e. at 10 minutes to the clock hour, march to be resumed at the hour.

7....... No smoking will be allowed until the first halt, and afterwards pipes only on the march.

8....... Uniformity of Dress must be obtained :- Full Marching Order, waterproof sheets will be carried under the flap of the pack, and Steel Helmets between the supporting straps of the pack. Rifle covers will not be carried on the rifles. Mounted Officers will wear Sam Browne equipment, all other Officers webbing equipment.

9....... A rear party consisting of 1 N.C.O. and 6 men from "A" Co., under 2nd Lieut. Wilcox will march in rear of the Bn., to collect all stragglers &c.

10....... Advance billeting party consisting of 1 N.C.O. per Co., H.Q. and transport will report to Asst. Adjt. at Orderly Room at 6-50 am and will proceed on bicycles to FREVILLERS.

The usual advance billeting party from 14th Worcester Regt. will report to Asst. Adjt, 2nd Bn., R.M.L.I.(Lieut.R. Burton) at the MARIE , FREVILLERS at 10-0 a.m.

11....... "B" Co., will provide a loading party of 1. N.C.O. and 8 men to be at Q.M. Stores at 7-0 a.m. This party is to take their equipment and be ready to march when stores are loaded.

12....... Officers' valises and Mess gear will be dumped as follows:-

ACQ :- At "D" Co.,s Cookers at 7-0 a.m.

FREVIN-CAPELLE :- At Q.M. Stores at 7-30 a.m.

continued.

Operation Order No., 86 (contd). 2.

13...... OC. Co.,s will ensure that billets vacated by them are in a clean and sanitary condition.
Senior Officer at ACQ will personally inspect all billets and obtain a certificate from the TOWN MAJOR or his representative that all billets were left ina satisfactory condition.
O.C. "A","B", Co.,s and Senior Officer of half "C" Co at FREVIN-CAPELLE will report "billets correct" to O.C. at Bn., H.Q. Mess before moving off.

14...... Dinners will be had on arrival at FREVILLERS.

G.A. Harling

Capt. and Adjt.
2nd Bn., R.M.L.I.

Copies to :-

No.,1. War Diary.
2 O.C. 14th Worcester Regt.
3 O.C. "A" Co.
4. " "B" "
5. " "C" "
6. ". "D" ".

Instructions regarding War Diaries and Intelligence Summaries are contained in F. S. Regs., Part II. and the Staff Manual respectively. Title pages will be prepared in manuscript.

WAR DIARY
or
~~INTELLIGENCE SUMMARY.~~
(Erase heading not required.)

Army Form C. 2118.

Sheet I

2nd Bn Royal Marine Light Infantry

Vol 17

Place	Date	Hour	Summary of Events and Information	Remarks and references to Appendices
Fravillers.	1-10-17	—	Battalion training.	R. B.
ditto	2-10-17	—	Battalion parade. Operation order No 87 issued.	Appendix I. RB
Tinques	3-10-17	—	Battalion marched to TINQUES, entrained & departed a. m. detrained HOUPOUTRE p. m. and marched to Brown Camp into Division reserve, transferred to XVIII Corps. Map reference. Belgium Sheet 28. A22d central.	R. B
Brown Camp.	4-10-17.		Divisional reserve. 73 O R's reinforcements joined battalion	R. B.
" "	5-10-17.		ditto " . Operation order No 88 issued. Battalion embussed & proceeded to Nouveau Monde area & relieved Hawke Bn.	Appendix II RB
Nouveau Monde.	6-10-17	—	Cleaning up etc.	R.B.
" "	7-10-17		Church parade. A/Capt F H Wrenn to R. F. C.	R. B.
" "	8-10-17		Bn in company training.	R B

Instructions regarding War Diaries and Intelligence Summaries are contained in F. S. Regs., Part II. and the Staff Manual respectively. Title pages will be prepared in manuscript.

WAR DIARY

or

~~INTELLIGENCE SUMMARY.~~

(Erase heading not required.) 2nd Bn Royal Marine Light Infantry.

Army Form C. 2118.

Sheet II

Place	Date	Hour	Summary of Events and Information	Remarks and references to Appendices
Nouveau Monde	9-10-17		Battalion training.	RB
" "	10-10-17.		" " . T/Capt B. G. Andrews to XIX Corps Reinforcement Camp	RB
" "	11-10-17		" " .	RB
" "	12-10-17		" " .	RB
" "	13-10-17		" " .	RB
" "	14-10-17		C hurch parades.	RB
" "	15-10-17		Battalion training.	RB
" "	16-10-17		" " . Sec Lt H L Hardisty to XVIII Corps School.	RB
" "	17-10-17		" "	
" "	18-10-17		" " . Sec Lt N. W. Spraggett joined Bn.	RB
" "	19-10-17		" "	
" "	20-10-17		" " .	RB
" "	21-10-17.		C hurch parade.	RB
" "	22-10-17		Battalion training. Operation order No 89 issued	Appendix III

A7092 Wt. W128 9/M1293 750,000. 1/17. D. D & L. Ltd. Forms/C2118/14.

Instructions regarding War Diaries and Intelligence Summaries are contained in F. S. Regs., Part II. and the Staff Manual respectively. Title pages will be prepared in manuscript.

WAR DIARY
or
~~INTELLIGENCE SUMMARY.~~
(*Erase heading not required.*) 2nd Bn Royal Marine Light Infantry.

Army Form C. 2118.
Sheet III

Place	Date	Hour	Summary of Events and Information	Remarks and references to Appendices
Nouveau Monde	23-10-17.		Battalion embussed & proceeded to Canal Bank area, debussed & proceeded Reigersburg Camp.	R.B.
Canal Bank.	24-10-17		Operation Order No 90 issued. Bn proceed by march route to Irish Farm.	R.B. Appendix IV
Irish Farm	25-10-17.		Operation Order No 91 issued. Battalion proceeded into line p.m., and took up position for attack.	R.B.
Front line	26-10-17.		5.40 a.m. Battalion attacked enemy's position opposite its front, in conjunction with other battalions of the 188th Infy Bde. Objectives gained & consolidated. Casualties: 7 officers and 301 O.R's.	Appendix V R.B.
" "	27-10-17.		Battalion consolidating position gained, relieved p.m. by Hawke Bn. & proceeded to Irish Farm.	R.B.
Irish Farm	28-10-17.		Battalion proceeded by march route to Sambre Camp. Map. Sheet 28. B27 c 9.4.	R.B.

A7092 Wt. W128_9/M1293 750,000. 1/17. D. D & L. Ltd. Forms/C2118/14.

Instructions regarding War Diaries and Intelligence Summaries are contained in F. S. Regs., Part II. and the Staff Manual respectively. Title pages will be prepared in manuscript.

WAR DIARY
or
~~INTELLIGENCE SUMMARY.~~
(Erase heading not required.)

Army Form C. 2118.

Sheet IV

2nd Bn Royal Marine Light Infantry

Place	Date	Hour	Summary of Events and Information	Remarks and references to Appendices
~~Sambre~~ Camp	29-10-17		Battalion. Reorganising, refitting ect.	R.B.
" "	30-10-17.		Ditto " " " baths	R.B.
" "	31-10-17		Battalion paraded in fighting order. Emergency companies told off. Lieut Col G. C. Wainwright R.M.L.I to XIV Corps Reinforcement Camp. Major C. G. Farquharson rejoined battalion. Major G. Llewelyn Parry assumed command of battalion	R.B. R.B.

G. Llewelyn Parry
Major R.M.L.I
Comd'g 2nd Bn R.M.L.I.

A7092 Wt. W125.9/M1293. 750,000. 1/17. D. D & L Ltd. Forms/C2118/14.

Issued at 10.45 A.M.

SECRET. 1. Copy. No 1

OPERATION ORDERS. No. 87.

BY LIEUT. COLONEL G. C. WAINWRIGHT. R. M. L. I.

COMMANDING 2ND Bn., ROYAL MARINE LIGHT INFANTRY.

Bn., Headquarters,
2nd October 1917.

Ref. Maps: LENS II. 1/100,000
HAZEBROUCK. 1/100,000.

1... ... The 63rd (R.N.) Division (less artillery) will be transferred from the XIIIth to the XVIIIth Corps by rail commencing on 2nd October 1917.

2... ... The 188th Inf., Bde. Group will entrain at TINQUES commencing 2nd Oct.

The 2nd Bn., R.M.L.I.(less "D" Co., one cooker and team) will entrain about 5-0 a.m. 3rd October in Train No., 14, serial No.12. "D" Co., will entrain about 5-0 p.m. 3rd Oct., in Train No., 23, serial No., 12a.

3... ... The Bn., will detrain at HOPOUTRE, half way between POPERINGHE and ABEELE stations, and will move by march route to DIRTY BUCKET CAMP (in woods 1¼ miles S.S.W. of ELVERDINGHE).

4... ... Billeting party consisting of 1 N.C.O. per Co., and H.Q. under Lieut. R. Burton proceeded in advance yesterday to arrange for the incoming of the Bn.

5... ... Transport will move off at 12-30 a.m. tomorrow in order to arrive at TINQUES 3 hours before train is due to leave.

Transport Officer will detailn one baggage wagon for conveyance of Officers' valises. The wagon will call at Co., H.Q. commensing with "A" Co., at 6-30 p.m.

Mess cart will collect Officers' mess gear, commencing with "A" Co., at 9-0 p.m. and limber will call for Orderly Room gear and Medical Stores at 7-0 p.m.

Horses to be watered before entraining. One breast rope per 4 horses is to be provided.

6... ... H.Q."A","B" and "C" Co.,s will fall in at 1-30 a.m. and will form up(in the order stated) at Cross Roads W. of the "F" in FREVILLERS ready to move off at 2-0 a.m. Route via CHELERS.

DRESS : Full marching order, steel helmets between supporting straps of pack - Mess tins hanging underneath packs.

"D" Co., will fall in at 11-30 a.m. 3rd inst, and move off at 12-0 noon arriving at rendezvous (see para 7) not later than 2-0 p.m. Dinner will be had before Co., moves off.

Water bottles will be filled before moving off and refilled at TINQUES station. Rations for the 3rd inst will be carried on the men - for the 4th inst in bulk on the train, under directions of Quartermaster.

Arrangements regarding Officers' chargers will be notified later.

Continued.

Operation Order No., 87 (contd).

7... ... On arrival at TINQUES the Bn., will rendezvous in stubble field immediately N. of and adjacent to TINQUES STATION, where orders in regard to entraining will be issued.

8... ... Lewis Guns and ammunition will be packed in the L.G. limbers by 4-0 p.m. today under supervision of Bn., L.G.O.

9... ... Entraining states, shewing number of personnel, will be forwarded by Co.,s to Orderly Room by 4-0 p.m. today.

10.. ... O.C.s Co.,s will ensure that both entraining and detraining is carried out expeditiously.

11.. ... All billets , latrines etc., are to be left clean and sanitary. Immediately on arrival in new area, a certificate will be rendered by Co.,s that these were inspected by an Officer before leaving and found clean.

G.A. Newling

Capt. and Adjt.
2nd Bn., R.M.L.I.

Copies to :

No., 1. File
2 O.C., "A" Co.,
3. O.C., "B" Co.,
4. O.C., "C" Co.,
5. O.C., "D" Co.,
6. War Diary.

SECRET.   COPY No. ...

OPERATION ORDERS No. 88.
BY LIEUT. COLONEL G. C. WAINWRIGHT. R.M.L.I.
COMMANDING 2nd Bn. ROYAL MARINE LIGHT INFANTRY.

Bn. Headquarters,
5th Octr. 1917.

Reference Maps. :- Sheet 27. 1/40,000.
" 28. "
HAZEBROUCK. 1/100,000.

1. The 188th Inf. Bde Group will move by Bus to the NOUVEAU MONDE area today (5th Octr).

2. Busses will be drawn up on the road running from A.18.d. to B.19.c. facing S.E.
The 2nd Bn. R.M.L.I. will commence embussing at 2.0. p.m. at A.18.d. and will debuss on the HERZEELE-HOUTKERQUE Road between HERZEELE and cross roads at D.18.b.2.4. Advance Billeting parties will meet their respective units on the road between these two points.

3. Transport will move by road and march independently. Lines to be cleared by 10.0. a.m. Route :- ELVERDINGHE - POPPERINGHE Rd. etc. as per 188th Inf. Bde. Order.

4. One Lorry will report at Bn. H.Q. at 11.0. a.m. for surplus kits etc.

5. On arrival in new area this Bn. will take over Camp at present occupied by HAWKE Bn. at D.16.a.1.0.

6. Cos. will parade at 1.0. p.m. and march off at 1.15. p.m. in the following order : H.Q. "A" "B" "C" "D" Cos.
DRESS. Full Marching Order, Caps to be worn, Steel Helmets between Supporting Straps of Packs, Waterproof Sheets under flap of Pack, Waterbottles to be filled before moving off.

7. O.C. Cos. will ensure that both embussing and debussing is carried out expeditiously.

8. All lines are to be left clean and sanitary. O.C. Cos. will report lines clean before moving off.

Capt. & Adjutant,
2nd Bn. Royal Marine Light Infantry.

Issued at

Copies to :- 1. Retained.
2. O.C. "A" Co.
3. O.C. "B" Co.
4. O.C. "C" Co.
5. O.C. "D" Co.

Addendum to Operation
Orders No 90.

The times referred to in paras
3 and 4, i.e. time for falling in
&c will be 1.15. p.m.
Move off at 1.30. p.m.

[signature]
Capt & Adjutant
2nd Bn RMLI

24. 10. 17.

Secret. Copy No. 7.

Operation Orders No 90.
by Lieut. Col. G. C. Wainwright RMLI
Comdg 2nd Bn Royal Marine Light Infy.

Reference Maps:- Bn Hdqrs.
Sheet 28. 1/40.000. 24th Oct. 1917.
St. JULIEN. 1/20.000

1. The 63rd (RN) Division will relieve the 9th Divn in Right Sector XVIII Corps today 24th inst.
The 188th Inf. Bde will relieve the 27th Inf. Bde, and the 2nd Bn RMLI. will relieve the 6th K.O.S.B's at IRISH FARM (C.27. a. 3.7).
2. Cos. of 2nd Bn RMLI. will relieve same Cos of 6th K.O.S.B's. Guides from the Battn to be relieved will report at these Hd Qrs at 1.30 pm.
3. The Bn will parade at time to be notified later in full 'Battle Order' with Packs. The following will be

4. The Bn will move off, at time to be notified later, by Platoons at 50 yards distance, in the following order. H.Qrs "A" "B" "C" "D" Coys

5. Greatcoats to be stacked, in bundles of 10, by Coys, at the Ration Dump by 12.0 noon.

6. Coys. will report "Relief complete" by Runner to Bn Hdqrs.

7. Small Box Respirators will be worn in the ALERT position during the Relief and during the whole time the Bn is in the Line.

8. All Trench Stores, Aeroplane photographs, Maps &c. will be taken over, and duplicate copies of receipts given to be forwarded to Bn Hdqrs by 6.0 p.m today.

[signature]

Capt & Adjutant
2nd Bn R.M.L.I.

Issued at 12.0 noon.

Copies to:-

No 1. Retained
2. O/C. "A" C.
3. " B. C.
4. " "D" C.
5. " ~~"D" C.~~ QM. & T.O.
6. ~~War Diary~~ O/C "C" C.
7. War Diary
8. Do.

carried :-

RATIONS - 24th (unconsumed portion)
25th & 26th
Iron Rations.

AMMn. 220 Rounds each man, excepting Lewis Gunners and Runners. (50 Rounds each)

BOMBS. Each man one Mills No. 5. Two Bombers per Platoon carry 12 Bombs each.

RIFLE GRENADES Three Rifle Grenadiers per Platoon carry 12 Hales No. 24 in Haversacks issued for the purpose.

SHOVELS. One every third man.

PICKS. One by every Section.

WATSON FANS. One to be carried by every fourth man.

SANDBAGS. Two per man.

S.O.S. sets. H.Q's & "A" Co. 9.
"B" & "C" Cos. 6.

1" VERY PISTOLS. "A" "B" & "C" Cos. 12 each

1½" " " One per Co & H.Q's

SECRET. COPY No. 1

OPERATION ORDERS No. 89.
BY LIEUT. COLONEL G. C. WAINWRIGHT. R.M.L.I.
COMMANDING 2nd Bn. ROYAL MARINE LIGHT INFANTRY.

Bn. Headquarters,
22nd Octr. 1917.

Reference Maps. Sheet 27. 1/40,000.
" 28. 1/40,000.

1\. ... The 188th Inf. Bde. Group will move to CANAL BANK AREA tomorrow, 23rd inst, taking over Camps of the South African Brigade.

The 2nd Bn. R.M.L.I. will take over the REIGERSBURG CAMP, (H.9.b.0.5) at present occupied by the 4th South African Infantry Regt.

2\. Dismounted personnel will move by Bus. Busses will be drawn up on the HERZEELE - OUDZEELE Road, facing N.N.W. with head of convoy at Road junction at D.16.c.0.2. (Sheet No.27). Vehicles allotted to this Battn. are Nos. 37 - 68. (all Busses). Cos. will be told off in parties of 25 per Bus when Cos. parade.

3\. The 2nd Bn. R.M.L.I. will commence embussing at 11.0. a.m. between the L. of Le NOUVEAU MONDE and junction of track with main Road at D.21.d.3.7., and will debuss on the BRIELEN - YPRES Road, XXXXXXXXXXX between BRIELEN and Cross Roads at B.29.d.8.4.

Advance Billeting parties will meet their respective units on the road between these two points.

4\. Transport will move by Road and will pass starting point at Cross Roads, D.10.d.1.6., at 9.15. a.m. Route :- HERZEELE - HOUTKERQUE ROAD, WATOU - SWITCH ROAD, turning North at about L.5.d.7.6., ELDERDINGHE ROAD as far as A.3.a.7.4., thence by Military Road to N. of VLAMERTINGHE to N.5.a.central.

Billeting N.C.Os will meet Transport on the POPERINGHE - YPRES ROAD at H.9.a.8.8. about 1.0. p.m., and direct it to the Lines.

5\. Three Lorries will be available for moving Stores etc.. One Lorry will call at Co.Hd.Qrs. for Blankets, (which should be rolled in Section bundles and tied with string), commencing with "A" Co. at 7.0. a.m.

Haversacks, which must be clearly marked, will be collected and returned to Q.M. Stores tonight.

6\. Cos. will parade at 9.45. a.m. and form up at 10.30. a.m. on the road running N.W. from road junction at the G. in GAEYENEST, (D.16.a.2.4) to D.15.b.8.2., facing S.E. in the following order :- "D" "C" "B" "A" & "H.Q" Cos.

DRESS. "Battle Order" with Steel Helmets, (all ranks). Great Coats to be worn. Haversack rations will be taken.

7\. O.C. Cos. will ensure that both embussing and debussing are carried out expeditiously.

8\. All Billets are to be left clean and sanitary. Extra tents drawn since the Bn. arrived in the area are to be struck by 6.30. a.m. tomr.

Transport Officer will detail a Limbered Wagon to call at Co. H.Qs. for these tents, commencing with "A" Co. at 6.45. a.m.

O.C. Cos. will report "All clear" to Officer Commanding before the Bn. moves from the point of assembly.

9\. Lewis Guns and Ammunition are to be loaded tonight under instructions already issued. Officers' Valises and Mess Gear will be collected from Co. H.Qs. commencing with "A" Co. at 7.30. a.m.

[signature]
Capt. & Adjutant,
2nd Bn. Royal Marine Light Infantry.

Issued at 6.40. p.m.
Copies to / Back.

COPIES TO :-

1.	Retained.
2.	O.C. "A" Co.
3.	O.C. "B" Co.
4.	O.C. "C" Co.
5.	O.C. "D" Co.
6.	War Diary.
7.	Do.

Continued. (2).

4. ... continued.

reach their objectives, O.C. Cos. must be prepared to form a defensive flank if required until a portion of the Reserve Co. is available for the purpose.

5. ... O.C. "A" Co. should obtain connection with the HOWE Bn. immediately on arriving at furthest limit of objective.

O.C. "C" Co. should maintain touch with the troops on his left by means of visual signalling.

6. ... The Bn. will assemble tonight on a line running 150 yards east of the BURNS HOUSE – VACHER FARM, "A" Co. with its right on two concreted emplacements at D.3.a.65.70., and "C" Co. with its left on V.26.b.5.1. "B" Co. will form up in rear of "A" and "C" Cos. as near as safety permits. All Cos. to be in line of Platoons in Column.

Cos. will be in their assembly positions at least one and a half hours before ZERO. Cos. are to report to Bn. H.Qs. as soon as they are in position. Necessity of silence in forming up on assembly lines must be impressed on all concerned.

7. ... At ZERO hour "A" "B" & "C" Cos. will move up behind the 1st Bn. R.M.L.I. and form up ~~xxxa xxxxxxxxxxxxxxxxxxxxxxxxxxxxxxxxxxxxxxxx barragexxxxxxxxxxxxfirstxobjective~~ 200 yards east of front assembly line, roughly from V.27.d.4.3. to V.27.a.3.2. Cos. will remain there until ZERO PLUS 50 mins. when "A" and "C" Cos. move through 1st Bn. R.M.L.I. and form up in attack formation behind the stationary barrage at limit of first objective.

At ZERO PLUS 116 mins. the barrage will lift and move forward at the rate of 100 yards per 8 mins. in lifts of 50 yrds.

"A" and "C" Cos. will follow barrage through second objective until limit is reached, dropping parties to consolidate in depth as they go forward.

8. ... The general bearing of advance from furthest limit of first objective is 65° true bearing.

All Officers will be in possession of Compasses and know their own magnetic variation. Bearings will be checked frequently during the advance. Steel helmets affect a Compass and should be taken off when reading a bearing. Iron Containers of Box Respirators also affect it.

9. ... O.C. Cos. will ensure that no orders, secret maps, documents or letters likely to be of information to the enemy are carried into action by an individual.

10. ... Watches will be synchronised at Bn. H.Qs. at 4.30. p.m.

11. ... The importance of passing back information, even of a negative nature, must be impressed upon all Platoon and Section Commanders.

12. ... At ZERO Bn. H.Qs. will be established at BURNS HOUSE.

At ZERO PLUS 1½ hours Bn. H.Qs. will move forward to PILL BOX at V.26.b.9.0.

Continued. (3).

13. ... Cos. will parade today at 4.30. p.m. and move off along ALBERTA TRACK by Platoons at 100 yards distance in following order, H.Q. "A" "C" and "B" Cos. Cos. will be met at BURNS HOUSE by their advance ~~xxx~~ parties who will lead them to the point of assembly.

Capt. & Adjutant,
2nd Bn. Royal Marine Light Infantry.

Issued at 3..30 pm

Copies to :-

1. Retained.
2. O.C. "A" Co.
3. "B" Co.
4. "C" Co.
5. "D" Co.
6. War Diary.
7. Do.

SECRET. COPY No. 17

OPERATION ORDERS No. 91.
BY LIEUT. COLONEL G. C. WAINWRIGHT, R.M.L.I.
COMMANDING 2nd Bn. ROYAL MARINE LIGHT INFANTRY.

Bn. Headquarters.
25th Octr. 1917.

REFERNCE MAPS. Poelcapelle. 1/5000.
St. Julien, 1/10000.

1. ... Earl y tomorrow morning at an hour to be notified later the 63 rd. (R.N) Division, in conjunction with the 8th Brigade, 3rd Canadian Divn. on its right and a Brigade of the 58th Divn. on its left, will attack the enemy's position opposite its front.

The attack will be made by the 188th Inf. Bde., with the "HOOD" Bn as Counter attacking Bn. and the HAWKE Bn. in Bde. reserve.

2. ... Two objectives are allotted the Bde. :- The first objective will be attacked by ANSON Bn. on the right, and 1st Bn. R.M.L.I. on the left : the second objective, by the HOWE Bn. on the right and 2nd Bn. R.M.L.I. on the left.

Farthest limit of first objective, is a line running from V.21.c.85.20. through H. of BANFF HOUSE to V.28.c.8.9., thence to V.28.d.1.3.

Farthest limit of second objective, is from point at V.21.d.8.8. to north end of house at V.22.c.9.0., thence dotted track to house due north of R. in TOURNANT FARM, V.28.b.4.3., thence to east end of SOURCE FARM.

Dividing lines between Battns.

First objective - A line ftom last S of INCH HOUSES to V.28.a.2.3.

Second objective. - From V.28.a.2.3. to PADDERBEEK Stream at V.28.a.5.5., thence by south side of dotted track to V.28.b.9.9.

3. DISPOSITIONS FOR ATTACK.

The 2nd Bn. R.M.L.I. will attack with two Cos. in front, each Co. with two Platoons in front line and two Platoons supporting.

One Co. Battn. Reserve ; one Co. carrying.

Frontage ; Approximately 800 yards.

Platoon frontages will be so arranged as to bring greatest strength against concreted positions about V.28.a.9.9.

No troops of the 2nd Bn. R.M.L.I. will cross to the North side of the LEKKERBETERBEEK stream but O.C. left Co. will arrange to cover the area north of the stream with Lewis Gun fire.

"A" Co. will be on the right of the Bn. front, and "C" Co. on the left. The dividing line between these Cos. will be a line running approximately from V.27.b.85.50. to junction of tracks at V.22.c.85.15.

"B" Co. will be i n Bn. reserve and "D" Co. will be the carrying Co.

4. ... The following strongpoints are shewn on the map in this Bn's area, and will be consolidated and held :-

STRONGPOINTS.	SUGGESTED GARRISONS.
5 organised shell holes. V.27.b.7.6.	Two sections.
8 Do. Do. V.27.b.6.7.	Do.
SOURD FARM. V.28.a.1.6. (Two buildings)	One platoon.
Concrete position. V.28.a.9.9.	Two platoons.

In the event of troops on either flank of the Bn. failing to

2ND BATTALION, ROYAL MARINE LIGHT INFANTRY. 13691

Sheet. NO. 1.

Instructions regarding War Diaries and Intelligence Summaries are contained in F. S. Regs., Part II. and the Staff Manual respectively. Title pages will be prepared in manuscript.

WAR DIARY
or
~~INTELLIGENCE SUMMARY.~~
(Erase heading not required.)

2nd Bn. Royal Marine Light Infantry

Army Form C. 2118.

VR 18

Place	Date	Hour	Summary of Events and Information	Remarks and references to Appendices
Dambre Camp	1st	NOV. 17.	Bn. parades. Inspection + Reorganisation of Coys.	JCW
" "	2nd	" "	" " " " " "	JCW
" "	3rd	" "	Parades. Baths. Inspection. Rev. Fr. W. Doran C.F. joined Bn.	JCW
" "	4th	" "	Inspection of Bn. by Divisional General. Church Parades. Operation Order NO. 92 issued.	appendix I. JCW
" "	5th	" "	Bn relieved DRAKE. Bn. in front line.	JCW
FRONT LINE	6th	" "	Holding line and working parties. 45 casualties. Operation Order 92/1 issued	JCW appendix II
" "	7th.	" "	Bn. relieved by 2/6th Bn. K.R.R.C. and proceeded to Irish Camp. operation order NO. 92/2 issued.	appendix III JCW
Irish Camp	8th	" "	Bn. entrained at Irish Camp and detrained at Poperinghe and marched to School Camp. 1. Casualty.	JCW.
School Camp	9th	" "	Bn. parade for baths. Cleaning up.	JCW.
" "	10th	" "	" " inspections etc. Lieut Monk joined Bn.	JCW.
" "	11th	" "	Church parades. Memorial Service. Operation Order NO. 93. issued.	appendix IV JCW
" "	12th	" "	Bn. proceeded by March Route to Winnezeele Area. Operation Order NO. 94. issued	" V JCW
Winnezeele.	13th	" "	" " " " Steenbrugge " . MAP Sheet. 27. I.14.b.3.3.	JCW.
Steenbrugge.	14th	" "	Bn parades. Inspections, baths etc. 132 reinforcements joined Bn.	JCW.
"	15th	" "	Platoon + Specialist Training	JCW.
"	16th	" "	" " "	JCW.
"	17th	" "		JCW.
"	18th	" "	Bn. Church Parade. ~~Presentation of Military Medal Ribbons to men who gained the award in the recent operations.~~ JCW	JCW JCW

A7092 Wt. W128 9/M1293 750,000. 1/17. D. D & L. Ltd. Forms/C2118/14.

Sheet. NO. 2.

Instructions regarding War Diaries and Intelligence Summaries are contained in F. S. Regs., Part II. and the Staff Manual respectively. Title pages will be prepared in manuscript.

WAR DIARY
or
~~INTELLIGENCE SUMMARY.~~
(Erase heading not required.)

2nd Bn. R. M. L. I.

Army Form C. 2118.

Place	Date	Hour	Summary of Events and Information	Remarks and references to Appendices
Steenbrugge	19th	Nov. 17.	Bn. in Platoon and Specialist Training. Major C. G. Farquharson R.M.L.I. to 1st Bn. R.M.L.I. to assume Command temporarily. Operation Order No. 95 issued.	Appendix VI. JCWS.
"	20th	Nov. 17.	Bn. inspected by Captain Oliver Backhouse C.B. R.N. The Commanding Officer presented ribbons to N.C.O's and men who won the Military Medal in the recent operations. (Bn. TRANSPORT moved independently to School Camp on 20th Nov. 17)	JCWS.
"	21st	" "	Parades inspections etc. addenda to operation order No. 95 issued. 26 reinforcements from base joined Bn.	Appendix VI. JCWS.
"	22nd	" "	Bn. embussed and proceeded to Reigersburg Camp. Map Sheet 28. H.6.a. (Bn. Transport, moved into lines in Reigersburg area independently on 21st Nov. 17.)	JCWS.
Reigersburg	23rd	" "	Parades: inspections etc. Lieuts. H. N. Pearse R.M. and G. Gibbons R.M.L.I. joined Bn.	JCWS.
"	24th	" "	Bn. working Parties. Specialists Training.	JCWS.
"	25th	" "	" " " " " . 19 reinforcements joined Bn.	JCWS.
"	26th	" "	" " " " " .	JCWS.
"	27th	" "	" " " " " .	JCWS.
"	28th	" "	" " " " " . Lieut. R. A. R. NEVILLE R.M.L.I. to Brigade H.Q.	JCWS.
"	29th	" "	" " " " " .	JCWS.
"	30th	" "	" " " " " .	JCWS.

[signature]
Lieut. Col. R.M.L.I.
Cmdg. 2nd Bn. R.M.L.I.

A7092 Wt. W128.9/M1293 750,000. 1/17. D. D. & L. Ltd. Forms/C2118/14.

SECRET. COPY. No. 1 .

OPERATION ORDERS No. 92.
BY MAJOR G. I. PARRY. R.M.L.I.
COMMANDING 2nd Bn. ROYAL MARINE LIGHT INFANTRY.

Bn. Headquarters,
4th Novr. 1917.

Reference Maps.
ST. JULIEN. 1/10000.
POELCAPPELLE. 1/10000.

1. The 188th Inf. Bde. will relieve the 189th Inf. Bde. in the Line on the night of the 5th-6th Novr.

2. The 2nd Bn. R.M.L.I., plus one Co. 1st Bn. R.M.L.I. will relieve the DRAKE Bn. in the left Sub Sector and will be known as "X" "Y" and "Z" Cos. respectively.

3. The Bn. will fall in at 1.0. p.m. and march off at 1.20. p.m. and will entrain at BRIELEN in the fore part of the Bde. Train. Detrain at ST. JEAN Station and proceed by March route via WEILTJE, WEILTJE – ST. JULIEN road as far as CORNER COT (C.17.b.6.4) thence by ALBERTA TRACK. By Platoons. 50 yards interval.

4. Guides of the 2nd Bn. R.M.L.I. will meet the Bn. at junction of BUFF ROAD with WEILTJE – ST. JULIEN Road on arrival. In order to ensure that Cos. proceed by the correct Duck Board Tracks, Guides from the HOWE Bn. will be posted on each junction of tracks.

5. Lewis Guns and ammunition will be loaded at Q.M. Stores by 12.0. noon and be conveyed from there by Limbers to Bde. Dump at C.18.a.0.7. Lewis Gun Officer will detail one N.C.O. and a Section to accompany Limbers. O.Cs. "X" and "Y" Cos. will detach eight men per Co. at Bde. Dump to assist in carrying Ammunition forward.

6. O.C. Cos. will ensure that greatest care is taken that every post at present held is properly taken over on relief.

7. Lists of Maps, Trench stores, etc. taken over on relief will be forwarded to Bn. H.QS. by 9.0. a.m. 6th inst.

8. Completion of Relief will be reported to Bn. Hd. Qrs. by the letter denoting the Co. relieving, e.g. "Y" Co. Relief complete, letter "Y" Will be sent by Runner.

9. Transport Officer will arrange to collect Officers' Valises and Mess Stores at 11.0. a.m. and remove Cookers and Water Carts at 1.0. p.m.
Q.M. will arrange for a party to clean up the Camp, under the R.S.M. after the departure of the Bn. He will report Camp Clean to the Camp Commandant.

A Burton

Lieut. & A/Adjutant,
2nd Bn. Royal Marine Light Infantry.

Issued at ... 8.30 am (5th).

Copies to /
Back.

Copies to :-

No. 1. Retain.
2. O.C., 1st Bn. R.M.L.I.
3. O.C., "DRAKE" Bn.
4. O.C. "X" Co.
5. O.C., "Y" Co.
6. O.C., "Z" Co.
7. Transport Officer and Qrmr.
8. War Diary.

Addenda to Operation Order No 92/1.

by Major G. L. Parry R.M.L.I.

Comd 2nd Bn. Royal Marine Lt Infy

Bn Headquarters
Nov. 7th 1917.

1. The Bn will parade at 9.0 a.m. & move independently to entraining point.
The Bn has been allotted the fore part of the train.
Transport will move by road independently

R Burton

Lieut & A/Adjt
2nd Bn RMLI.

SECRET

Operation Orders No. 92/1
by Major A. R. [illegible], RMLI
Comdg 2nd Bn Royal Marine Light Infy.

Reference Maps.
SPRIET.
POELCAPELLE.

Bn Headquarters.
6th November 1917.

1. The 188th Inf. Bde will be relieved in the line on the night of 7/8th inst. by Units of the 2nd & 3rd Infantry Brigades.

2. "X" & "Y" Coys. will be relieved by two Coys. of the 60th Rifles.

3. O/C Coys will ensure that greatest care is taken that all [illegible] held by us are handed over properly to the incoming Units.

4. Co. Representatives of the relieving Units are proceeding into the line tonight to take over the line and to arrange actual details of relief.

5. Guides. O/C Coy. will arrange to send a Guide from each Platoon to guide the incoming Units. They will report at Bn HQrs at [illegible]

6. O/C "HOWE" Bn has been detailed to furnish Guides to bring relieving Coys. up to Bn HQrs.

(Continued). 2.

7. "Z" Co. will not be relieved by any Unit & will leave the line as soon as the Relieving Cos. of "X" & "Y" Cos. have moved forward. To ensure this O/C "Z" Co. will send a representative from each Platoon to wait at the end of the Duckboard track. As soon as the Relieving Cos. have passed them they will go back to their Platoons and send them down.

8. Completion of Relief. O/C Cos will report personally to the O/C at Hqrs. when relief is complete.

9. Route. Via HUBNER and alternative track CORNER COT then by Duckboard track to IRISH FARM where the Batt. will camp for the night. A hot meal will be ready upon arrival.

10. Bn will proceed to back Area by train leaving ST JEAN Station about 9.30 a.m.
Detailed Orders will be issued on arrival at IRISH FARM

R Burton

Lieut & Adjutant
2nd Bn RMLI.

Operation Orders No. 93
by Major. G. L. Parry. RMLI.
Commandg. 2nd Bn. Royal Marine Light Infy

Reference Map :-
Belgium & France
Sheet 27 1/40,000.

Bn. Headquarters
11th Novr. 1917.

1. The 188th Inf. Bde. Group will move on the 12th inst, and proceed by march route to WINNEZEELE.

2. Transport will march with the Battn.

3. Attention is drawn to "Brigade Standing March Orders" the instructions contained therein will be strictly complied with.

4. An Advance Billeting Party, consisting of one NCO per Co., Hdqrs, & Transport, under 2nd Lt. J. C. Lee, will proceed on Bicycles at 7.15 am. Lieut. Lee will report to the Staff Captn at the Area Commandants' Office at Winnezeele at 8.30. am. He will also arrange to send a Guide to J.10 central by 4.0 pm to meet details left behind at the Reinforcement Camp.

5. "A" Co. will detail a party of one NCO & six OR's, who will remain behind to clear up the Camp after the departure of the Battn, in addition to the Bn. Sanitary Corps & eight HQ. Pioneers.

"B" Co. will detail a party of one NCO & six OR's who will work as Carrying Party under Lieut. Hore.

"C" Co. will detail a party of one NCO & six OR's. This party will be under command of the Assist Adjutant & will march in rear of Battn to collect Stragglers &c.

2nd Lt. Proffitt will remain behind to ensure that the Camp is thoroughly cleaned up. He will then report to the Camp Adjutant & obtain from him a Certificate stating that the Camp has been left in a satisfactory condition. On completion of this duty he will march the Clearing up and Loading Parties by march route to Winnezeele

6. Cos. will parade under O/C Cos. at 8.20 am with all gear. Rifles to have covers. Waterproof Sheets to be strapped under Flap of Packs. Steel Helmets between Supporting Straps.

Every effort is to be made to ensure that all gear is carried in the Pack & not hanging on the Equipment in an untidy manner.

6. (continued).

The Battn will march as two Parade Cos. in the following order :- H.Q; "D" Co; Composite Co. made up from "A" "B" & "C" Coys

500. yards distance will be maintained between Battns 100 yards between each Co. & Transport.

Head of Column to pass starting point, Road junction at L.3 a.6.3. at 9.25. am.

Route. From L.3 a.6.3. via ST JAN — BIEZEN road — WATOU — WINNEZEELE.

7. Guides. The Battn will be met by Billeting Officer & guides at J.17 a.7.5.

The Battn will march in Column of Route, but, if traffic met is too heavy, then in file, not threes.

Halts. The usual Halts at 10. mins. to the hour will be observed, the march being resumed at the hour.

No Co. is to halt within 200 yards of a Village, if necessary closing up to the next Co. Cos will get there correct distances as soon as the march is resumed.

8. As soon as possible after arrival at destination O/C Cos will report their Cos in Billets to the C.O.

9. Officers Valises. Officers' Valises are to be dumped at the bottom of the Duck-board track leading to Transport Lines by 7.20. am. & reported to Quartermaster.

Blankets, tied tightly in bundles of 10. are to be dumped at bottom of Duckboard Track by 7.0. am.

Officers' Mess Gear is to be loaded in the Mess Cart by 8.0. am. Medical Cart to be ready to move off by 8.0. am.

Orderly Room gear to be dumped at bottom of Duckboard track by 7.0. am.

Additional Transport. One Motor Lorry will be supplied and will make three trips.

10. All Billets, Latrines, &c. are to be left in a clean & sanitary condition. O/C Cos will report that this is so at 8.30. am.

Issued at. 6.0 p.m.

N Burton

Lieut & A/ Adjutant,
2nd Bn. RMLI

Operation Order No. 5?.
by Major ? C. ?, RMLI.
Commandg 2nd Bn. Royal Marine Light Infy.

Reference Map.
Belgium & France.
Sheet 27. 1/40,000.

Bn. Headquarters.
12th Nov. 1917.

1. The march of the 188th Inf. Bde. Group will be resumed tomorrow. The 2nd Bn. RMLI. will move to Area L.?

2. As [illegible] in Operation Orders No. ? of yesterday.

3. Do. Do.

4. An Advanced Billeting Party of one NCO per Co. HQrs & Transport under 2/Lt ? will proceed on Bicycles at 8.0 am. & will report to [illegible] outside Bn. Hdqrs, Billet No. 130. at 7.45 am.

Guides will meet the Bn. at STEENBRUGGE. I.14.6.3.8.

5. "C" Co. will detail a party of one NCO. & six ORs, who will remain behind to clean up the Camp after the departure of the Bn., in addition to the Bn. Sanitary Sergt. & eight HQ. Pioneers.

"D" Co. will [illegible] [illegible] Loading Party [illegible] by the QM., who will inform O/C. "D" Co. of his requirements & the time at which the party will be required.

2/Lt Trappitt will remain behind to ensure that the Camp is thoroughly cleaned up. He will report to the Area Commandant WINNEZEELE & obtain from him a Certificate stating that the Camp has been been left in a satisfactory condition. (Vide ✱).

Lieut. Williams will detail a party of one NCO & six ORs. This party will be under the command of the Assist. Adjutant & march in rear of Bn. to collect Stragglers &c. They will report to the Assist. Adjutant at [illegible] Point at 7.25 am.

✱ On completion of these duties 2/Lt Trappitt will march the Cleaning Up and Loading Parties to destination.

6. Cos. will parade under O/C Cos. at 8.45 am. Rifles to have covers. Waterproof Sheets to be strapped under flap of Packs, Steel Helmets [illegible] Supporting Straps.

Every effort is to be made to get all [illegible] in [illegible] & not [illegible] in Equipment in an untidy manner.

Continued (2).

6. The Battn will march in three Company Cos. in the following order:– HQrs. (Composite Co. made up from A. B & C Cos.), D Co., Details from Reinforcement Camp in command of 2nd Lieut. Williams.

Same distances as today. Head of column to pass Starting Point, Road junction at J.11.c.2.0. at 9.25 am.

A Guide will be detailed to lead the Leading Co. to Starting Point & will report to Capt. [illegible] at 8.45 am.

Route. From J.11.c.2.0. – HARDIFORT. – Crossroads at I.29.b.6.6. thru L'ANGE. Crossroads I.33.b.8.5. – ZERMEZEELE. to STEEN. BRUGGE, where Guides will meet the Battn.

7. As per Operation Orders of yesterday

8. Do.

9. Officers Valises & Mess Gear. Officers billeted near QM Stores are to have their Valises & Mess Gear dumped there by 7.30 am.

Transport Officer will supply a limber to collect outlying Officers Valises. O/C "D" Co. will send a Guide to Transport Lines by 6.20 am. who will guide the limber to D Co. [illegible] will also report there at 6.30 am. & will guide limber to Bn. HQrs. after he has collected Valises & Mess Gear from D Co.

10. Blankets. Blankets are to be tightly rolled in bundles of 10, & carefully labelled & dumped at QM Stores by 7.30 am. Today Blankets were very loosely rolled & not labelled, [illegible] they should have done. No bundles will be received if these orders are not complied with.

11. All Billets, Latrines &c. are to be left in a clean and sanitary condition. O/C Cos. will report to that effect to the Adjt. before Starting Point.

Issued at.

N Burton
Lieut. & A/Adjutant
2nd Bn. RMLI.

Operation Order No 96.
by Major C. L. Harvey, RMLI
commandg 2nd Bn Royal Marine Light Infy.

Reference Maps:- Bn Headquarters.
Sheet 27. 1/40.000. 19th Novr 1917.
— 28. 1/40.000.

1 The 188th Inf Bde, less MG Co, LTM Batty, & 148th FA will probably move to the forward Area tomorrow 20th inst.
The Bn will be located at REIGERSBURG CAMP. H.6.a. Sheet 28.

2. Dismounted Personnel will move by train. Detailed Orders as to place and time of entraining (probably ARNEKE) will be issued later.

3. Transport will move by Road. Head of Column will pass starting point, (I.8.central. Sheet 27) at 7.25 am.
All Cookers & Co Chargers are to be at Transport Lines by 7.0. am.
Three Dixie Kettles ~~[illegible]~~ will be retained by each Co & two by HQrs. All necessary cooking is to be done in these.
One Co Cook will remain behind with the three Dixies. The other one will

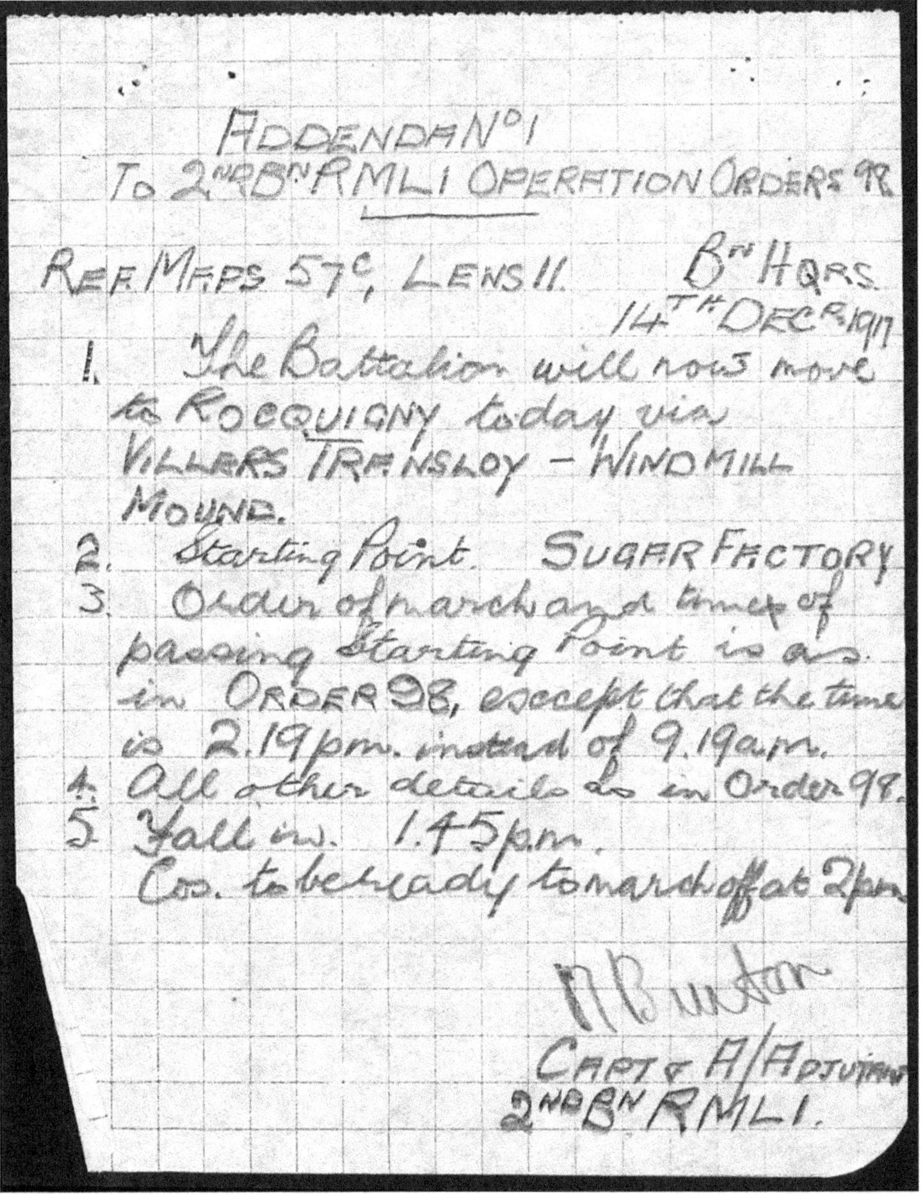

ADDENDA No 1
TO 2nd Bn RMLI OPERATION ORDERS 98.

REF. MAPS 57c, LENS 11.
Bn HQRS.
14TH DECR 1917

1. The Battalion will now move to ROCQUIGNY today via VILLERS TRANSLOY – WINDMILL MOUND.
2. Starting Point. SUGAR FACTORY
3. Order of march and times of passing Starting Point is as in ORDER 98, except that the time is 2.19 pm. instead of 9.19 a.m.
4. All other details as in Order 98.
5. Fall in. 1.45 pm.
Cos. to be ready to march off at 2 pm.

R Buxton
CAPT & A/ADJUTANT
2nd Bn RMLI.

3. (continued)
accompany the Cookers. Detailed Orders regarding these have been issued separately to Transport Officer.

4. Advance parties to take over Camp proceeded forward today.

5. Transport will not rejoin Bn until 21st inst. Rations for tomorrow are to be carried on the person. Rations for the 21st will be brought to the Bn by N.Z.C.

(Sgd) R Benton
Capt & A/Adjutant.
2 Batt. RMLI.

Addenda to

Operation Order No 95.

by Major G. C. Pavry. RMLI

Commanding 2nd Bn Royal Marine Light Infy.

Reference Map
Sheet 27. 1/40,000.

Bn Headquarters
21st Nov. 1917

1 The 188th Inf Bde will proceed by Bus to the forward area tomorrow. The Column will be drawn up on the ARNEKE – L'ANGE road facing SE. with the Head of Column at Cross Roads I 26. d.0.4.

All Vehicles (Busses or Lorries) will be numbered consecutively from front to rear throughout the Column. The number of Vehicles allotted the Batt will be notified later.

2. The Bn will parade on the road running from I.14. b. 3.8. to I.19. c 6.4. Head of "A" Co to be in line with the Gate at the entrance to HQ Mess Billet facing S.W. at 8.15 am. No interval between Cos.

3 The Bn will embuss between the following points approximately. I. 25. b 2.9. and the second E in LE. COFFRE. Cos will move independently to the assembly point via RATTE BREUGGE road junction at I.13. d. 8.1

A Brigade Staff Officer will be at the Embussg Point

DRESS. Full Marching Order with all gear. One Blanket rolled on top of Pack.

4. O/C Cos. will render a Certificate to the Commanding Officer at the point of assembly stating that their Billets and Latrines have been left in a clean & sanitary condition.

5. On arrival in the forward Area tomorrow the Bn will debuss on the YPRES – VLAMERTINGHE road. Head of Column will halt at Asylum.

The Bn will proceed to Camp via YPRES road to Cross Roads at I.7. c 8.9. thence by the BRIELEN road.

200 yards distance will be maintained between Cos. The Bn will move in file. Co. Commanders will ensure that Cos keep well closed up & that the pace is not too fast.

6. Orders regarding work will be issued on arrival by the 35th Division.

N. Burton

Capt & A/Adjutant.
2nd Bn RMLI.

CONFIDENTIAL.

188/63

Headquarters.
2nd Bn. ROYAL MARINRS LIGHT INFANTRY.
1st. January 1918.

W A R D I A R Y

(vol. XlX)

of

2nd Battn. ROYAL MARINES LIGHT INFANTRY.

from

1st DECEMBER 1917
to
31st DECEMBER 1917

To:-
Headquarters,
63rd (R.N.)Division.

for Lieut.Colonel. R.M.L.I.
Commanding 2nd Bn. ROYAL MARINES LIGHT INFANTRY.

SHEET. NO. 1.

Instructions regarding War Diaries and Intelligence Summaries are contained in F. S. Regs., Part II. and the Staff Manual respectively. Title pages will be prepared in manuscript.

WAR DIARY

or

~~INTELLIGENCE SUMMARY.~~

(*Erase heading not required.*)

Army Form C. 2118.

2nd Bn. R. M. L. I.

Place	Date	Hour	Summary of Events and Information	Remarks and references to Appendices
Reyersburg Camp	Dec. 1st 1917		Battn working parties + Specialist Training	[illegible]
" "	" 2nd	"	" parades, inspections etc. 10 reinforcements joined from Base.	[illegible]
" "	" 3rd	"	" working parties and Specialist training	[illegible]
" "	" 4th	"	" " " "	[illegible]
" "	" 5th	"	" inspections etc. " O.O. No 96 issued.	Appendix I [illegible]
" "	" 6th	"	" marched to Schools Camp	[illegible]
Schools Camp	" 7th	"	Battn Training. 2/Lt. Egan to F.A.	[illegible]
" "	" 8th	"	" " O.O. No. 97 issued	Appendix II [illegible]
" "	" 9th	"	Battn Church parades etc. Entrained p.m. at Peselhoek.	[illegible]
Achiet-le-Grand	" 10th	"	Battn detrained and proceeded by MARCH ROUTE to BEAULENCOURT AREA	[illegible]
Beaulencourt	" 11th	"	" parades, inspections etc	[illegible]
"	" 12th	"	Battn Training	[illegible]
"	" 13th	"	" + Specialist training. Capt B.C.V. Weeks to F.A. O.O. No. 98 issued.	Appendix III [illegible]
"	" 14th	"	" proceeded by march route to camp at ROCQUIGNY. O.O. No 99 "	Appendix IV [illegible]
Rocquigny	15th	"	" " " " ETRICOURT. Lts. Braid, Vance, Perry + 2/Lts Collier, Bowden, Smith, Albany + [illegible] joined Battn	[illegible]
ETRICOURT	16th		" Church parades, inspections etc.	[illegible]
"	17th	"	" " " " O.O. No. 100 issued	[illegible]
METZ	18th		" proceeded by march route to METZ. 2/Lt Boucher to F.A.	[illegible]
"	19th		" and Specialist training. 2/Lt Egan rejoined Battn	[illegible]
"	20th		" " " "	[illegible]
	21st		" " " O.O. No. 101 issued.	[illegible]
	22nd	"	" " "	[illegible]
Front Line	23rd	"	" relieved 2/8 Worcesters and 1 Coy 2/4 Gloucesters in front line. Nil Casualties	[illegible]
"	24th	"	" working + Salvage parties etc.	[illegible]

A7092 Wt. W125 9/M1293 750,000. 1/17. D. D & L. Ltd. Forms/C2118/14.

Sheet. No. 2

WAR DIARY
or
~~INTELLIGENCE SUMMARY.~~

2nd Bn. R.M.L.I.

Army Form C. 2118.

Instructions regarding War Diaries and Intelligence Summaries are contained in F. S. Regs., Part II. and the Staff Manual respectively. Title pages will be prepared in manuscript.

(Erase heading not required.)

Place	Date	Hour	Summary of Events and Information	Remarks and references to Appendices
FRONT Line	25th	Dec 1917	Batn working + Salvage Parties etc. O.O. No. 102 issued	appendix V [illegible]
" "	26th	" "	Batn relieved by 1st Bn. R.M.L.I. + proceeded to METZ in reserve. 1 casualty	[illegible]
METZ	27th	" "	" inspections, cleaning up etc.	[illegible]
"	28th	" "	" " " " " 50 reinforcements joined Bn	[illegible]
"	29th	" "	" " " " " Baths, + Specialist training	[illegible]
"	30th	" "	" " . O.O. No. 103 issued. Batn Stand by in Billets. O.O. No 103 in abeyance.	appendix VI [illegible]
"	31st	" "	Amendment to O.O. No. 103 issued. Batn relieved 1st Bn. R.M.L.I. in front line.	[illegible]

[illegible signature]
Lieut Colonel RMLI
Comdt 2nd Bn RMLI

A7092 Wt. W128_9/M1293 750,000. 1/17. D. D & L. Ltd. Forms/C2118/14.

Addendum to.
Operation Orders No 96.

Caps will be carried between Supporting Straps, so that they may be worn when the Batt: is out of the danger area.

H Burton

Capt & A/Adjutant.
2nd Batt RMLI.

SECRET

Operation Orders No 96.
by Lieut Colonel G. R. Parry R.M.L.I.
Commanding 2nd Bn Royal Marine Light Infantry.

Reference Maps: -
Sheets 27 & 28.
1/40.000.

Bn Headquarters.
5th December 1917.

1. The Battn will move by march route to SCHOOLS CAMP tomorrow. 6th inst DRESS. Full Marching Order. Steel Helmets will be worn.

First Line Transport will move with Unit.

Transport, less Cookers, Maltese Cart & Mess Cart, will join Battn at BRIELEN Cross Roads, B.29. central at 10.45 am.

2. Blankets. All mens Blankets are to be tightly rolled in bundles of 10, labelled, & dumped alongside Area Commandant's House by 7.0 am.

Officers' Valises, spare Mess Gear & Orderly Room Boxes to be dumped as above by 7.20 am. (These will be loaded on the first Lorry to arrive)

3. Loading Party. O/C "C" Co. will detail a loading party of 30 ORs. They will work under the command of Capt. Williams, to whom orders have been issued separately.

In addition to the above the Battn Sanitary Sergt and 8 HQ Sanitary Section will remain behind to clear up Latrines &c.

O/C "C" Co will also detail one NCO & six ORs to act as "Stragglers' Party" under Lieut. Slaughter.

4. The Battn will march in the following order. Head of Column to pass Area Commandants House at 10.15 am. – HQ Co "C" Co, Band, "D" "A" "B" Cos. Transport, Stragglers' Party.

5. Route. Camp – to BRIELEN Cross Roads — BRIELEN-VLAMERTINGHE road as far as road junctions at H.3.d 2 3 — thence via SWITCH ROAD to main VLAMERTINGHE-POPERINGHE road at H.8.b 4.9. — road junction at G.3.c 7.3 — SWITCH ROAD — thence via POPERINGHE – WATOU road.

Continued. 2

6. East of VLAMERTINGHE – ELVERDINGHE road the Battn. will move in file, not in fours. It will close up into fours when clear of the road junctions at H 3 d. 2 3.

Intervals. The following intervals will be maintained on the march. 200 yards between Cos. 100 yards between rear Co & Transport. 25 yards after every six Vehicles.

7. The usual halts will be observed at 10 mins. to the clock hour; the march being resumed at the hour. First halt being at 11 50. am.

8. Transport Officer will arrange to send Officers' Mess & Maltese Carts to Camp by 9.0. am. Teams for Cookers to arrive by 9 20. am. These will move in rear of Battn. from Camp to BRIELEN Cross Roads and then take up their proper positions in the column.

9. Attention is called to "Brigade Standing March Orders".

10. An Advanced Billeting Party under command of Lieut. Lee will proceed to SCHOOLS CAMP by cycles. Each Co. HQrs & Transport will send one representative. They will report at Orderly Room at 6.15. am.

Guides will meet the Battn. at SCHOOLS CAMP.

H Burton

Capt. & Adjutant.
2nd Bn. RMLI.

Copies to:-

No. 1 Retain
2. War Diary
3. O/C "A" Co.
4. " "B" Co.
5. " "C" Co.
6. " "D" Co.
7. Transport Officer.

SECRET

Operation Orders No 97
by Lieut Colonel G. R. Parry, RMLI.
Commandg 2nd Bn Royal Marine Light Infantry.

Reference Maps:-
Sheets 27. & 28.
and LENS 11.

Bn Headquarters
8th Dec 1917.

1. The Battn will move to the new area by march route and train, pm tomorrow. Entraining Station PESELHOEK.

2. QM Stores will be transported by Motor Lorries tomorrow between 8.0. am & 3.0. pm.

O/C "B" Co will detail a Guard to proceed with the first Lorry to the entraining Station. They will report to the QM at the bottom of the Duck board track at 8.30. am. Dress. Marching Order. Rations for the 9th & 10th to be carried. Strength of Guard. One NCO. & three men.

3. Officers Valises &c. Officers Valises, spare Mess Gear and Orderly Room Gear are to be dumped outside Nissen Hut at the bottom of the Duckboard track leading to the main road by 11.0 am.

Medical Cart will call at Medical Inspection Room at 11.0. am to be loaded and then return to Transport Lines.

Blankets. All Blankets are to be tightly rolled in bundles of ten, clearly labelled, and dumped at the bottom of the Duckboard track by 8.0 am.

4 Lieut Spraggett will report to RTO. at PESELHOEK. at 4.45. pm. to ascertain the situation. He will report to the O/C. before leaving Camp.

5. An Advance Billeting Party consisting of one NCO. per Co. & one representative from Transport will report to Lieut. Lee at the Orderly Room at 1.0. am tomorrow. Dress. Less Great Coats. All gear. Rations for 9th & 10th.

6 Officers Mess Gear. The Officers Mess Cart will call at the Camp at 2.30. pm tomorrow to collect Mess Gear.

Gear required on the journey is to be carried in Sandbags.

7. Water. Water Carts, Petrol Tins & Water Bottles will be entrained full. Horses to be watered at the Station.

Continued. (2)

8 Transport. Transport will move off at 4.0. pm, and proceed by the ST. JEANTER BIEZEN road → POPERINGHE road – SWITCH ROAD to A 25. d. 4 1., thence to road junction at A 20. d. 3 1., and from thence proceed by the left hand fork to Station which is situated between A. 20. b. and A. 21 a. (Bread ropes to be taken).

Cookers & Water Carts to be withdrawn from Camp in sufficient time to allow them to join the Column.

To enable the men to be supplied with Tea, Soyer Stoves & Dixie Kettles are being arranged for by the Cook Sergt.

9. Battn will parade at 5.0. pm. Dress. Loose Great Coats. All gear. Unconsumed portion of Rations for the 9th and Rations for the 10th. Men are to be warned that no further food will be supplied on the 10th.

O/C. Cos. will report their Cos present to the O/C.. Bn will then be formed up on the road leading from Camp to the main road in Column of Route without intervals.

Bn will then proceed by march route to the entraining Station in the following formation:- HQ. Band "A" "B" "C" "D" Cos. 200 yards distance will be maintained between Cos. O/C. Cos. are to keep touch by Connecting Files.

10. Route. As laid down for the Transport with the exception that at the fork at A 20 d. 3.1. the Bn will proceed by the right fork and not the left.

No Officers' Chargers will be available for riding.

11 Entraining. Train Serial No 6312. This train will convey the whole Battn. It consists of 30 covered trucks, 17 flat trucks & one Officers' Coach.

Lieut. Greaggett will arrange details.

It is hoped to allot 4 covered trucks to each Co.

Plan of the Station and Approaches can be seen on application at the Orderly Room.

Entraining is to be completed by 8.15 pm.

Troops are to be cautioned against using the Chinese Latrine at the Station.

Continued. (3)

12. Pickets on the Train. O/C. HQ & 'D' Cos. will each detail a Picket of 3. NCOs & 12 men who will travel on the front and rear compartments respectively. Their duty will be to prevent men leaving the train at halts.

All doors of covered trucks and carriages on the right hand side of the train are to be kept closed.

No men are to be allowed to travel in the Brake Compartments or on the roofs of the carriages, nor to interfere with the Brake arrangements on the trucks.

13. Detraining. No orders regarding detraining are yet available.

14. Billets are to be left in a clean & sanitary condition. O/C Cos are to report their Billets correct or otherwise to the O/C at 5.0. pm.

A Burton

Capt & A/ Adjutant
2nd Bn RMLI.

SECRET

Operation Order No 98.

by Lieut. Colonel G. R. Parry, RMLI.
Commandg 2nd Bn Royal Marine Light Infy.

Reference Maps:-
LENS. 11 and
FRANCE. 57.C

Bn Headquarters.
13th Decr 1917

1. The 2nd Battn RMLI. will move on 14th Decr 1917 to ETRICOURT. L.6. (LENS.11) and V.8. (57C)

2. Route. The Route will be VILLERS — AU-FLOS — BARRASTRE — BUS — LECHELLE — ETRICOURT.

3. An Advance Billeting Party of one NCO per Co. Hdqrs, & a representative from Transport will report at Orderly Room at 7.45. am. and proceed by cycle under the charge of Lieut. J. C. Lee to the destination. They will report to the Town Major, ETRICOURT at 9.0. am Billeting States to be taken.

4. Officers' Valises are to be dumped outside Orderly Room at 8.30. am

Orderly Room Gear and Officers' Spare Mess Gear to be dumped outside Battn Hdqrs by 7.15. am.

Officers' Mess Cart will call for remainder of Officers Mess Gear at 8.15. am. and remain in Camp and await arrival of Transport.

Blankets, tightly rolled in bundles of ten & labelled, are to be dumped outside Orderly Room by 7.0. am. It is suggested that a wooden tally be substituted for the usual paper one, as the latter invariably gets torn off.

Medical Cart will call at Medical Inspection Room at 7.45. am and await arrival of Transport.

Transport will move with Battn. Orders regarding move have been issued separately to the Transport Officer.

5. Dress. Mounted Officers. Sam Browne.
Dismounted Officers Full Marching Order.
O.R's Full Marching Order, all Gear, Steel Helmets between Supporting Straps.

Packs & Rifles of the Band will be carried on Motor Lorry. Q.M to arrange accordingly.

6. Battn will fall in by Cos. on their private Parades at 8.45. am. & be ready to move off at 9.0. am.

Order of March. HQ. Band. B. C. D. A. Cos.

Continued (2)

7 The Batt. will pass Starting Point. Road junction at N.18.a.1.0. at 9.19 am.

8. The following distances will be maintained:-
Between Units 100 yards. Between HQ & "B" Co. Nil.
Between Cos. 50 yards. Between Cos & Transport 50 yards.

9 The usual halts on line of march will be observed, the first halt being at 9.50 am.

10. Extra Transport. Two Lorries are being provided. They will make two trips each.

11. * A Loading and "Clearing up Camp" Party of 4 NCOs & 20 men will be detailed by O/C "C" Co.
In addition to the above the Bn Sanitary Sergt. & HQ Sanitary Squad will remain behind to clean up Latrines &c.
Lieut. Gibbons will remain behind in charge of the above parties, and will obtain a Certificate from the Area Commandant, or his representative, stating that the Camp has been left in a clean and satisfactory condition. He will then march the above parties to ETRICOURT.

12 O/C "C" Co. will detail a party of 3 NCOs, and 6 men, who will march in rear of the Transport under the command of 2nd Lieut. Slaughter.
No man is to fall out unless he is in possession of a Pass signed by an Officer.

13 Attention is called to Brigade Standing March Orders.
It was observed on the last march that an excessive number of men were marching behind the Co. Cookers. The only men allowed there are the Co. Cooks.

---

* Loading Party will report to QM. at 7.0 am.

R. Burton
Capt & A/Adjutant
2nd Bn Royal Marine Light Infantry.

SECRET.

OPERATION ORDERS Nº 99.

BY LIEUT. COLONEL G.LL. PARRY, RMLI.
COMMANDING 2ND BN ROYAL MARINE LIGHT INFANTRY

REF MAPS LENS 11. 57c.

BN HEADQUARTERS
14TH DECR 1917

1. The march of the Battn will be resumed tomorrow. Destination. V.1.c. (N of ETRICOURT).
2. Advance Billeting Party. The usual advance billeting party will precede the Battn. They will report to Lt. Lee at Bn HQrs at 8 a.m, and proceed by cycle to ETRICOURT, at V.7.d.5.4. They will meet the Battn on road 150 yds west of Crossroads at V.1.b.3.7.
3. Route. Via LE MESNIL – thence by road through O.35.d. to crossroads O.35.d.9.9. thence by road S.E. to cross roads at V.1.b.3.7. – thence South to camp.
4. All blankets tightly rolled in bundles of ten and labelled to be dumped at Q.M. Stores by 7 a.m. All officers' spare mess gear and Orderly Room gear to be dumped at QM Stores by 7.15 a.m. Officers mess cart will call for officers mess gear at 7.45 a.m. Officers Valises to be dumped at Q.M. Stores by 8.30 a.m.
5. Dress. Mounted Officers, Sam-Browne. Dismounted Officers, full marching Order. Other Ranks full marching order, steel helmets to be carried between supporting straps. To ensure uniformity no covers to be carried on rifles.
6. Parade. Fall in 8.45 a.m. Cos. to be ready to move off at 9 a.m. Order of march. H.Q. Band, "C" "D" "A" "B" Cos.
7. First line Transport will move with unit. It will branch off after passing LE MESNIL and proceed thence by road through U.11.b., over the Railway to MANANCOURT – cross roads at V.13.c.5.4 – V.7.d. – ETRICOURT. – BEET-ROOT SUGAR FACTORY – crossroads at V.1.b.3.7. thence South to Camp.
8. All other details as for todays march.

N. Dunston

CAPT & A/ADJUTANT.
2ND BN RMLI.

SECRET   Copy No 100

Operation Orders No 100

by

Lieut Colonel [illegible] R.A. [illegible]
Commanding 2nd Bn Royal [illegible] L.I.

Reference Map
Sheet 57c 1/40,000.

Bn Headquarters
December 17th 1917

1. The 2nd Battalion [illegible] will move today by march route to quarters in Q.20.c
2. Advance billeting party. The usual advance billeting party will precede the Battn. They will report to [illegible] at Battn H.Q. at 10 am and proceed by [illegible] METZ. They will meet the Battn at Cross Roads at Q.19 D.7.2
3. Route via EQUANCOURT thence by road running N.E through V.4.b. and P.35. Central to METZ.
4. Orders concerning the dumping of blankets have already been issued.
All officers mess gear, Officers valises, and Orderly Room gear to be dumped at Q.14 [illegible] by 10.30 am. Officers mess carts will call for surplus mess gear at 11.30 am.
Medical Stores will be loaded on Medical Cart by 11.30 am.
5. Dress. Mounted Officers [illegible]
Dismounted Officers Full marching order
O.R. Full marching order. No covers will be carried on rifles.
Steel helmets will be worn by all ranks.
6. Parade. Fall in 11.45 am. Coys to be ready to move off by 12.0 noon.
Order of march HQ Band D A B & C Coys
200 yards distance [illegible] between Coys.
7. Travelling Kitchens and Water Carts will accompany the Battn. Other first line transport will move at 11.30 am to LECHELLE under orders of Battn Transport Officer.
[illegible] Coy will detail a party of 20 O.R. to remain behind to clean up the camp under orders of the Officer of the day who will obtain a certificate from the Camp Commandant at ETRICOURT that the camp was vacated in a clean condition. He will then conduct

the

Contd. 2

[illegible] to METZ by [illegible] and [illegible] the [illegible] [illegible] from the Camp Commandant at ETRICOURT to 2nd H.Q. [illegible] on [illegible]

[illegible] one N.C.O. and [illegible] O.R.s [illegible] to 2 Lieut [illegible] to act as [illegible] party

8 [illegible] details as for [illegible] 10th inst

9 [illegible] at METZ [illegible] of the following [illegible]:

(a) Trench running E from TRESCAULT to [illegible]

(b) TRESCAULT – BEAUCAMP – VILLERS PLOUICH Road.

J. Lee [illegible]

Lieut & Adjutant

2nd [illegible]

SECRET   Copy No 6

Operation Order No 101
by Lieut Colonel [illegible] RMLI
Commanding 2nd Bn Royal Marine Light Infantry.

Bn Headquarters
21st Dec 1917

Reference Map:
BEAUCAMP. 1/10000

1 The 188th Infantry Brigade will relieve the 189th Infantry Brigade and one Co. of the HOOD Bn on the night 22/23rd Dec 1917.

2 The 2nd Bn RMLI will relieve the 2/8th WORCESTERS and one Co of the 2/4th GLOUCESTERS.

3 The 9th Division will be on our right and the ANSON Batt on our left.

4 'A' Co will relieve C & D Cos. 2/8th Worcesters.
B Co will relieve A Co. Do.
C Co will relieve B Co. Do and No 2 Co of the 2/4th Gloucesters.

D Co will be in support to A Co.
Bn HQrs will be located in FARM RAVINE.
RAP. will be located at Q 20.a.10.80.

5. Advance parties, to whom separate instructions were issued, proceeded into the line this morning to take over Trench Stores etc.

6 Small Box Respirators will be worn in the ALERT position during the relief and during the tour in the trenches.

7 Cos will report "Relief complete" to Bn HQrs by telephone code word "VERTICAL".

8 Cos will parade at 1.0 pm and move off at 1.15 pm in the following order 'A' C D B & HQ Cos. 200 yards distance between Cos 100 yards between Platoons, touch being maintained by connecting files.

9. Route. TRESCAULT ROAD — Q.20.b.20.60. — Q.22.a.10.87. — CHARING CROSS. — BEAUCAMP — VILLERS PLOUICH — FARM RAVINE.
One Guide per Platoon will meet Bn at Q.14.d.50.10.

10 Dress. Fighting Order with Steel Helmets (Caps to be left behind in Packs) Jerkins will be worn. Great Coats & Waterproof Sheets en bandoleer.

11 Officers Valises, Surplus Mess Gear, Packs & Blankets (tightly rolled in bundles of 10 & labelled) to be dumped at QM Stores by 11.0 am.

12 Lewis Guns, with [illegible] Magazines per Gun will be carried by Lewis Gun teams. Transport Officer will arrange for teams to draw Lewis Gun Limbers, Water Carts & Cookers to Transport Lines.

Continued (2).

12. (continued). Medical Cart & Officers' Mess Cart will be provided to convey Officers' Mess Gear, Medical Stores & Orderly Room Gear; Gear must be ready for loading by 12.45 pm.

13. O/C Cos. will ensure that Billets vacated by them are clean and tidy, reporting same to the O/C before moving off. The QM will obtain a Certificate from the Town Major concerning state of Billets vacated and forward same to Bn. Hqrs.

J C Lee

Lieut & A/Adjutant
2nd Bn. RMLI.

Copies to –

No. 1	Retain
2	O/C 'A' Co.
3	" B
4	" C
5	" D
6	War Diary.

OPERATION ORDERS No 102. Copy No 1

By Lieut. Colonel G L Parry RMLI
Comdg. 2nd Bn ROYAL MARINE LT INFY

1. On the night 26/27th. 1st Bn RMLI will relieve 2nd Bn RMLI in the Front Line.

2. Relief will be carried out in daylight if visibility is poor.

3. A.A. Gun (L.G.) posts will be handed over. Two. A.A. L.Gs have been sent to relieve 2 L.Gs of 1st Bn RMLI at A.A. post at YTRES.

4. Trench stores, schemes of work, aeroplane photos & secret maps will be handed over to advanced parties of 1st Bn RMLI. Receipts will be obtained and duplicates forwarded to Bn H.Q by 2-0 pm 26-12-17.

5. 63rd (RN) Division Trench Standing Orders as far as they affect the relief, will be strictly adhered to.

6. "B" Co. 1st Bn will relieve "C" Co 2nd Bn RMLI
"A" " " " "A" " "
"C" " " " "D" " "
"D" " " " "B"

7. The following guides will be supplied –
"A" Coy – Three. "B" Coy. Three. "C" Co. Three
"D" Coy – Three. "H.Q." – One.
2nd Lt. Albury (who will be in charge) and the above guides will report to Bn. H.Q. at 2.0pm.

8. The H.Q. Ser Co, will report, with all gear, at Bn. H.Q. at 9-0 am. to proceed to METZ and take over billets vacated by 1st Bn RMLI.

9. On relief, Co's will move independently to METZ. Os. C. Cos. will report at Bn. H.Q. on their way out of the line.
ROUTE VILLERS PLOUCH – BEAUCAMP – TRESCAULT – METZ. 200 yds distance between Co's, & 100 yds distance between platoons will be kept & touch maintained by connecting files between platoons.

10. Transport Officer has received separate instructions re blankets, packs, surplus Mess Gear, officers' valises etc. All details at present at Q.M. Stores will join Bn on arrival at METZ.

Contd.

11 All food containers, dixies, Officers Mess gear, Medical Stores and Orderly Room Gear will be dumped at the Quarry by 5.0 p.m.
Lewis Gun Panniers will be dumped in the Quarry as Co.s pass that point and loaded on to limbers under the supervision of Bn. L.G. Sgt. Lewis Guns will be carried to METZ by L.G. Teams.

12 OsC Co's. will report to Bn H.Q. when their Companies are in billets.

13 Code word for "Relief complete - SUPER"

14 Acknowledge

J Gee
Lt. & A/Adjt.
2nd Bn R.M.L.I.

Issued at ____

Copies to:
No 1 - Retained
2 - O.C. 1st Bn R.M.L.I
3 - O.C. "A" Co
4 " "B" "
5 " "C" "
6 " "D" "
7 War Diary
8 FILE

AMENDMENT TO OPERATION ORDERS No.103.
issued 30th December 1917.

For all dates read one day later. Leading Co. will not reach VILLERS PLOUICH before 5.0.pm.

Lieut. & A/Adjutant,
2nd Bn. R.M.L.I.

31.12.17.

SECRET. OPERATION ORDERS No. 103
BY LIEUT. COLONEL G. Ll. PARRY. R.M.L.I.,
COMMANDING 2nd Bn. ROYAL MARINE LIGHT INFANTRY.

Bn. Headquarters,
30th Decr. 1917.

1. The 2nd Bn. R.M.L.I. will relieve the 1st Bn. R.M.L.I. in the right sector on the night 30/31st Decr. 1917.

2. "A" Co. 2nd Bn. R.M.L.I. will relieve "D" Co. 1st Bn. R.M.L.I.
"B" Co. -- -- "A" Co. --
"C" Co. -- -- "C" Co. --
"D" Co. -- -- "B" Co. --

Bn. Headquarters and R.A.P. will be located as before.

3. Advance Parties proceeding into the Line to take over Trench Stores etc will parade at Bn. Orderly Room at 11.0.a.m.
Advance Party will consist of one Officer per Co. one N.COO. from H.Q., Bn. L.G. Sergt., one N.C.O. per Platoon, one Signaller to take over Signals for the Bn., one representative from M.O.
Officers giving receipts for Trench Stores will render duplicates to Bn. Hdqrs in the Line by 9.0.a.m. 31st inst.
S.B.Rs will be worn in the "ALERT" position during the relief and during tour in the Trenches.
Code words concerning relief will be as follows :-
RELIEF. "JERRY"
RELIEF COMPLETE. "JERRY DONE"

4. Cos. will move off in the following order :- "B" "D" "C" "H.Q" & "A" Cos. 200 yards distance between Cos. 100 yards between Platoons. Touch will be maintained by connecting files.
Cos. are to be ready to move off qt 3.0.p.m. The exact time will be notified later.

5. Route. Route is left to the discretion of Co. Commanders. No guides will meet the Battn.

6. Dress. "Fighting Order" with Steel Helmets. Caps to be left behind in Packs. Jerkins will be worn. Great Coats and Waterproof Sheets en banderole.

7. Lewis Guns, with 16 Magazines per Gun, will be carried by Lewis Gun Crews. Transport Officer will arrange for Medical Cart and Officers Mess Cart to be at Orderly Room at 2.0.p.m. Officers' Mess Gear, Medical Stores and Orderly Room Gear will be ready for loading by 2.30.p.m.

8. Two Cooks per Co. and the Cook Sergt. will proceed into the Line after dinner today. Dixies and Food Containers will be brought up by Limber.

9. Officers' Valises, Spare Mess Gear, Packs, and Blankets tightly rolled in bundles of ten and labelled, will be dumped in the house immediately in front of H.Q.Huts (No.22.Billet) by 2.0.p.m.

10. O.C. Cos. will ensure that all Billets vacated by them are clean and tidy, reporting same to the O.C. before moving off. Q.M. will obtain a Certificate from the Town Major concerning state of Billets vacated and render same to Bn. Orderly Room.

Lieut. & A/Adjutant,
2nd Bn. R.M.L.I.

Copies to/ Back.

COPIES TO :-

No. 1. Retain.
2. O.C. 1st Bn. R.M.L.I.
3. O.C. "A" Co.
4. "B" Co.
5. "C" Co.
6. "D" Co.
7. Transport Officer.
8. War Diary.

CONFIDENTIAL.

Headquarters,
2nd Bn. Royal Marine Light Infantry.

1st February 1918.

W A R D I A R Y

(VOL. XIX)

2nd Battn. ROYAL MARINE LIGHT INFANTRY.

from

1st JANUARY 1918
to
31st JANUARY 1918.

Major. R.M.L.I.,
Commdg 2nd Bn., Royal Marine Light Infantry.

To :- Headquarters,
63rd (R.N) Division.

Instructions regarding War Diaries and Intelligence Summaries are contained in F. S. Regs., Part II. and the Staff Manual respectively. Title pages will be prepared in manuscript.

WAR DIARY
or
~~INTELLIGENCE SUMMARY.~~
(Erase heading not required.)

Sheet number — Army Form C. 2118.

2nd Bn Royal Marines Light Infantry

Place	Date	Hour	Summary of Events and Information	Remarks and references to Appendices
Front line	1-1-18		Working, salvage and carrying parties.	R.B.
" "	2-1-18		Ditto " " " " . One casualty.	R.B.
" "	3-1-18		" " " " " . Two casualties. Operation Order 104 issued.	R.B. Appendix I
" "	4-1-18		" " " " " . Battalion relieved by Howe Bn & moved into support at VILLERS PLOUICHE.	R.B.
Support	5-1-18		Working, salvage & carrying parties. Capt C H Goode, R.M.L.I joined Bn. T/Capt B.C.V. Weeks & T/Lieut M.W. Curtis struck off strength. S.R.O. 3466 & 3455 respectively. 20 reinforcements joined battalion. One casualty.	R.B.
" "	6-1-18		Working, salvage & carrying parties. One casualty	R.B.
" "	7-1-18		" " " . Operation Order No 105 issued.	Appendix II R.B.
" "	8-1-18		" " " . Battalion relieved 1st R.M.L.I in the front line. (Left of H- sub sector)	R.B.
Front line.	9-1-18		Working, salvage & carrying parties. Operation Order No 106 issued.	Appendix III. R.B.
" "	10-1-18		Battalion relieved by Howe Bn in the front line & moved into support. One casualty.	R.B.
Support	11-1-18		Working, salvage & carrying parties.	R.B.

A7092 Wt. W128 9/M1293 750,000. 1/17. D. D. & L. Ltd. Forms/C2118/14.

Instructions regarding War Diaries and Intelligence Summaries are contained in F. S. Regs., Part II. and the Staff Manual respectively. Title pages will be prepared in manuscript.

WAR DIARY

or

~~INTELLIGENCE SUMMARY.~~

(Erase heading not required.)

Sheet II

Army Form C. 2118.

2nd Bn Royal Marines Light Infantry

Place	Date	Hour	Summary of Events and Information	Remarks and references to Appendices
Support	12-1-18		Operation Order 107 issued. Bn. relieved by Anson Battalion & proceeded to Metz (Divisional Reserve).	Appendix III RB
Metz.	13-1-18		Battalion cleaning up, baths ect. Major C G Farquharson R.M.L.I rejoined Bn & assumed duties as Second in Command.	RB
"	14-1-18		Battalion cleaning up. Specialists parades ect.	RB
"	15-1-18		" Battalion parades. P.T & Specialist Instruction. 23 reinforcements joined battalion. Operation Order 108 issued.	RB
"	16-1-18		Battalion relieved 1st Bn R.M.L.I in the front line. (Right sub sector) T/2nd Lieut H L Hardisty struck off strength to XVIII Corps School. 18 reinforcements joined battalion.	Appendix V RB. RB.
front line	17-1-18		Battalion working & carrying parties. Major Act Lieut Col G L Parry wounded & 2 O R's casualties. Operation Order 109 issued.	Appendix VI RB
"	18-1-18		Battalion working & carrying parties. Major Farquharson assumed command of battalion. Capt Goode assumed duties of Second in Command. Inter company relief.	RB RB
"	19-1-18		Battalion working & carrying parties. Operation Order 110 issued. 2 casualties.	Appendix VII RB

A7092 Wt. W128.9/M1293 750,000. 1/17. D. D & I. Ltd. Forms/C2118/14.

Instructions regarding War Diaries and Intelligence Summaries are contained in F. S. Regs., Part II. and the Staff Manual respectively. Title pages will be prepared in manuscript.

WAR DIARY
or
INTELLIGENCE SUMMARY.
(*Erase heading not required.*) 2nd Bn Royal Marine Light Infantry.

Army Form C. 2118.

Sheet number III

Place	Date	Hour	Summary of Events and Information	Remarks and references to Appendices
20-1-18 Front line	20-1-18		Battalion relieved by H.A.C. Bn & moved into support. 1 Lieut A H H Sayer joined Bn.	RB
Support	21-1-18		Battalion working & carrying parties. Operation Order 111 issued. 2 casualties	Appendix VIII RB
" "	22-1-18		Battalion working, carrying & salvage parties. Relieved 1st Bn R.M.L.I in the front line (Left sub sector). Operation Order 112 issued	Appendix IX
Front line	23-1-18		Battalion relieved by 1st Bn K.R.R. & proceeded to camp in Havrincourt Wood. One casualty.	RB RB
Havrincourt Wood	24-1-18		Battalion proceeded by route march to Metz. Entrained & proceeded to Rocquigny Station. Detrained & moved into camp "B". (Corps Reserve).	RB
Rocquigny	25-1-18		Battalion refitting, cleaning up ect.	RB
"	26-1-18		" baths ect.	RB
"	27-1-18		working parties fatigues ect.	RB
"	28-1-18		training. Major Farquharson to leave. Capt Goode assumed cmd of battalion.	RB

A5834 Wt. W4973 M687 750,000 8/16 D. D. & L. Ltd. Forms/C.2118/13.

Army Form C. 2118.

Sheet number IV

Instructions regarding War Diaries and Intelligence Summaries are contained in F. S. Regs., Part II. and the Staff Manual respectively. Title pages will be prepared in manuscript.

WAR DIARY
or
INTELLIGENCE SUMMARY.

(*Erase heading not required.*) 2nd Bn Royal Marine Light Infantry

Place	Date	Hour	Summary of Events and Information	Remarks and references to Appendices
Rocquigny	29.1.18		Battalion training.	R.B.
"	30.1.18		" " & working parties ect. Major N. S. Clutterbuck joined battalion & assumed command.	R.B. R.B.
"	31.1.18		Battalion working parties ect.	R.B.

N S Clutterbuck
Major RMLI
Comdg 2nd Bn RMLI

A5834 Wt. W4973 M687 750,000 8/16 D. D. & L. Ltd. Forms/C.2118/13.

SECRET. COPY. No.

OPERATION ORDERS No. 104,
BY LIEUT. COLONEL G. Ll. PARRY. R.M.L.I.,
COMMANDING 2nd Bn. ROYAL MARINE LIGHT INFANTRY.

Bn. Headquarters,
3rd January 1918.

1. On the night 4/5th January 1918 the HOWE Bn. will relieve the 2nd Bn. R.M.L.I. in the right sector. After relief the 2nd Bn. R.M.L.I. will move into Support.

2. On completion of Relief RIFLE ALLEY (inclusive to right sector) will be the boundary between the right and left sectors.

3.

HOWE Bn.		2/R.M.L.I.			1/R.M.L.I.
"C" Co.	will relieve	"B" Co.	who will take over quarters vacated by		"B" Co.
"D" Co.	"	"D" Co.	"	"	"D" Co.
"A" Co.	"	"C" Co.	"	"	"A" Co.
"B" Co.	"	"A" Co.	"	"	"C" Co.

4. Co. Cooks with their Dixies, will return to their Cos.and remain with them whilst the Bn. is in Support. Three German and five Denison Food Containers will be used and taken on charge by "D" Co.

5. Advance parties have come into the Line tonight to take over Trench Stores etc. O.C. Cos. will obtain receipts for all Stores etc. handed over and forward same to Bn. H.Q. not later than 12.0. noon 4th inst.

6. Each Co. will detail one N.C.O. to act as Advance Party together with one H.Q. Signaller and one M.U. Rating. This party will report at Bn. H.Q. 9.0.am 4th inst. They will take over quarters, and return to the Line in time to guide their respective Cos. into Support. 2nd Lieut. BUCKLEY will be in charge of the Advance Party.

O.C. Cos. will also detail four guides per Co. for the incoming Unit. They will report at Bn. H.Q. at 2.0.pm. 2nd Lieut. COLLIER, to whom separate instructions will be given, will be in charge of the guides.

7. All Food Containers are to be returned to the QUARRY by 4.30.pm. The Cook Sergt. will arrange to send up Tea to the Cos. at 3.30.pm.

Medical Stores and Officers' Mess Gear will be ready for loading at 5.0.pm at the QUARRY. Officers' Mess Gear will only be carried as far as the new Dump (opposite Bde. H.Q). The disposal of extra Lewis Gun Ammunition will be arranged by B.L.G.O.

8. O.C. Cos. (with the exception of "D" Co) will report to the O.C. at new Bn.H.Qs(next Bde.H.Qs) when their Cos. have arrived in their new quarters.

9. Code words :- Relief. "PORK"
Relief complete. "PORK AND BEANS"

(sgd) J.C.LEE.
Lieut.&.A/Adjutant,
2nd Bn. R.M.L.I.

SECRET. Operation Order No 105. Copy No 1

By Lt. Colonel G. L. Parry R.M.L.I.
Commanding 2nd Bn Royal Marine Lt. Infantry.

Bn Headquarters
4th January 1918

1.. On the night of 8th/9th January 1918 the 2nd Bn R.M.L.I. will relieve the 1st Bn R.M.L.I. in the left sector.

2... The Battn. front extends from RIFLE ALLEY, NORTH to CORNWALL SUPPORT.

3.... 2nd Bn R.M.L.I. — 1st Bn R.M.L.I.

"A" Co will relieve "A" Co. (3 platoons in front line, 1 in close support)
"B" " " " "B" Co. (2 " " " " , 2 in CORNWALL Trench)
"C" " " " "C" Co. & will occupy NEWPORT & TRURO Trenches (Carrying Co.)
"D" " " " "D" Co. & will occupy PRENTICE Trench.

4.. All cooking will be done alongside the CEMETERY, West of FARM RAVINE, Co. cooks reporting to Cook Sergt after tea. "D" Co. will return food containers to R.S.M. tomorrow forenoon.

5... All extra S.A.A. and bombs drawn from Brigade Dump is to be returned tomorrow forenoon.

6.. Advance party of 1 officer per Co, 1 N.C.O. per platoon and 1 N.C.O. from H.Q. will proceed into the line tomorrow to take over line, trench stores etc, reporting to 1st Bn R.M.L.I. H.Q. at 9-0 am. Duplicate receipts for Trench Stores taken over to be rendered to Bn. H.Q. by 3.0 pm.

7.. One guide per platoon will be supplied by 1st Bn R.M.L.I. who will report to these H.Q. by 5-0 pm. Co.s will move into the line in the following order by the routes specified.

5-0 pm. "A" Co will move ~~by~~ VILLAGE ROAD, & NEWPORT Trench, followed by "B" Co. a distance of 50 yds between platoons, & 100 yds between Co.s to be maintained. "D" Co. will move in sufficient time to admit them passing Bn. H.Q. at 5.30 pm and will then move via POPE Avenue into PRENTICE Trench. "C" Co. will follow "D" Co, maintaining the same distances as laid down for "A" & "B" Co.s.

8.. Medical Officer will make his own arrangements for taking over the R.A.P. of 1st Bn R.M.L.I.

9... Bn. Headquarters will be located in FARM RAVINE.

10... Disposition map to be rendered to Bn. H.Q. by 10-0 am 9th inst.

11 -- Code word for "RELIEF" - "BULLY"
" " " "RELIEF COMPLETE" - "BULLY" - followed by code name of Company.

Issued at —

Copies to / overleaf.

C. Buxton
Capt. Adjt.
2nd Bn R.M.L.I.

Copies to:-

No. 1. War Diary
" 2. O.C. 1st Bn RMLI
" 3. " "A" Co
" 4/5. " "B" "
" 6. " "C" "
" 7/8 " "D" "
File
Do.

SECRET

COPY No 1

OPERATION ORDERS No 106

BY LIEUT. COLONEL G.LL PARRY, R.M.L.I.
COMDG 2ND BN ROYAL MARINE LIGHT INFANTRY

BN HEADQUARTERS,
9. 1. 18.

1. On the night of the 10/11TH JANUARY 1918, the HOWE BN will relieve the 2ND BN RMLI in the LEFT SUB-SECTOR.
After relief the BN will move into Support at VILLERS PLOUICH, "A" & "B" Cos. occupying the same billets as before. "D" Coy will take over "C" Cos. billets and "C" Coy will be located in LINCOLN AVENUE.
1 N.C.O. per Coy is to be sent down at 2 p.m to take over billets. "C" Coy will also detail an officer in addition to take over the billets in LINCOLN AVENUE. The RSM. will detail 1 N.C.O. to take over Stores and H.Q. billets.

2. "C" Coy. HOWE BN will relieve "A" Coy 2ND BN RMLI
"A" " " " " "B" " " "
"D" " " " " "C" " " "
"B" " " " " "D" " " "
Advance parties of the HOWE BN are proceeding into the line tomorrow to take over Trench Stores &c., reporting to these HQrs. at 10 a.m.

3. Greatest care is to be taken that all posts and Trench Stores are turned over correctly. Duplicate receipts of all Ammunition, Stores &c, turned over are to be sent to BN H.Qrs by 2 p.m.

4. 1 Guide per platoon will be sent to the HOWE BN H.Qs. reporting there at 4.45 p.m.

5. ROUTE. "C" & "A" Cos HOWE BN relieving "A" & "B" Cos. 2ND BN RMLI will proceed via VILLAGE ROAD, NIEUPORT TRENCH, RIFLE ALLEY and PRENTICE TRENCH. "D" & "B" Cos HOWE BN relieving "C" & "D" 2ND BN RMLI will proceed by POPE AVENUE, Times and distances being arranged by O.C. HOWE BN.

6. After relief, Cos will proceed to VILLERS PLOUICH under Os. C. Cos arrangements.

7. The last meal to be served in the trenches will be dinner. All food containers are to be returned to BN DUMP after that meal.

8. The M.O will make his own arrangements for moving to support BN R.A.P.

9. CODE WORD for relief "TIN"
" Relief complete "TIN EYE".

10. Officers billeted at VILLERS PLOUICH report to O.C after their Cos. are in billets.

R B Burton

CAPT & A/ADJUTANT
2ND BN RMLI

Copies to/over

Issued at

Copies to No 1 War Diary
2 O C [illegible] Bn
3 A Coy.
4 B
5 C
6 D
7 File
8 [illegible]

SECRET. COPY Nº 1

OPERATION ORDER Nº 104.

By Lieut Colonel G. H. Parry, R.M.L.I.
Commanding 2nd Bn Royal Marine Light Infantry.

Reference maps:- BEAUCAMP 1/10,000. SHEET 57C

Bn. Headquarters
12th January 1918.

1 INFORMATION. The 1st Bn R.M.L.I. will relieve the ANSON Bn in the right Sub-sector on the night of the 12/13th inst. After relief, the "ANSON" Bn., will move into SUPPORT.

2 OBJECT The 2nd Bn RMLI. will move into billets vacated by 1st Bn R.M.L.I. at METZ.

3 INSTRUCTIONS An advance billeting party of 1 NCO. from H.Q. and each Co, will proceed to METZ this day, leaving Bn. H.Q. at 10-0 a.m.

4. All Lewis Guns, Ammunition and Officers' Mess gear is to be dumped opposite Bn. H.Q. by 4-30 p.m. O.C.s Cos will detail 2 Lewis Gunners to remain in close proximity to the dump to load the above, on the arrival of transport. Two limbers & the Officers' Mess cart will be available to carry stores down. The Medical cart will carry Medical Officer's stores down, who will arrange for loading of same at R.A.P.

5. CO. COOKS & COOKING ARRANGEMENTS One cook per Co. will proceed to METZ after the mid-day meal. The other cooks will remain behind and prepare tea. After that meal, all cooking utensils will be loaded on a limber opposite Bn. H.Q. The Cook Sergt. will make arrangements accordingly. The Co. cooks will follow the transport. A hot meal will be served on arrival of the Bn. at METZ.

6. ORDER & TIMES OF MARCH "H.Q." "A" "B" & "D" Cos. H.Q. will move off at 5.0 p.m "A" Co, at 5.15 p.m., "B" Co at 5.30 p.m., "D" Co at 5.45 p.m. A Distance of 100 yds will be maintained between platoons. "C" Co, will move off independently, leading platoon leaving at 5.0 p.m. O.C. Cos will make their own arrangements as to the route to be followed.

7. Before moving off, O.C. Cos will report their Co. billets as having been left in a sanitary condition. "C" Co. will report by wire, using the code word "CAN-DOO"

8 On arrival at METZ O.C. Co.s will report their Co.s in billets to O.C. or his representative Lt. Lee.

9 Orders relating to tomorrow's routine will be issued after arrival at METZ.

N Burton
Capt & Adjt.

Issued at 12.50 p.m. Copies to/over.

Copies to:-

No	1	Retained
	2	O.C. "A" Co.
	3	" "B" "
	4	" "C" "
	5	" "D" "
	6	War Diary
	7	Do Do
	8	File.

SECRET

COPY No 1.

OPERATION ORDERS No.108.
BY LIEUT. COLONEL G. Ll. PARRY, R.M.L.I.,
COMMANDING 2nd Bn. ROYAL MARINE LIGHT INFANTRY.

REFERENCE MAP SHEET 57.c

Bn. Headquarters,
15th January 1918.

INFORMATION.

The 1st Bn. R.M.L.I. is holding the Right sub-sector.

OBJECT.

On the night 16/17th January the 2nd Bn. R.M.L.I. will relieve the 1st Bn. R.M.L.I.

INSTRUCTIONS.

1. An Advance Party will preceed the Bn. into the Line tomorrow, reporting at Bn. Orderly Room at 10.0.a.m. This party will consist of one Officer and one Runner per Co., one N.C.O. from H.Q. and each Platoon, Bn.Lewis Gun Sergt., one Signal N.C.O., and one representative from Medical Unit.

Two Trench Store Lists per Co. will be issued by the Adjutant. One copy is to be retained for information of the O.C. Co. and the other sent to the H.Q.Sergt, who will be found at H.Qs. 1st Bn. R.M.L.I.

Officers taking over Stores are to ensure that the Stores signed for are actually in the trenches. This particularly applies to Boots Gum.

2. Blankets tightly rolled in bundles of ten and clearly labelled are to be dumped at Bn. Orderly Room by 10.0. a.m. tomorrow.

3. Officers' Valises, Spare Mess Gear, Packs, etc., are to be dumped at Bn. Orderly Room by 2.0. p.m. tomorrow. The Band will be responsible for the storage of the above.

4. Billets. O.C. Cos. will ensure that all Billets vacated by them are clean and tidy, reporting same to the O.C. before moving off. The Q.M. will obtain a Certificate from the Town Major concerning state of billets vacated by the Bn. and render same to the Rear Orderly Room.

5. "D" Co. 2nd Bn. R.M.L.I. will relieve "D" Co. 1st Bn. R.M.L.I. in the right of the sub-sector.
"C" Co. 2nd Bn. R.M.L.I. will relieve "A" Co. 1st Bn. R.M.L.I. in the left of the sub-sector.
"A" Co. 2nd Bn. R.M.L.I. will relieve "C" Co. 1st Bn. R.M.L.I. in the centre and immediate support of the sub-sector.
"B" Co. 2nd Bn. R.M.L.I. will relieve "B" Co. 1st Bn. R.M.L.I. in the Quarry.
Details will be arranged at the O.C's Conference tomorrow.

6. Order of March. "D" "C" "A" "H.Q" "B" Cos.
"D" Co. will pass Starting Point, Cross Roads, METZ, Q.20.c.7.7., at 3.30.p.m. 100 yards distance will be maintained between Platoons. Quarter of an hour's interval between Cos.

7. Route. (By Road) METZ -- TRESCAULT -- BEAUCAMP -- VILLERS PLOUICH. No Guides will be supplied.

8. Dress. "Fighting Order" with Steel Helmets. Caps to be left behind in Packs. Jerkins will be worn. Great Coats and Waterproof sheets en banderole round Haversacks. Small Box Respirators will be worn in the "ALERT" position during the relief and during the tour in the trenches.

9. Lewis Guns and 16 Magazines per Gun will be carried by Lewis Gunners

CONTINUED. 2.

10. Transport Officer will arrange for Medical Cart and Officers' Mess Cart to report at METZ by 2.30. p.m.

11. Cooking arrangements. All Cooking will be done in the Quarry. Two Cooks per Co. and the Cook Sergt. will proceed into the Line after dinner tomorrow. O.C. Cos. will arrange for Dixies to be dumped outside Bn. Orderly Room by 2.30. p.m. Transport Officer will arrange for one Limber to convey above to the Quarry, reporting at Bn. Orderly Room by 3.0. p.m.

12. Bn. Headquarters and R.A.P. will be located as before.

13. Relief complete will be reported by Wire and Runner. Code words for relief will be :-

RELIEF. "THING"
RELIEF COMPLETE. "OLD THING"

N Burton

Capt. & A/Adjutant,
2nd Bn. R.M.L.I.

Issued at 9.0. p.m.

Copies to :-

No. 1. Retain.
2. O.C. 1st Bn. R.M.L.I.
3. O.C. "A" Co.
4. "B" Co.
5. "C" Co.
6. "D" Co.
7. War Diary.

SECRET Copy No 1

OPERATION ORDER No 109
by
Major C. C. Farquharson R.M.L.I.
Commanding 2nd Bn Royal Marine Lt Infy

Ref. Maps 57c. Bn. H.Qrs
17-1-18

1 ------- On the night of the 18/19th inst. an inter-Co. relief will take place.

2 ------- Advance party of 1 officer & N.C.O. from POUNDS & SHILLINGS will precede their Cos. into the line tomorrow forenoon. Great care is to be taken that all posts & Trench Stores are taken over correctly.

One N.C.O. from PENCE and FARTHINGS to be sent down to take over billets and Trench Stores.

3 ------- POUNDS will relieve FARTHINGS, SHILLINGS will relieve PENCE.

4 - - - Guides One guide from each post will report to the Co. H.Qs of the relieving Cos. by ~~4~~ 3 p.m. tomorrow.

5. - - - Relieving Cos will move into the line independently after the arrival of rations tomorrow night.

6. — — Meals. The Cook Sgt will arrange to supply a hot meal to the relieving Co's before they move up. This meal is to be ready by 4.0 pm. He will also arrange to supply relieved Cos. with a similar meal on their return.

7. Lewis Guns. Farthings will detail 1 L.G.s crew to take over the supporting Lewis Gun on the right Co. section. PENCE will detail 2 L.G's crews to take over 2 supporting Lewis Guns on the left supporting section.

8. — — All posts are to be self contained as regards ammunition, food & stores as arranged at the O.Cs conference this afternoon.

9. — — Relief complete will be reported by OC Cos of the relieved Cos on return of their Cos to their billets.

10. — — Arrangements re supply of food after relief. Hot meals will be sent up as far as possible as hitherto. FARTHINGS will be responsible for the supply of food to the right Co & PENCE to the left Co. It is not considered possible to supply the mid day meal to FOSTER SAP Garrison. OCs POUND & SHILLINGS will send guides to the cookhouse at the usual times to guide up carrying parties & also arrange distribution of food to their various posts.

J.C. Lee 2/Lt

Issued at 8.25 pm

Asst FILM

Copies to /one

NUTRIMENT

Copies to

No. 1 R.Harned

2 Pounds

3 Shillings

4 Pence

5 Farthings

6 War Diary

SECRET

Copy No. 1

OPERATION ORDERS No. 110

by

Major C. G. Farquharson M.C., R.M.L.I.

Commanding 2nd Bn. Royal Marine Light Infantry

Reference Maps
Parts of 57C.

Bn. Headquarters
Jany 19th 1918.

1. Information. On the night of the 20/21st Jany 1918 the HOWE Bn will relieve the 2nd Bn. R.M.L.I. in the right Sub Sector.

2. Object. After relief the 2nd Bn. R.M.L.I. will become Support Bn. & move into billets (H.Qrs & 4 Coys) at VILLERS PLOUICH

3. Advance Billeting Party. An advance billeting party consisting of Lieut. YANCE "PENCE" Coy, 1 N.C.O. from H.Qrs & each Coy will report to FILM at Bn. H.Qrs. at 10 a.m. tomorrow to receive instructions.

4. An advance party of the relieving Bn. will move up tomorrow to take over the line, Trench Stores &c. Great care is to be taken that all posts, work in hand, Trench Stores &c. are handed over correctly. 2 Trench Store lists per Co will be issued by FILM to O.C. Coys concerned. One copy is to be rendered to the Orderly Room as soon as possible after stores have been handed over.

5. ORDER OF RELIEF

C Coy HOWE Bn.	will relieve	A Coy. 2nd Bn RMLI
A "	" " "	B " "
B "	" " "	C " "
D "	" " "	D " "

6. GUIDES All guides will be under the command of 2nd Lieut PROFFITT "Farthings" Co. He will report to FILM at 4 p.m. tomorrow for instructions.

POUNDS & SHILLINGS will supply one guide from each post occupied. In addition to the above "Farthings" will supply guide for each of the posts held by him. (i.e. 41 & 42.)

PENCE will similarly supply guides from each of the posts held by him (i.e. 43, 44 & 61). All these guides are to report to FILM at Bn. Orderly Room by 4 o p.m.

The leading platoons of the relieving Bn will arrive at the

Railway Crossing at VILLERS PLOUICH about 5 pm.

Co's will be relieved independently by posts

7. Relief After relief each post will proceed independently to billets in VILLERS PLOUICH. N.C.Os in charge of posts will report personally to their O.C. Coys on their way down at their respective Co. H Qrs.

O.C. Coys will report relief complete by wire & afterwards personally to the O.C. at the present Bn H Qrs.

They will also report their Coys "in billets" to O.C. at Support Bn. H.Qs.

8. Arrangements of Meals The last meal to be sent up to the trenches of the Left Coy will be dinner, to the Right Co. breakfast. O.C. [illegible] will arrange to send 1 Food Container at dinnertime to posts 2 & 4. F.K.M. will supply a guide

9. Code word for relief HALL

relief complete NOBBY HALL

10. Lewis Guns All Lewis Guns, Ammunition, & Gear are to be carried down to support by their crews.

11. Gum Boots Gum Boots will be worn down from the line. Each man is to be in possession of one pair

H Burton

Capt: F.K.M

Issued at 9.15 pm. 2nd Bn R.M.L.I.

Copies to
1 Retained
2 O.C. Howe Bn.
3. POUNDS
4. SHILLINGS
5. PENCE
6 FARTHINGS
7 War Diary

SECRET Copy No

OPERATION ORDERS No 111
by
Major C. G. Farquharson M.C. R.M.L.I.
Commanding 2nd Bn. Royal Marine Lt. Infy.

Reference Maps
Parts of 57c

Bn Headquarters
Jany 21st 1918

1. Information The 1st Bn R.M.L.I. are holding the left Sub Sector.

2. Object On the night of the 22/23rd inst. the 2nd Bn R.M.L.I. will relieve the 1st Bn R.M.L.I. on the left Sub Sector.

3. Owing to the Brigade Order "that no movement is to take place on the top by daylight" it will not be possible to send the usual advance party.
O.C. Coys. will ensure that the routes to their respective Co. positions are known to all Officers.

4. Order of relief C Coy. 2nd Bn R.M.L.I. will relieve B Coy 1st Bn R.M.L.I. & will take over posts 26–34 inclusive
A Coy will attach 2 Lewis Guns with crews to O.C. C Coy for duty during the tour in the line. They will report to him at 11 a.m. tomorrow for instructions
1st Bn R.M.L.I. will supply one guide to each post. They will meet C Coy at the junction of CORNWALL Avenue & the new duckboard track.
D Coy 2nd Bn R.M.L.I. will relieve D Coy 1st Bn R.M.L.I. & will take over posts 21 to 25 inclusive & 65 to 67 inclusive.
1st Bn R.M.L.I. will also supply one guide per post. They will meet D Coy at the junction of CORNWALL ~~ROAD~~ AVENUE & the duckboard track.
'A' Coy will detach 2 Lewis Guns with crews to O.C. D Coy. They will report to O.C. 'D' Coy at 11 a.m. tomorrow.
B Coy 2nd Bn R.M.L.I. will relieve C Coy 1st Bn R.M.L.I. & will take over posts 61 to 64 inclusive and the dug outs in POPE AVENUE One guide per post will be supplied & will report to the Support Bn. H.Qrs.
Personnel of the posts will move via Village Rd.
The remainder of 'B' Coy will move via Pope Avenue (all

routes are overland.)

A Coy 2nd Bn RMLI will relieve A Coy 1st Bn RMLI & take over billets in FUSILIER Reserve Trench. No guides will be supplied.

5. All posts are to be self contained. All rations for the 24 hours are to be taken up in a sandbag for each post. No hot meals will be supplied during this tour in the trenches each man of each post is to take up 6 sandbags which will be used in improving his post. Each post will also take up 1 Petrol tin of water under Co. arrangements. A hot meal will be served at 7.30 pm. After this meal all cooks will be returned to the Transport Lines & Coys will be left to their own resources re cooking. The meat ration for the 23rd will be supplied cooked. Other details will be arranged at the O.C.s conference.

6. Method of taking over & accounting for Trench Stores. Each post has its own supply of its own ammunition & bombs; in addition to those in the Coy Dumps.

Each post Commander will send a chit to his O.C. Coy showing ammunition & any Trench Stores at his post. O.C. Coys will enter these on their Trench Store lists in addition to those taken over in the Company Dump. This is most necessary in order to facilitate the relief of the Bn the following night.

, No gum boots are to be taken over. The 1st Bn RMLI are responsible that all gum boots in the left Sub Sector are returned to the Brigade Drying Room.

7. Code word for relief WHITE

relief complete DODGER WHITE

Issued at 8.45 pm.

A Burton

Capt & A/Adjt.
2nd Bn RMLI

Copies to/ No 1. Retained
- 2. OC 1st Bn RMLI
- 3 OC 'A' Coy
- 4 " B "
- 5 " C "
- 6 " D "
- 7 War Diary

SECRET

Copy No. 1.

OPERATION ORDERS No. 12

by

Major C. G. Farquharson M.C. R.M.L.I.

Commanding 2nd Bn. Royal Marine Light Infantry

Reference Maps.
Parts of 57c

Bn. Headquarters.
Jany 22nd 1918

1. Information On the night of 23rd/24th Jany 1918 the 1st Bn. K.R.R.C. will relieve the 2nd Bn. R.M.L.I. in the left Sub Sector. After relief the 2nd Bn. R.M.L.I. will move to a camp in HAVRINCOURT WOOD (Q.15.a)

2 Advance parties from the relieving Bn. are already in the line.

3. Advance billeting parties of 1 N.C.O. from each Co. & H.Qrs. will report at Bn. H.Qrs. by 8 a.m. tomorrow. This party will be required to take over the camp at Q.15.a. In addition to the above another advance billeting party consisting of 1 N.C.O. from H. Qrs. & each Coy. will be required to take over billets at ROCQUIGNY. This party will also report at Bn. H.Qrs. at 8 a.m. In the case of Front Line Coys. it will be necessary to send these N.C.Os. down before dawn.

4. Trench Stores. Receipts for Trench Stores are to be sent down to the Adjt. as soon as they have been taken over.

A Coy 1st Bn KRRC will relieve	A Coy 2nd Bn RMLI
B	B
C	C
D	D

This is as far as is known at present.

6 Guides 2nd Lt Buckley will be in charge of all guides. He will report to the Adjt. at 3.30 p.m. for instructions. One guide from each Coy. H.Qrs. & post occupied will report to the Adjt. by 4 p.m. but in the case of Front Line posts where it is not possible to get down through the trenches these guides will not be sent down till dusk. The head of the relieving Bn. is expected to arrive at VILLERS PLOUICH about 5 p.m.

7 Relief Great care is to be taken in handing over each individual post. All information possible is to be given to the relieving troops. After relief each post will proceed independently to the left Bn. Drying Room in Village Rd. Gum boots will be taken off & ankle boots put on at this point. O.C. Coys will ensure that no man proceeds west of this point wearing gumboots.

8 Lewis Guns All Lewis Guns, Panniers & Spare ~~Parts~~ Parts (Bn. Stores) are to be carried down to the drying room by their teams. 3 limbers will be in position there by 8 p.m. All Lewis Gun gear is to be loaded into these, under the supervision of the Bn. L.G.O. (5 Guns to 1 Limber)

- 2 -

9 Officers Mess Gear & Orderly Rm Gear is also to be loaded in these limbers

10 Medical Stores will be loaded into the Medical Cart under M.O's arrangements.

11 ROUTE On completion of loading limbers the Coy will proceed independently via ~~[illegible]~~ VILLERS PLOUICH - BEAUCAMP - TRESCAULT - METZ RD. Coy billeting N.C.O's will meet their Coys at Q.13.b.35.90.

12 MEALS A hot meal has been arranged for on the arrival of the Bn in the Camp.

13 CODE WORD for relief BEEF
Complete BULLY BEEF

Relief complete is to be reported as arranged at O.C's Conference

N Burton

Capt & A/Adjt
2nd Bn RMLI.

Copies to

1. Retained
2. O.C. 1st Bn KRRC.
3. O.C. A Coy
4. " B "
5. " C "
6. " D "
7. War Diary

SECRET. COPY. No. .

ADDENDUM TO OPERATION ORDERS No. 112.
BY MAJOR C. G. FARQUHARSON, M.C., R.M.L.I.
COMMANDING 2nd Bn. ROYAL MARINE LIGHT INFANTRY.

Bn. Headquarters,
23rd January 1918.

---

1. The move of the 188th Inf. Bde. to the rest Area will be continued tomorrow.

2. The 2nd Bn. R.M.L.I. will move by march route and train to ROCQUIGNY Camp "B".

3. Lieut. BRAID and a Loading Party of three N.C.Os and fifty O.Rs. will proceed to METZ to superintend the entraining, and loading of Stores etc..

4. The Bn. will parade under O.C. Cos. arrangements at 1.0.pm. and proceed via METZ to the entraining station. A distance of 200 yards will be maintained between Cos.; 100 yards between Platoons.

(sd) R. BURTON.
Capt. & A/Adjutant,
2nd Bn., R.M.L.I.

CONFIDENTIAL.

Vol 21

Headquarters,
2 nd Bn., Royal Marine Light Infantry

1ST MARCH, 1918.

W A R D I A R Y.

(Vol. XX)

2nd Battn. ROY AL MARINE LIGHT INFANTRY.

from

1ST FEBRUARY, 1918,
to
28th FEBRUARY, 1918.

C G Ingoldsby

Lieut. Colonel, R.M.L.I.
Comdg. 2nd Bn., Royal Marine Light Infantry.

To :- 1. H.Q., 63r d (R.N.) Division.

Instructions regarding War Diaries and Intelligence Summaries are contained in F. S. Regs., Part II. and the Staff Manual respectively. Title pages will be prepared in manuscript.

WAR DIARY
or
INTELLIGENCE SUMMARY.
(*Erase heading not required.*)

Army Form C. 2118.

Place	Date	Hour	Summary of Events and Information	Remarks and references to Appendices
ROCQUIGNY.	1 Feb		Bn training-musketry. Diarrhoea prevalent, committee formed to combat it. Cross country run.	Ew
			Capt. L. H. Wrangham, Lt. J. C. Lee, leave to England.	
"	2 Feb		Po/15464 Sgt W. J. O'Donnell reduced to the ranks by F. G. C. M. – Major (Act Lt. Col.) G. H. Parry died of wounds	Ew
"	3 "		Church parade etc. Nominal roll of long service N.C.Os who have served two & a half years with Bn. who are desirous of returning home for service afloat, rendered. – 5 reinforcements.	Ew
"	4 "		Bn. training. Baths. Div. Gas Officer lectured in Recreation Hut. – Sgt O'Donnell's sentence promulgated. Div. Gen. visited lines of Bn. 21 Reinforcements.	Ew
"	5 "		Duty Bn., Guards and working parties supplied. P. H. Helmets returned to ordnance. Paper chase. Experimental firing with 20 rounds magazine.	Ew
"	6 "		Bn. passed through Gas Chamber (Lieut P. S. Watts + 1 O.R. accidently gassed) Bombing instructions. Stocktaking of canteen goods. 10 Reinforcements.	Ew
"	7 "		Duty Bn., Guards and working parties supplied. Instructions issued in the event of E.A. being forced to descend. Allotment for leave to AMIENS.	Ew
"	8 "		Bn. training. Cross country run. 25 Reinforcements	
"	9 "		Duty Bn., Guards and workings parties supplied. Lieut P. Ligertwood granted rank of A/Capt with pay by Lords Commissioners of Admiralty dated 22nd Oct 1917 (subsequently killed in action 26th Oct 1917.	Ew
"	10 "		Church parades. Baths. 2nd Lieuts Saunders and Whitting R.M. joined Bn. 2nd Lieut F. W. Slaughter leave to England.	Ew
"	11 "		Duty Bn. Guards and working parties supplied. Lieut P. S. Watts leave to England. Div. works Bn. formed. S. B. R's tested by Div. Officer. Div. cross country run, team supplied by Bn. Sub. Lieut. Moorcroft R.N.V.R. to England, struck off strength. 2nd Lieut Bing R.M. joined Bn. – Sub Lieut Pryor and 102 O.Rs joined Bn. on disbandment of HOWE Bn.	Ew
"	12 "		Bn. training. Musketry etc. Capts Coode R.M.L.I and Williams R.M. attended a TANK demonstration. Inspection of Howe Bn draft by O.C.	Ew
"	13 "		Duty Bn. Guards and working parties supplied. Wiring etc. 2nd Lieut F. A. Proffitt appointed O.C. "D" Coy. Requiem Mass for the late Lieut Col. Parry. Lieut C. W. F. Feldham leave to England.	Ew
"	14 "		Presentation of Co. + Platoon Flags. Baths. Operation order No 113 issued. 2/Lt. C. V. Egan appointed Bn Lewis Gun Officer. 2nd Lieut F. W. Slaughter to M.G. School Grantham. Lewis Guns A.A. teams supplied to YTRES dump. Lieut Col. C. G. Farquharson R.M.L.I. from English leave and assumed command of the Bn.	Ew Appendix No 1
"	15 "		Bn proceeded by march route to camp in VALLULART WOOD. Major H. S. Clutterbuck R.M.L.I. to 1st Bn R.M.L.I.	Ew
VALLULART WOOD	16 "		Bn. now in Bde. Reserve. Revetting hutments etc. G. R. O. 3376 Intercourse with the enemy read on parade. 2 casualties E.A. bomb	Ew
" "	17 "		Church parades – work continued round hutments. Application of whale oil. Operations Orders No 114 issued. 2nd Lieut Ewick's performed duties of Officer i/c Rear Orderly Room.	Ew Appendix No 2

Instructions regarding War Diaries and Intelligence Summaries are contained in F. S. Regs., Part II. and the Staff Manual respectively. Title pages will be prepared in manuscript.

WAR DIARY
or
~~INTELLIGENCE SUMMARY.~~

Army Form C. 2118.

Sheet NUMBER 2.

(Erase heading not required.) 2ND BN ROYAL MARINES LIGHT INFANTRY.

Place	Date	Hour	Summary of Events and Information	Remarks and references to Appendices
VALLULART WOOD	18th Feb		Bn. relieved "HAWKE BN" in support. 25 Reinforcements.	EW
(IN THE LINE COLLVIET WOOD	19th "		MARCOING SEC. working - carrying and salvage parties.	
" " "	20 "		Ditto Ditto Rev. Father Davey to Hospt. Operation Orders No 115 issued	Appendix No 3. EW
" " "	21 "		Bn relieved by 2nd Bn OXF & BUCKS L.I. and proceeded by train from TRESCAULT to YTRES. thence by march route to VALLULART WOOD CAMP.	EW
VALLULART WOOD	22 "		BN parade in fighting order. Operation orders 116 issued.	
" "	23 "		Bn. proceeded by march route ~~to~~ YTRES and entrained. proceeding to TRESCAULT. ~~by train~~ - detrained and proceeded into the line relieving the 18th and 20th London Regt.	appendix No 4. EW
(IN THE LINE. FLESQUIERES	24 "		RIBECOURT SEC. working, carrying and wiring parties. Lieut A. H. H. Sayer to Hospt.	EW.
" " "	25 "		Ditto Ditto. 28 Reinforcements joined. 1 casualty	EW.
" " "	26 "		Ditto Ditto. 2 Casualties.	EW.
" " "	27 "		Ditto Ditto. Operation Orders 117 issued. Bn. relieved by "ANSON BN" in front line. Bn marched to TRESCAULT and entrained, detraining at EASTWOOD CAMP, HAVRINCOURT WOOD. 1 casualty	EW.
EAST WOOD CAMP	28 "		Bn in Rear Reserve. Baths & clean clothing. Lt. H. Daw R.M.A.C. to 148th F.A. for duty. T/SURG. A. L. PEARCE GOLD R.N. joined Bn.	Appendix No 5. EW EW

A. G. Ingelrason
Lieut. Colonel RMLI
Comdg 2nd Bn RMLI

A7092' Wt. W128.9/M1293 750,000. 1/17. D. D & I. Ltd. Forms/C2118/14.

SECRET.

Copy. No.

OPERATION ORDERS NO.113.
BY LIEUT.COLONEL. C. G. FARQUHARSON, R.M.L.I.
COMMANDING 2nd Bn ROYAL MARINE LIGHT INFANTRY.

Bn Headquarters,
14th FEBRUARY, 1918.

Reference Maps:-
Sheet 57c.1/40000.

---

1. The Bn. will move by march route to a camp located in Vallulart Wood, P.33.a., tomorrow, 15th inst.
DRESS. Full marching order. Steel helmets will be carried between supporting straps.
Orders for First Line Transport will be issued separately.

2. BLANKETS. All men's blankets are to be tightlt rolled in bundels of ten, labelled and dumped on a tarpaulin near the RECREATION HUT by 7 a.m.
Officers Valises, Spare Mess Gear and Orderly Room Gear to be dumped as above by 9 a.m.
The Medical Cartwill report to Bn. Orderly Room at 8.30 a.m.
The Mess Cart will report to Bn. Orderly Room to laod up Officers Mess Gear, etc.

LOADING PARTY. The O.C."B" Co. will detail a party of thirty O.Rs to work as a loading party. They will report to BnQ.M.S.,Q.M.Stores at 7 a.m. O.C."B" Co. will also detail an unloading party of ten to unload stores at YTRES. This party will ride in the first lorry.
The Bn. Sanitary Sergt., and eight H.Q. Sanitary Section will remain behind to clear up latrines etc.
2nd Lieut. Smith will also remain behind after the Bn. has vacated the Camp and obtain from the Town Major, Rocquigny, a certificate stating that the Camp has been left in a clean and sanitary condition.
O.C."B" Co., will also detail N.C.O and six O.Rs as a "Stragglers Party" Lieut. Spragget will be in command.

4. The Bn. will parade on the Bn. Parade Ground at 10.40 a.m.
Officers Call 10.5 5 a.m.

5. The Bn. will march in the following order. Head of Column to pass the starting point D.27.d.8.8. at 11.25 a.m. Band, H.Q.Co., "A", "B" "C" "D" Cos., Stragglers Party.

6. ROUTE. Via BUS-YTRESto Camp.

7. INTERVALS. Two hundred yards distance will be maintained between Cos.

8. The usual halts will be observed at ten minutes to the hour, the march being resumed at the hour.

9. Attention is called to "Brigade Standing March Orders."

10. An advance Billeting Party under the command of Capt. Coode will be sent to the new Camp by cycle. One representative will be sent from H.Q. "A","B""C" & "D" Cos.and the trasnport. They will report to the Orderly Room at 8.30 a.m.

sgd.R.BURTON.
Capt. & A/Adjutant.
2nd Bn R.M.L.I.

Issued at 8.0 p.m.
Copies to/over
By runner.

SECRET. Copy No.

2nd Bn ROYAL MARINE LIGHT INFANTRY.
OPERATION ORDERS NO.114.

Reference Maps:- 57c, La Vacquerie.

Bn Headquarters, 17th FEBRUARY, 1918.

INFORMATION. The 189th Inf. Bde are holding portion of the front line running North and South through R.4.a & c.
INTENTION. On the night of the 18/19th inst., the 188th Inf.Bde will relieve the 189th Inf. Bde.
The 2nd Bn R.M.L.I. will relieve the Hawke Bn in Support.

1. An advance billeting party of one officer per Co., and one N.C.O from each platoon and Bn Headquarters proceeded into the line this day.

2. The Bn. will parade for inspection in fighting order at 10.0 a.m. tomorrow.

3. The O.C., will meet O.C. Cos. in Bn. Hd.Qrs Mess at 10.30 a.m.

4. All blankets tightly rolled in bundles of ten and clearly labelled, spare Officers' Mess Gear, Offie rs' Valises, Spare Orderly Room Gear and men's packs will be dumped outsi e the Guard Room by 10.30 a.m.
O.C."A" Co., will detal a loading party of two N.C.Os., and twenty O.rs who will load and unload the above.

5. LEWIS GUNS AND AMMUNITION. Lewis Guns and 10 magazines of S.A.A., per gun will be carried by the teams from the Camp. Twenty magazines per gun will be carried by the Transport. O.C. Cos. are to arrange to collect the same from the Bn. Dump on arrival in the trenches.

6. TRANSPORT. The Transport Officer will arrange to supply limbers to carry Lewis Gun Ammunition, Medical Stores, Officers Mess Gear and Orderly Room Gear. These limbers will report opposite the Guard Room at 2 p.m.

7. MOVE. The Bn. will parade by Cos. in fighting order at 4.30 p.m. and move off in the following order:- HdQrs, "B", "C", "D", "A"., to the entraining station at P.20.b A distance of 200 yards will be maintained between Cos. 2nd Lieut. Smith will be the Entraining and Detraining Officer. He will report at the Station at 5 p.m. O.C. Cos. will detail one O.R. to reconnoitre t he route to the Station. These guides will report to the Orderly Room at 9.30 a.m.

8. ROUTE. The Bn. will proceed by light railway to TRESCAULT and thence by March Route to a point located at Q.12.c.o.6., where they will be met by guides from the "HAWKE" Bn, who will conduct them to their position in the line. The usual distances will be maintained between platoons.

9. RELIEF. "A" Co. will relieve "A" Hawke Bn in Wood Trench between R.3.c.20.80 and R.3c.40.50
"B" Co.will relieve "B" Hawke Bn in the trecnhes round R.3c.8.8. and R.3.c.55.30.
"C" Co. will relieve "C" Hawke Bn in the trecnhes round R.2.b.4.5 and R.2.b.7.35.
"D" Co. will relieve "D" Co. Hawke Bn. in the trecnhes round R.3.a.40.50.

10. RATIONS The unconsumedp ortion of the rations for tomorrow and the rations for the 19th inst., will be carried on the person. The Q.M. to arrange accordingly.
Eighty tins of water will be carried up by the Transport and issued to Cos. from the Bn. Dump

Contnd. 2.

All cooking in the line will be done under Co. arrangements.
The Cook Sergeant will arrange to send up five dixie kettles per Co. and one large dixie for the use of Bn.Headquarters.

11. BILLETS. O.C.Cos. will report to the O.C. at 3 p.m. that their hutments are in a clean and sanitry condition.

12. RELIEF. Code words for relief:-
RELIEF:- UNCLE.
Relief Completed:- YES UNCLE.

" Relief Complete" will be reported by wire and runner.
Bn.Headquarters will be located at R.3.c.10.85.
R.A.P. will be located at R.3.c.1.o.90.
Bn Dump Do. R.3.c.1.5.75.

---

sgd.R.BURTON.
Capt. & A/Adjutant.
2nd Bn R.M.L.I.

Issued at 9.30 p.m.
Copies to :- No.1 O.C.nd Retain.
By runner. 2 O.C. "A" Co.
3 O.C. "B" Co.
4. O.C. "C" Co.
5. O.C. "D" Co.
6. War Dary.
7. War Diary.

Secret.   Copy No.

2nd Bn ROYAL MARINE LIGHT INFANTRY.
OPRATION ORDER NO.115.

Reference Maps.
La Vacquerie, Special Sheet.
France 57c.1/10000.

Bn. Headquarters,
20TH FEBRUARY, 1918.

1. INTENTION. (a) The 5th Inf. Bde. will relieve the 188th Infantry Bde on the night 21/22th February, 1918.
(b/ The 2nd Bn Oxford and Bucks Lt. Infy(less 1 Co.) will relieve the 2nd Bn R.M.L.I.

2. RELIEF. "A" Co.2nd Bn Oxford & Bucks L.I. will relieve "A" Co.2nd Bn. R.M.L.I.
"C" Co. 2nd Bn Oxford and Bucks L.I. do. "A" & "B" Cos. R.M.L.I.
"D" Co. Do. do. "D" Cos. 2nd Bn R.M.L.I.

3. MOVE. On relief the Bn will take over Camp at VALLULART WOOD proceeding by train from TRESCAULT to YTRES. Cos. will move from the Line to TRESCAULT and from YTRES to camp indpendently. Lieut. Vance will perform the duties of Entraining Officer and will arive at TRESCAULT STATION at 7.0 p.m. O.C.Cos. will detail one officer to report the O.C. "Relief Complete" on their way down from the line and again when their Cos. are in billets.

4. ADVANCE BILLETING PARTIES. An advance billeting party consisting of 1 N.C.O per Co. will report to the Adjutant, Bn.Headquarters at 7.0 a.m. 21st inst.

5. TRENCH STORES. Trench Maps, Defence schemes, work schemes, Aeroplane Photographs and Trench Stores are to be handed over to the relieving unit and receipts obtained for same forwarded forthwith to Bn.Headquarters.

6. Lewis Guns and Ammunition. Lewis Guns and 10 magazines of S.A.A. per gun will be carried by the teams to the Camp. 20 magazines per gun will be carried by the Transport O.C. Cos. are to ensure that these magazines are loaded on the way down from the line into the limbers which will be waiting at the Bn. Dump.

7. TRANSPORT. The Transport Officer has received instructions to provide Limbers to carry down Lewis Gun Ammunition, Medical Stores, Officers Mess Gear and Orderly Room Gear. These stores with the exception of Lewis Gun Ammunition will be at Bn.Dump by 6.30 p.m.

8. WATER TINS. Water tins will not be turned over to the relieving unit but are to be brought to the Bn. Dump by 6.30 p.m.

9. KIT. Men are to be warned that any man arriving in camp deficient of any part of his kit will be charged for replacement of same.

10. SALVAGE. All salvage collected during the day will be at Bn.Dump by 6.30 p.m.

11. CODE WORD for Relief. PUSH.
Do. complete PUSH AND GO.

sgd.R.BURTON.
Capt.& A/Adjutant.
2ns Bn RM.L.I.

Copies to/over.

Copies to:-

No. 1 Retained.
2 O.C. "A" Co.
3 O.C. "B" Co.
4 O.C. "C" Co.
5 O.C. "D" Co.
6 War Diary.

SECRET..   Copy No.

2nd Bn ROYAL MARINE LIGHT INFANTRY.
OPERATION ORDERS NO.116.

Reference Maps:-
Moeuvres 1/20000.
France 57c 1/40000.

Bn.Headquarters,
22ND FEBRUARY,1918.

INFORMATION. The 63rd (R.N.) Division is extedning its front to the left and taking over the 47th Divisonal Sector.

The 188th Inf. Bde will relieve the 141st Inf. Bde in the line on the night of the 23/24th February, 1918.

Disposition.	The 2nd Bn R.M.L.I.	Front Line.
	Anson Bn.	Support.
	1st Bn. R.M.L.I.	Reserve.

Boundaries. Right. L.15.d.40.30.
Left. K.17.b.80.50.

The 189th Inf. Bde will be on our right and the 50th Inf. Bde on our left.

INTENTION. The 2nd Bn R.M.L.I. will relieve the 18th and 20th Bns. of the London Regiment in the front line and will take over the H.Qrs of the 20th London Regiment located at K.24.b.3.7.

Disposition. The relief will be carried out as follows:-

"B" Co.	2nd Bn R.M.L.I.	will relieve	"A" Co.	20th	London Regt.
"A" Co.	Do.	Do.	"D" Co.		Do.
"D" Co.	Do.	Do.	"B"	18th	Do.
"C" Co.	Do.	Do.	"C"	18th	Do.

1\. INSTRUCTIONS. Advance Parties. An Advance Party consisting of O.Cs "A","B" "C" and "D" one N.C.O per platoon, one N.C.O from Hdqrs., six men from the Intelligence Squad will precede the Bn. into the Line tomorrow. A lorry for the above party will report at 8 a.m.

All blankets tightly rolled in bundles of ten and clearly labelled to be dumped outside the Guard Room by 9.0 a.m. If wet, these will be stacked inside the Guard Room.

Officers Mess Gear, Officers Valises, Orderly Room Gear and Men's packs will be dumped outside the Guard Room by 2.0 p.m.

O.C."B" Co. will detail a working party of 2 N.C.Os and 20 O.Rs who will act as a loading and unloading party for the above.

2\. LEWIS GUNS AND AMMUNITION. Lewis Guns and ten magazines of S.A.A per gun will be car ried by theteam from the Camp. Twenty magzines per gun will be carried by the Transport. O.C.Cos are to arrange to collect the same from the Bn.Dump on arrival in the trecnhes.

10\. TRANSPORT. The Trasnport Officer will arrange to supply limbers to carry to carry Lewis Gun Ammunition, Medical Stores, Officers Mess Gear and Orderly Room Gear. These limbers will report opposite the Guard Room at 2 p.m.

4\. MOVE.AND ROUTE. Parade. The Bn. will parade by Cos. on their respective parade grounds at 3 p.m. O.C.Cos. will report to the Officer Commanding that their Cos. are preent or otherwise and hand in a marching state.

The Bn.will then proceed by march route to the Entraining Station at B.w.29., Map Reference P.20.a.

Order of March. H.Q."C", "D", "A". "B", Two hundred yards distance will be maintai ned between Cos. The first train will leave at 3.30 p.m.

2nd Lieut. Collier will be the entraining officer and will report to the ~~Entraining Officer at 3.0 p.m.~~ R.T.O., at 3.0 p.m. The Bn will detrain at TRESCAULT and will proceed by platoons to the forward area.

Cos will be met by their Co. Commanders at the CROSS ROADS TRESCAULT. One ~~XXXXXXXX~~ guide per platoon is being supplied by the Bns. now in the line.

5. COOKING ARRANGEMENTS. 40 Dennison Food Containers will be carried up the Transport and dumped on the Bn. Dump. These will be issued ten to ea each Co. All Cooking will be done in the line under O.C. Cos. arrangements. To Co. Cooks per Company will accompany their respective Cos. into the line. Five dixie kettles or their equivalent per Co. will be taken up by the Transport. The Cook Sergeant will generally supervise the cooking.

6. RATIONS. The unconsumed portion of the rations for tomorrow and the rations for the 24th will be carried on the person. The Quartermaster to arrange accordingly.

100 tins of water will be carried up by the Transport and issued to Cos. from the Bn. Dump.

x7. BILLETS. O.C. Cos. will report to the O.C. at 3 p.m. that their hutments are in a clean and sanitary condition.

8. RELIEF. Code Words for relief:- FOLLOW.
Relief Complete:- FOLLOW THE CROWD.

Relief complete will be reported by wire and runner.

Sgd. R. BURTON.
Capt. & A/Adjutant.
2nd Bn R.M.L.I.

Issued at 11.45 p.m.
Copies to :- No.1 O.C. and Retain.
By Runner 2 O.C. "A" Co .
3 O.C. "B" Co.
4 O.C. " C" Co.
5 O.C. "D" Co.
6. War Diary.
7 Do.

SECRET. Copy No.

2nd Bn ROYAL MARINE LIGHT INFANTRY.
OPERATION ORDER NO.117.

Refeeence Maps:- 57c.
Premy. Special Sheet.

Bn. Headquarters,
27THFEBRUARYb1918.

1.INFORMATION. The Anson Bn. now in support will relieve the 2nd Bn R.M.L.I on the night 27th/28thi nst.

2.INTENTION. After relief the 2nd Bn R.M.L.I. will proceed by march route and train to EASTWOOD CAMP, HAVRINCOURT WOOD.

3.INSTRUCTIONS. Advance Billeting Party under the command of the Second in Command, will proceed to take over the new camp this morning. This party will consist of one N.C.O per Co. and Bn. Hdqrs and will report to Bn.Orderly Room at 8.30 a.m. An advance party of the relieving unit will be reporting to these Hdrs. at about 12.15 p.m. today.

4.RELIEF.

"A" Co.	Anson Bn.	will relieve	"A" Co, 2nd Bn	R.M.L.I.
"B" Co.	Do.	Do.	"B" Co.	Do.
"C" Co.	Do.	Do.	"C" Co.	Do.
"D" Co.	Do.	Do.	"C" Co.	Do.

5.TRENCH STORES &c. All Trench Stores are to be carefully entered on the attached list, signed nd countersigned, then forwarded to Bn.Orderly Room No petrol tins will be handed over on relief but are to be returned to the R.S.M by 5.30 p.m.

6.All posts are to be very carefully handed over togëther together with any information gained during XXXXXX this tour of duty in the line concerning the enemy. Programmes of wiring and work on the trecnhes are also to be prepared and handed over.

7.Co. Commanders will make their own arrangements with the relieving Unit Co. Commanders regarding guides to be supplied.

8.TRANSPORT. Three G.S.Libered Wagons will arrive at Bn.Dump at about 7.15 p.m. All salvage, Officers Mess Gear, Orderly Room Gear are to be dumped there by 7.0 p.m. 20 magazines per L.G will also be carried down by the Transport. No magazines, however, are to be brought out of the line by any Co. until it has been relieved.

9.After relief Cos. will proceed independently to the entraining station, TRESCAULT. A distance of 100 yards to be maintained between platoons. 2nd Lieut. Fielden will be the entraining officer. He will report to the entraining officer, TRESCAULT at 8.30 p.m. Trains will proceed as soon as loaded.

10.Relief Complete will be reported by wire and personally by O.C.Cos. O.C.Cos. will also report their Cos. in billets to the Officer Commanding on arrival in Camp.

Code Word for Relief. ZIG.
Do. complete ZAG.

sgd R. BURTON.
Capt. & A/Adjutant,
2nd Bn R.M.L.I.

Issued at 7.10 a.m.

Copies to:- No.1 Retained.
2 C.C."Anson Bn".
3 C.C."A" Co.
4 C.C."B" Co.
5 C.C."C" Co.
6 C.C."D"Co.
7 War Diary.

188th Brigade.

63rd Division.

2nd BATTALION

ROYAL MARINE LIGHT INFANTRY

M A R C H 1 9 1 8

Attached:-

Battalion Operation Orders.

SECRET

CONFIDENTIAL.

WAR DIARY
of
2nd Bn. Royal Marine Light Infy.
Volume ?
from
March 1st 1918
to
March 31st 1918

A 670

To. A.Q. 63rd (R.N.) Division

N.S. Clutterbuck
Major RMLI
Comdg 2nd Bn RMLI.

Instructions regarding War Diaries and Intelligence Summaries are contained in F. S. Regs., Part II. and the Staff Manual respectively. Title pages will be prepared in manuscript.

WAR DIARY
or
~~INTELLIGENCE SUMMARY.~~
(Erase heading not required.)

Sheet. NO. 1.

Army Form C. 2118.

2nd Bn R. M. L. I.

Place	Date	Hour	Summary of Events and Information	Remarks and references to Appendices
EASTWOOD CAMP	1/3/18		cleaning up, Baths, working parties etc.	JGW
"	2/3/18		" " " " " . O.O. NO. 117 issued.	appendix I. JGW
"	3/3/18		" " . Batt. entrained at Camp, detrained at TRESCAULT + proceeded into trenches to relieve 1st Bn. R.M.L.I. in support.	JGW
Support	4/3/18		Wiring + working parties.	JGW
"	5/3/18		" " " . LT. ROBERTS, 2/LTS. BOUCHER - DEAN joined Bn.	JGW
"	6/3/18		" " " . O.O. NO. 118 issued	
"	7/3/18		Relieved 1st Bn. R.M.L.I. in front line. LT Roberts. to F.A.	appendix II JGW
FRONT LINE	8/3/18		working parties, patrols etc. 6 casualties	JGW
" "	9/3/18		" etc. A raiding party under command of 2/LTS FIELDEN + Collier raided the enemy's positions. The raid was successful, one prisoner being captured. casualties 2/LT. H. Fielden + 2. O.Rs killed. 6. O.Rs wounded. other casualties. 3.	JGW JGW
" "	10/3/18		working parties, patrols etc. Capt. B. G. Andrews rejoined from [illegible]	JGW
" "	11/3/18		" " " " O.O. NO. 119 issued. Bn, relieved by ANSON Bn, proceeded by march route to Divisional Reserve, Eastwood Camp.	appendix III JGW
Eastwood Camp	12/3/18		Bn parades, cleaning up etc.	JGW
" "	13/3/18		" " " " . Capt. B. G. Andrews to F.A. ~~O.O. No.~~ JGW	JGW
" "	14/3/18		" " O.O. NO. 120 issued.	JGW appendix IV
" "	15/3/18		" relieved ANSON Bn in front line. Capt + A/Adjt R. Burton to F.A. 2/Lt. Wilcot to M.G training centre. GRANTHAM.	
FRONT LINE	16/3/18		working parties, wiring, patrols etc.	JGW
" "	17/3/18		" " " etc.	JGW JGW

A7092 Wt. W128 9/M1293 750,000. 1/17. D. D & I. Ltd. Forms/C2118/14.

Instructions regarding War Diaries and Intelligence Summaries are contained in F. S. Regs., Part II. and the Staff Manual respectively. Title pages will be prepared in manuscript.

WAR DIARY
or
~~INTELLIGENCE SUMMARY.~~
(Erase heading not required.)

Army Form C. 2118.

Sheet. NO. 2. 2nd Bn. R.M.L.I.

Place	Date	Hour	Summary of Events and Information	Remarks and references to Appendices
FRONT LINE	18/3/18		A raiding party under command of 2/LT SAUNDERS raided the enemy's position. No identification was obtained. Casualties. 1 officer (2/LT Saunders wounded) + 12 O.Rs. other casualties: MAJOR C.H. COODE wounded. 2/LT Dean transferred to 1st Bn. R.M.L.I.	J.C.W.
" "	19/3/18		Relieved by 1st Bn R.M.L.I. and proceeded into support O.O. No 121 issued.	appendix V J.C.W.
Support	20/3/18		Working parties etc.	J.C.W.
"	21/3/18		Enemy attacked on flanks after heavy Gas bombardment of our positions. Bn "STANDING TO".	J.C.W.
"			1st Bn. R.M.L.I. ordered to withdraw through 2nd Bn. R.M.L.I., causing Support Position to become FRONT LINE	J.C.W.
FRONT LINE	22/3/18		ordered to evacuate. Bn proceeded to HAVRINCOURT WOOD. Lt/Col. C.G. FARQUHARSON wounded. Lt/Cmdr. J. COOTE, ANSON Bn, assumed command of Battn.	J.C.W.
HAVRINCOURT WOOD	23/3/18		Bn proceeded to prepared line in front of BERTINCOURT	
FRONT LINE	24/3/18		Bn ordered to withdraw from BERTINCOURT + took up position. Proceeded to BAPAUME–PERONNE Rd + thence to MARTINPUICH. Took up position in SUPPORT to ANSON Bn.	J.C.W.
SUPPORT	25/3/18		Reinforced ANSON Bn + then ordered to withdraw. Bn in conjunction with the remainder of BRIGADE fought a rear guard action to THIEPVAL, where brigade took up positions	J.C.W. J.C.W.
FRONT LINE	26/3/18		Ordered to withdraw. Bn proceeded into Support behind MESNIL. relieved by Bn. Buffs. Regt + proceeded to ENGELBELMER. Thence proceeded to MARTINSART into billets.	J.C.W.
MARTINSART	27/3/18		In conjunction with ANSON Bn, counter-attacked along MARTINSART–MESNIL Road + the AVELUY WOOD, repulsing enemy. Returned to MARTINSART. Bn took up position just outside AVELUY WOOD as precautionary measure.	J.C.W.

Army Form C. 2118.

WAR DIARY
or
~~INTELLIGENCE~~ SUMMARY.

(*Erase heading not required.*)

Instructions regarding War Diaries and Intelligence Summaries are contained in F. S. Regs., Part II. and the Staff Manual respectively. Title pages will be prepared in manuscript.

Sheet No. 3. 2nd Bn. R.M.L.I.

Place	Date	Hour	Summary of Events and Information	Remarks and references to Appendices
AVELUY WOOD	28/3/18		Relieved by Bn. Royal Fusiliers & proceeded to MAILLY-MAILLET & thence later in the day to FORCEVILLE into billets.	JCW.
FORCEVILLE	29/3/18		Cleaning up etc & reorganising	JCW
"	30/3/18		" " " " " . Bn. inspected by G.O.C. 188th Infy Brigade	JCW.
"	31/3/18		" " " " Church parades etc.	JCW.
			Orders issued during operations 22/3/18 to 28/3/18 inclusive were destroyed after perusal. APPENDIX. No. 1. was destroyed by fire at YTRES. Casualties during operations 22/3/18 to 28/3/18 inclusive were:–	

Killed.

A/Capt. G. Gibbins.
T/2/Lts. E.W. Collier,
T/2/LT. S. N. Tilbury.
+
13. O.R.S.

WOUNDED

LT/COL. C.G. Farquharson M.C.
T/CAPT L.H. WRAMGHAM
T/LT. A.S.R. PERRY
2/LT C.V. EGAN.
2/LT. J.A. Smith.
2/LT. A.H. MITCHELL
+
83. O.R.S.

UNACCOUNTED for.

T/CAPT. R. J. WILLIAMS.
T/LT. P.S. WATTS.
Sub/Lt. R.G. GRAY.
2/LT. F. DEATON.
+
213. O.Rs.

N. Chitterbuck MAJOR R.M.L.I.
Cmdg. 2nd Bn. R.M.L.I.

A7092 Wt. W128 9/M293 750,000. 1/17. D. D & L Ltd. Forms/C2118/14.

SECRET

Copy No 1

2nd Bn. R.M.L.I. Operation Order No 118

Ref Maps
FRANCE 57c.
" RIBECOURT Special Sheet.

Bn. Headquarters
March 7th 1918.

1.---- On the night 7th/8th inst the 2nd Bn. R.M.L.I. will carry out a double relief as follows :-
ANSON BN will relieve 2nd Bn R.M.L.I. in Support.
2nd Bn R.M.L.I. will relieve 1st Bn R.M.L.I. in Front Line.

2.----- Dispositions. Coys will take up the following positions in the front line viz:-
"B" Coy Right Front Coy "C" Coy Left Front Coy
"A" Coy Right Counter Attack Coy "D" Coy Left Counter Attack Coy.
Bn. H.Qrs, ~~&~~ R.A.P, & Bn. Dump will be located as previously

~~3.---- Bky~~

3.--- Relief (a) "A" Coy Anson Bn. will relieve "A" Coy 2nd Bn R.M.L.I.
"B" " " " "B" " "
"C" " " " "C" " "
"D" " " " "D" " "

(b) "B" Coy 2nd Bn. R.M.L.I. will relieve "A" & "B" Coys 1st Bn R.M.L.I. in the front line.
"C" Coy Do Do Do "C" & "D" do do do.
The location of "A" & "D" Coys will be explained to officers proceeding with advance party this morning.

4.--- Move. On the completion of the first relief Coy Commanders will report by wire & personally to the O.C. at Support. Bn. H.Qrs. & will move their Coys independently to the forward position, reporting the second relief ~~by wire~~ complete by wire. Guides for this move will not be supplied.

5.----- Advance Parties (a) Advance Parties are coming into this area this morning to take over Trench Stores &c. Each Coy will send one guide to meet representatives of the incoming unit at 10 a.m. at the fork of the light railway lines in K.29.c
(b) An advance party consisting of 1 officer per Co., 1 N.C.O. per platoon & H.Qrs & 1 Bn Signalman will proceed into the front line to reconnoitre & take over Trench Stores. This party will rendezvous at Bn H.Qrs at 10 a.m. & report to the Adjutant.

6.--- Trench Stores. Greatest possible care is to be taken in the handing over & taking over of Trench Stores (a) Receipted lists of Trench Stores handed over to the ANSON Bn. will be forwarded to these H.Qrs by 2 p.m. (b) Receipted lists of Trench Stores taken over ~~from~~ in the forward area will be forwarded to Bn. H.Qrs as soon as possible

7----- Lewis Guns & all ammunition will be carried by the L.G. Crews.

No petrol tins, other than those taken over as trench stores, are to be handed over to the incoming unit.

8----. CODE WORD for [illegible] relief JERRY.

Do 1st Do complete JERRY DIZZY.

Do 2nd Do Do JERRY COLLAPSED.

J. Lee

By Runner.

Issued at 1.50 am.

Lieut & a/Adjt.

2nd Bn R.M.L.I.

Copies to :-

1. Retained.
2. O.C. 1st Bn R.M.L.I.
3. O.C. ANSON Bn.
4. O.C. 'A' Coy
5. O.C. 'B' Coy.
6. O.C. 'C' Coy.
7. O.C. 'D' Coy
8. War Diary

SECRET

COPY No. 1

2nd Bn. R.M.L.I. Operation Order No 119

Reference Maps
France 57c 1/40.000
Ribecourt Special Sheet.

Bn. Headquarters
March 10th 1918.

1.------INFORMATION. The "ANSON" Bn. will relieve 2nd Bn. R.M.L.I. in the Front Line RIBECOURT LEFT-SUB-SECTOR. On the right of the 11/12th unit.

2.------INTENTION. On the completion of the relief the 2nd Bn R.M.L.I. will move by march route to TRESCAULT & thence by light railway to EASTWOOD CAMP (P. 18. d).

3.------INSTRUCTIONS. Advance parties – An advance party of the "ANSON" Bn will precede that unit into the line tomorrow morning to take over Dispositions, Trench Stores &c.

An advanced billeting party consisting of 1 N.C.O from H.Qrs & 1 N.C.O from each Coy. will report to the Orderly Rm. Bn. H.Qrs at 2 pm. They will proceed under the command of Major C.H.COODE R.M.L.I. to take over Eastwood Camp.

4.------DISPOSITIONS "A" Coy Anson Bn will relieve "A" Coy. 2nd Bn R.M.L.I.

B ————	B ————
C ————	D ————
D ————	C

Coy. H.Qrs. The headquarters of "A" & "B" Coys. "Anson" Bn will be located in the dug-out now occupied by "A" Coy 2nd Bn R.M.L.I. The headquarters of "C" & "D" Coys "Anson" Bn will be located in the dug-out now occupied by "C" & "D" Coys. 2nd Bn R.M.L.I.

5.------TRENCH STORES ETC. Duplicate receipts signed by the officer of the relieving unit taking over will be forwarded to Bn. H.Qrs as early as possible. The O'sC. C & D. Coys will each send a party to the Coy. H.Qrs occupied by them when last in the front line to collect any area stores & ammunition which may be remaining there. These are to be entered on the T.S. Lists & handed over to the relieving unit.

6.------WORK &c Work Reports & programmes of suggested works are to be prepared for the relieving Coys; & a copy of same forwarded to Bn. H.Qrs. The greatest care is to be taken in that part of the report concerning the existing wire. All possible information regarding known enemy posts, movements &c is to be given to the relieving unit.

7.------GUIDES No guides will be required.

8.--- RELIEF. On the completion of relief Coys will move independently to the entraining Station BW. 54. TRESCAULT. Distances of 100 yds between platoons to be maintained.

9.--- ENTRAINING. 2nd Lt E.E. Bing. will perform the duties of entraining officer. He will report to the R.T.O TRESCAULT at 9.0 pm. Trains will move off as soon as loaded.

10.--- TRANSPORT ARRANGEMENTS. Officers Mess Gear, Medical Stores, 20 Magazines per Lewis Gun, Denison Food Containers &c. will be carried down by first line transport. All the above, less L.G. magazines, will be dumped at the Bn. Dump by 7.30pm. L.G. magazines will be dumped by Coys. as they pass the Bn dump after the completion of relief.

Lewis Guns & the remainder of L.G. Magazines will be carried down by their teams.

Administrative Instructions to the Transport Officer & Quartermaster are being issued separately.

11. RELIEF COMPLETE will be reported by wire & personally by an Officer of each company at present Hd.Qrs & to the Officer Commanding on completion of billeting in camp.

CODE WORD for relief — BETTER

" " " complete — BETTER-'OLE.

——— " ———

[signature]

Capt & 9/Adjt.

2nd Bn. R.M.L.I.

By Runner

10-25 pm

COPIES to :-

No 1. O.C. [illegible] ✓
2 O.C. ANSON. Bn
3 O.C. 'A' Coy.
4 OC 'B' Coy.
5. OC 'C' Coy
6. OC. D. Coy
7. WAR DIARY.

SECRET. COPY No. .

2nd Bn. ROYAL MARINE LIGHT INFANTRY.
OPERATION ORDERS No. 120.

REFERENCE MAPS :-
FRANCE. 57 c. 1/40,000.
RIBECOURT. 1/20,000.

Bn.Headquarters,
14th MARCH 1918.

1. The 2nd Bn., R.M.L.I. will relieve the ANSON Bn. in the front line trenches on the night of 15/16th March 1918.

2. DISPOSITIONS. The relief will be carried out as follows :-
"A" Co. 2nd Bn., R.M.L.I. will relieve "B" Co. ANSON Bn., in the front line.
"B" Co. 2nd Bn. R.M.L.I. will relieve "A" Co. ANSON Bn. in Immediate Support.
"C" Co. 2nd Bn., R.M.L.I. will relieve "C" Co. ANSON Bn., in Immediate Support.
"D" Co. 2nd Bn., R.M.L.I. will relieve "D" Co. ANSON Bn., in the front line.

3. ADVANCE PARTIES. An Advance party consisting of one Officer per Co. one N.C.O. per Platoon, one N.C.O. and one Signalman from H.Q. Co. will report to the Adjutant at the Bn. Orderly Room at 10.0.am tomorrow.
This party will proceed into the line to take over Trench Stores Defence and Work Schemes, accommodation, etc. Duplicate lists of Stores etc. taken over are to be forwarded to Bn. H.Q. in the Line as early as possible.

4. LEWIS GUNS AND AMMUNITION. Lewis Guns and ten Magazines of S.A.A. per Gun will be carried by the teams into the Line. Twenty Magazines per Gun will be carried by the Transport. O.C. Cos. will detail one O. R. per Co. to accompany the L.G. Ammunition carried by the Transport and to remain at the Bn. Dump until it has been drawn.

5. STORES. Blankets tightly rolled in bundles of ten and clearly labelled, spare Officers Mess Gear, Officers Valises, and Surplus Orderly Room Gear, and men's Packs, will be dumped at the junction of the plank road and main road by 12.0.noon.
O.C. "D" Co will detail a party of 2 N.C.Os and 20 men for loading the above.
Stores and Ammunition for the Line will be dumped at the above mentioned point at 4.0.pm. One servant from each Mess will accompany the Mess Gear up the Line and O.C. "D" Co. will detail one O.R. to accompany the Transport. This man will act as a Guard over Petrol Tins at the dump until the Bn. arrives.

6. TRANSPORT. The Transport Officer will arrange :-
(a) To supply Limbers to convey L.G. Ammunition, Medical Stores, Officers Mess Gear and Orderly Room Gear to the Line.
(b.) To supply Limbers to convey surplus gear to the Q.M. Stores.
(c) To draw out the Cookers at 5.0.pm.

7. MOVE. The Bn. will fall in by Cos. on the plank road at 5.15 .pm and will move off by march routs at 5.30.pm, maintaining distances as follows :- Between Cos. 200 yards. Between Platoons, 100 yards.
O.C. Cos. will report before moving off to the O.C. that their billets have been left in a clean and sanitary condition.

CONTINUED . 2.

8. COOKING ARRANGEMENTS. Cooking arrangements will be the same as during the last tour in the line. Two large Dixies per Co. will be carried up the line by Transport. Two Cooks per Co. will be detailed for duty in the Line one of whom will accompany the Transport.

9. RATIONS. The unconsumed portion of tomorrow's Rations will be carried on the person. The Quartermaster will arrange for the Rations for the 16th to be carried up by the Transport.

10. LOCATIONS. Bn. Headquarters will be located in the late Support Bn. H. Qs. in SCREW TRENCH. Other locations as previously.

11. RELIEF. During the Relief, the following code words will be used.
Code word for RELIEF. "FROZO".
Do. RELIEF COMPLETE. "FROZO GONE"
Relief complete will reported by wire and Runner.

J. Lee

Lieut. & A/Adjutant,
2nd Bn., R.M. L.I.

Issued at 10.20.pm.

COPIES TO :-

No. 1. O.C., and Retain.
2. O.C. ANSON Bn.
3. O.C. "A" Co.
4. "B" Co.
5. "C" Co.
6. "D" Co.
7. Transport Officer and Quartermaster.
8. War Diary.

SECRET. COPY No. 1

2nd Bn Royal Marine Light Infantry
Order No. 121.

Reference Maps:-
FRANCE 57c 1/40000
RIBECOURT 1/20000.

Bn Headquarters
18th March 1918.

1. On the night 19th/20th March 1918 the 2nd Bn RMLI will be relieved by the 1st Bn RMLI and will then proceed into Support.

"A" Co.	1st Bn RMLI.	will relieve	"A" Co.	2nd Bn RMLI.
"B" Co	do	do	"D" Co	do
"C" Co.	do	do	"C" Co	do
"D" Co	do.	do.	"B" Co	do

After relief "B" Co 2nd Bn RMLI will move into quarters at present occupied by "B" Co 1st Bn RMLI in SCREW TRENCH and the vicinity. "A" "C" & "D" Cos. will move into the area at present occupied by the Support Bn.

Relief complete will be reported by Wire and also to the O/C personally by an Officer from each Co.

2. Advance Parties (a). Advance Parties from the incoming Unit will arrive at the respective Co Hdqrs at about 10.0 am. 19th inst. Receipts for all Trench Stores, Defence & Works Schemes &c handed over to the 1st Bn RMLI will be forwarded to these Hdqrs not later than 2.0 pm

(b). An Advance Party consisting of 1 Officer per Co. one NCO from Hdqrs, one NCO per Platoon, Cook Sergt, Lewis Gun Sergt, one Signalman and one MU Rating, will report at these Hdqrs at 9.0 am. They will proceed to Hdqrs 1st Bn RMLI for the purpose of taking over the accommodation, Trench Stores, Work & Defence Schemes, &c.

Lists of Stores &c taken over are to reach these Hdqrs by 5.0 pm. After having taken over this advance party will return to the Bn for the purpose of acting as Guides.

3 Lewis Guns. Lewis Guns and ten Magazines per Gun will be carried by the Crews. 20 Magazines per Gun will be loaded on Limber at the Bn Dump on the way down from the Line. One OR per Co will proceed with this Limber and act as Guard over the Ammunition until it is redrawn from the Support Bn Dump.

4 Transport. Transport Officer has received separate instructions. Mess Gear, Medical Stores, Orderly Room Gear and Boxes will be dumped at Bn Dump by 7.30. pm.

5. Administration. Arrangements will be issued later.

6. Code words. During Relief the following Code words will be used - "Relief" "PELMANS"
"Relief complete" "INSTITUTE"
"Established in Support Area". "THREE PIPS".

J. Lee
Lieut & A/ Adjutant
2nd Bn RMLI.

Issued at

Surgeon Lt. A L P Gould
2/RMLI. 1918

D I A R Y
of
Surgeon-Lieutenant A.L.P.Gould, R.N., attached 2/R.M.L.I.

63rd (Naval) Division, V Corps, Third Army.

In Front Line, Fesquieres?.

Thursday March 21st 1918. Woke at 10 minutes to 5 a.m. by the noise of a terrific bombardment. The Commanding Officer woke at the same time, and at once rushed to the mouth of the dug-out, remarking to me "This is the beginning of the real thing". Two minutes later he ran back shouting "gas", and as the alarm was given we detected phosgene already streaming through dug-out. All gas masks on promptly - Commanding Officer and Adjutant then went up to explore but all was black fog with gas shells bursting all round and gas pervading everything. The next four hours were sheer misery - we sat like caged rats with fear upon us all and a sense of hideous impotence. Fires were lit and fans blown and about 9 a.m. we found atmosphere sufficiently clear to leave off masks below, but above all was still thick. All this time no news was available. About 11 a.m. the sun burst through the morning mist, and the gas slowly cleared out of the ravine. Never was sunshine more welcome! Gas bombardment had now stopped some two hours, but high explosives were falling behind us near the batteries, and barrage could still be heard in front. We got news from the Brigade of an attack on Premy Salient with a slight loss of trench on our front and of further dent to left of Flesquieres on 17th Division front. About noon I got an urgent call to attend wounded at a battery behind us, and went off with Wormald. Found a horrible shambles, about 8 men in deep dug-out with but the scantiest first aid since 8 a.m. I did what I could for them - amputated a hanging arm with jack knife, doped with morphia all round and got all away to Power at Havrincourt. Returned about 1.30. The rest of the day was quiet with us. We had a few minor wounded only. Evening situation reported to be (1) Dent to left of Flesquieres, (2) Dent in front of Ribecourt, (3) Dent in La Vacquerie Sector, re-gained, (4) Voluntary retirement to take place at nightfall from Flesquieres and Ribecourt to H.defences, leaving us occupying front line in Bilhem Chapel Switch and Intermediate Brown Line. This made our Headquarters unsuitable and late at night Spraggett and I were sent to look for new Headquarters and Regimental Aid Post. My search unsuccessful, but Spraggett thinking he had found a place, Headquarters and Company were led off at 4.30 a.m., wandered for 1-1/4 hours in pitchy darkness, failed altogether to identify the spot and finally returned at 5.45 jaded and dejected, and thoroughly unprepared by any rest for the next day's attack. Altogether a black ending to a black day. Commanding Officer appears distinctly unnerved.

Friday, March 22nd. Barrage started early in the left distance. After this fitful sleep, I got up about 7, and had tea and toast with Wrangham. A new search was to be made for Headquarters, but before this was done an alarm was given at 8.30 that Hun was coming over on the "left". The Commanding Officer promptly summoned Headquarters Company and started leading them over via Brown Line to the left where he thought the attack was coming. Morning misty and visibility poor. After crossing Bapaume-Havrincourt road and getting into Brown Line again we came into heavy shell fire; passed poor Collier and Wittey killed, and on through a devilish fire to find Williams. I got separated a little from the Commanding Officer but heard his whereabouts and ran into a Cabouche to find him. With a shock I came upon him there lying badly hit, pale, collapsed, and in great pain. Left arm badly smashed close to shoulder - a second wound in buttocks. Dressing it very difficult, but we did what we could and after a painful half hour I got him fixed up on a stretcher ready for carrying to Havrincourt Village. Then had Wrangham to see to with broken right arm and leg - he was a brick. Together we formed a slow party along a narrow trench on to the Flesquieres road and to the village - a very painful half hour, shells rather thick and both men in pain. However, we arrived without harm at Havrincourt Brewery, where I found Broadhurst. We got them some hot drink and more morphia and packed both off in ambulance to Trescault. I decided to make Regimental Aid Post here and sent back word to Williams, now commanding Battalion, and to men of medical unit. These joined me about 11 a.m., and we rigged up a fairly satisfactory Regimental Aid Post - acetylene still burning, water short. Some wounded drifted in during morning and also a runner with news that Major Coote of Anson Battalion was coming from Anson to command Battalion, but I could get no contact with Battalion. Village shelled continuously and heavily and for 20 minutes about 2 p.m. Brewery was bombarded furiously. We all sheltered under concreted floor, and no harm done, not even to cars standing outside!. These ran intermittently all day, through heavy fire. I was rather anxious about my whereabouts as we could get no news of Battalion or of battle, and about 5 p.m. started off to 1st Marine Light Infantry Headquarters to get news. Here I met runner with note from Medical Officer to return to Ravine. I went straight on, sending my own runner back to fetch Medical Unit. We went a long way round via Brown Trench but arrived safe about 7.30. Found Coote, Lee, Egan, Spraggett and White all there - no great events had occurred on our front but owing to trouble elsewhere we had orders to retire in night to St.Hubert's Cross (in Havrincourt Wood) where eventually we all fetched up and got into billets very tired and hungry - though rations had arrived all right. Here we were to occupy support line with "Anson" in front and 1st Royal Marine Light Infantry to our left. I turned in about 3.30 and slept heavily till dawn.

<u>Saturday, March 23rd.</u> Woke to a bright, sunny, peaceful morning. Hunted round for a Regimental Aid Post and had just fixed up a good hut when news came that we were all to retire again! So had a hasty shave and wash, followed by a welcome breakfast, and at 11 a.m. both battalions started off by companies to Bertincourt. It was a strange scene, columns of men all retiring through the wood and across the open country, forming wonderful targets but for some mysterious reason absolutely unmolested! The battle seemed far enough away from us and our only trouble was the heat of the day.

We passed between Ruyalcourt (now Burning) and Hermes, and so to the front of Bertincourt - by irony of fate the very ground where Thomas and I had been shooting partridges a month ago! Eventually about 2 p.m. we got settled into our bit of the "Green Line", two companies just below the railway embankment in front of Bertincourt, two in reserve behind the Bank; Headquarters took a large drain pipe running through the Bank and I got an excellent hut on the rear side, protected from everything but a direct hit. Line was well dug and excellently wired, and everyone felt confident of holding it. Rations arrived almost as soon as we did and we settled down to a quiet afternoon. Stragglers from other divisions kept coming through us - chiefly 51st, 17th, and 47th Divisions most of the afternoon, but we saw no Huns, and the battle was only close to us on the left where the line took a sharp bend and the Hun was in Velue Wood. We had some casualties from shell fire during the day - Gibbons killed - and these I could only get away in various opportunist methods, directing them vaguely to Bus and Barastre. I was quite out of touch with Field Ambulance and in spite of repeated notes got no bearers from them and no reply. All quiet on our front till evening, after a gloomy meal in Headquarters drain pipe ugly rumours began to arrive about the Boche breaking into Bus on our right. Commandant therefore threw out C Company to act with "Hood" as defensive flank and himself withdrew to Bertincourt about 4 a.m. I remained in hut with Medical Unit and got what sleep I could, wondering much what the morrow would bring and how long our withdrawal would have to go on without a fight.

<u>Sunday March 24th</u>. <u>Dies Nefasta!</u> Had very little sleep, disturbed by wounded passing through and by worrying rumours. Had to keep one poor fellow with gunshot wound of the spine and paraplogia in the hut. Turned out at 7 a.m. could glean little news from Company Headquarters (now in a drain pipe). All was quiet round us and I had just finished a welcome cup of tea with Profitt when without a word of warning "S.O.S" went up from front line at 7.55 a.m. B.Company (in reserve)

dashed up to top of embankment and fire started, while I hurried back to Regimental Aid Post. In less than a minute there were cries of "cease fire" -"Boche is coming in with his hands up". This seemed incredible and a minute later Perry passed me shouting "Boche is in our front line - A and 2 Companies have surrendered, run for your life". We dived for our packs and gear and I leading the way we ran like rabbits across the field and village. I arrived breathless and hot, Perry and others close behind - no machine guns had started yet, but suddenly a hellish barrage came down on Bertincourt Village. The others not appearing and it being apparently a case of sauve qui peut, I dropped my pack and took to my heels straight through village and out the other side, heading for Barastre. By amazing luck I got through safe, and reached opposite slope. Pulling up here, I could see no one behind me and could only believe them fallen in the barrage. I decided to carry on till past the support line and then try to find the remnants of the Battalion, so went on now quite alone, over hill and valley, to edge of Barastre. Just behind this I found 17th Division occupying a line, and met a Brigadier who told me 63rd Division was retiring on Villers au Flos and probably Beaulencourt. Bus, Bertincourt and probably Rocquigny had fallen. I passed on to sugar factory between Le Transloi and Beaulencourt. Here to my joy I found the Staff Captain and odd remnants of the Battalion and Brigade and heard Brigade would be reformed here. I was frightfully hot, thirsty and not a little weary after the morning, which had been disturbing enough. Battle still appeared to be well on both flanks, and rumours came of Boche holding Lechelle, Sailly Saillisel and Haplincourt! Apparently for the moment we were in full retreat, and all seemed black enough. I got some food with Staff Captain and in early afternoon, to my joy, substantial remnants of 1st and 2nd Royal Marine Light Infantry Battalions came in - Coote, Lee, Egan, Spraggett, White, all my Medical Unit, except Wormald and my servant Stamp(?) - about 120 all told! We were all as surprised as pleased to see each other. Their story was very similar to mine - a sudden late order to withdraw, a retreat, then a ghastly barrage, and a gathering up of remnants at Villers au Flos, followed by orderly march to the sugar factory. It seemed that large parts of A and B Companies must have been caught by Boche breaking in on our right and working down the trench before any warning could reach us, but substantial remnants of other companies had got through. Poor Broadhurst and all his medical unit missing. Clutterbuck and West safe with about 120 of the 1st Royal Marine Light Infantry. We all spent an hour resting on the grass waiting for news and orders. We heard that tanks had gone in from Haplincourt and had temporarily pushed Hun back from Bus and Ytres, but situation was still very ugly and we were nearly surrounded! About 5 p.m. we reformed as a slender remnant of the 188th Brigade and started retiring across Somme battlefield for Martinpuich, "Ansons" in front, ourselves as rearguard. We Had a long and weary, but fortunately unmolested march through the gathering dusk, passed 17th Division holding a temporary line near Gueudscourt and fetched up about 9.30 p.m. at Martinpuich. Here we found some huts left by Chinese Labour Corps, and Brigade took up its position. By some marvellous means our rations were there, and we all fell to with a will, getting fires and food. Then late at night the Battalion turned out to hold a guarding line. I stayed in the huts with Headquarters officers of Worcesters, the Colonel, Ladd, Dunlop, Medical Officer of Worcesters, etc., and endeavoured to sleep, but with very little success.

Monday March 25th. Had an early breakfast with the Worcesters; spent the morning in Martinpuich with the 1st Royal Marine Light Infantry and Worcesters - our Battalion holding the line about 1 mile out in support of "Anson". For two or three hours things went well, and on our own front Boche made no advance. Some dozen wounded or so came through and we directed them on to Pozieres - no news from Field Ambulance. About midday Brigade withdrew to Courcelette and we with them. From this time onwards all the battle was absolutely confusion. Our left and right were wildly in the air and no one knew anything -

General Lowrie, G.O.C., of Division in Courcelette up to dangerous hour. Then everyone started slowly withdrawing on Thiepval. Dunlop and I kept together in front of them, believing that all must be cut off and being able to do nothing. We slowly backed across the hideous old battle field till we reached Thiepval ridge. Here there was a terrible scene - long lines of straggling and demoralized troops streaming in. Fortunately Brigadier of 189th Brigade was on the ridge and he held everyone up and slowly reorganized the Division. Our own Battalion turned up about 6 p.m., all still safe and in good order, and good moral. Boche still some way off. Defence of Thiepval ridge was organized, 188th Brigade to hold ridge, 189th and 190th to retire across Ancre. Rations mysteriously arrived in galloping limbers together with ammunition after dusk. For a time there was free interchange of machine-gun fire and we had several casualties, but both sides were absolutely lacking guns, and there was no shelling. We settled down to a strange night - weather very cold, men all "dohe" and a hopeless feeling of isolation and despair on us all. I joined up with O'Neill (Medical Officer of Bedfords) and Dunlop, and together we made a very comfortable Regimental Aid Post in two huts close to a bridge over the Ancre behind Thiepval ridge. Col.Kirkpatrick of "Ansons" came through badly hit in abdomen. We made a good fire and cooked tea, etc., and did our best to sleep for an hour ot two.

Tuesday March 26th. Had only one or two wounded through during night. Slept fitfully, woke about 3 a.m. to hear movement outside, and on going out found Brigade Staff (189th) preparing to move. Found Brigadier who told us Thiepval was to be evacuated at 4.30 a.m., and a new line to be taken up across river, roughly Aveluy-Hamel. We three Medical Officers therefore left with our men about 3.45 a.m., crossed the bridge and made our way to Mesnil Village, where we temporarily installed ourselves in a cellar just being vacated by Royal Field Artillery. A fire and tea here helped to keep out the cold and we slumbered till daylight. Then I set off with Meadowcroft to find Battalion, and was lucky in meeting them close at hand, just taking up their designed position in reserve line just east of Mesnil Village. This consisted of a sunken road near a railway, with one or two inferior dug-outs near, one of which we took for Headquarters. I then returned to find a Regimental Aid Post, which I fixed up much to my satisfaction in the railway station - a two-storey cottage sandbagged on top floor, and with a fair cellar. Having settled here, I went along to Headquarters for breakfast - fried ham and toast eaten with the fingers! During the morning units of the 12th Division came marching in - telling they had been hurried down from Armentières - and evidently coming to reinforce our line. One of the battalions settled in the road near us, and about tea time news came that they were to relieve us, and we were to go to Englebelmer. Day passed quietly - some shelling near us, and one alarm of an attack on our left, which came to nothing. Medical Officer of Buffs joined us in Regimental Aid Post, and took over. Staff Captain looked in for a meal. Village shelled rather heavily at times, but we got no wounded from our own unit. Soon after 6, the Medical Unit (now consisting of Hargreaves and Meadowcroft only) and I set off in advance of Battalion, and walked to Englebelmer. We arrived there to find more "wind" about Hun being in Mailly, which proved quite untrue! Battalion followed soon, and we had just settled into fairly comfortable billets and were looking forward to a night's sleep, when an amazing counter-order came for us to go back to Martinsart! Fortunately cookers and rations had arrived, so all troops got a hot meal at 11 p.m. and foot-sore, jaded and bitterly disappointed, Battalion resumed the road and wearily marched to Martinsart. We arrived at midnight and billetted in the square, where two terrible things happened: (1) an agitated platoon commander came running in with a story that the Boche had broken through into Aveluy Wood, and was close to the village "in force" - his own company surrounded - (2) a few minutes later a high explosive and high velocity shell burst right in the middle of one of our companies - a horrible scene followed, shrieks and groans, men scattering etc. There was a perfect shambles, but everybody turned to with a will to clear, providentially there was an Advanced Dressing Station of the 37th Brigade right at hand, and we had got all the cases dressed and away in 45 minutes! Casualties from this one shell were 5 killed and 18 wounded, including poor "Old Gentleman" among the latter, but fotunately not bad. While this was doing, a frantic buzz was going on at the joint 37th and 188th Brigades. Our function appeared plain, i.e. we had been dragged back to reinforce the morally weak and futile 12th Division. We turned into our billets frightfully tired, for a short time, but in vain - within half an hour the Battalion was ordered out and with our Commandant in command, a joint mob of 20 Royal Marine Light Infantry and "Anson" dashed off, literally shouting with joy to drive back the Hun! The story of what actually happened is difficult to determine, but all the Huns that had got footing were driven headlong back right through Mesnil and across to the other side of the railway, the line was re-established, and the wood was cleared by 4 a.m! This little achievement was due entirely to the jaded ranks of the 2nd Royal Marine Light Infantry and "Ansons" and under the circumstances was little short of miraculous. It had the instant effect of giving a great "buck-up" to the moral of the Battalion. We took 5 machine guns and 12 prisoners, mostly wounded. We had a string of wounded up to about 5.30, but I felt so utterly exhausted that I turned in about 4.30 and left Hargreaves to carry on. Finally all was quiet, and we slept till morning.

Wednesday, March 27th. The morning broke calmly after the feverish night. We had some welcome breakfast in our billets - a large cellar under a farm, lined with potatoes and straw - and dozing among the former, Lee, of course, being totally inert with sleep. There was some shelling of the village, one or two coming unpleasantly close, and the men were moved out of the barn into the fields, but we had no casualties. The day slowly slipped on, and we all slumbered at intervals till tea time, when orders came for the Battalion to move out and hold a reserve line behind Mesnil, to prevent a repitition of last night's trouble. I was left with the Medical Unit and

Headquarters servants. During the evening we had stray casualties coming past from the 12th Division who talked of their men "Falling back" and were all in a state of miserable moral, but evidently no attack was on, though to our right some brisk machine gun fire was audible in the evening, and we heard that the Boche was trying to push forward towards Bouzincourt. Power turned up in the evening bringing Morris, a new Medical Officer (U.S.A.) for 1st Royal Marine Light Infantry, and he stayed with me. Power told me the location of his Advanced Dressing Station on the Englebelmer Road, and left two squads and runners, so we again felt in touch with Field Ambulance. He returned later with news that we were to be relieved by 2nd Division and about 10 p.m. the Medical Officer of the 24th Royal Field Artillery appeared with his men. They had had 24 hour's rest at Englebelmer and were returning to take our place. We all spent a long and weary night together by the fire, keeping ourselves going with tea at intervals, and all dead tired. At last about 4 a.m. the definite order of relief came through and about 4.30 Coote and Lee appeared. Never did a relief seem slower, but at last we got away in driblets - Morris and I started off with Headquarters servants, and we wearily dragged our way along to Englebelmer, and so to Mailly-Maillet, where we arrived completely done, just as dawn was breaking. However, there we found our own principal medical officer with billets ready, and it seemed as though at last we were really to get some rest. I turned in at once, between two large mattresses, and dropped into a heavy sleep.

Thursday,March 28th. Slept till 11 a.m.,turned out for breakfast - lunch and back again to bed. Woke about 4.30 p.m. to hear we were to move back to Forceville, and at 5 p.m. we started, in better spirits than we had been for many a day, and already better for a day's sleep. The march was not long, and we all got in by companies before 7 p.m., to find good billets in an estaminet for ourselves, barns and houses for the men. Other units of the 2nd Division were vacating them for Engelbelmer, and we felt really out of things at last - with beds to sleep on, a village full of splendidly fit New Zealand troops, and not a shell to be heard. We all turned in as soon as we had had some dinner, and slept the sleep of the just - our first undisturbed night for 8 days! Weather broke to-day, and it was raining hard at intervals during the evening, but we little cared for such minor afflictions as this, and felt utterly happy and content.

SECRET. CONFIDENTIAL.

Vol 23

WAR DIARY.

— of —

2nd Bn Royal Marine Light Infy.

Volume 22.

— from —

April 1st 1918

— to —

April 30th 1918.

N B Clutterbuck

Lieut Col: RMLI.

Comdg 2nd Bn R.M.L.I.

2/ A.D.s 63rd RN Division

Instructions regarding War Diaries and Intelligence Summaries are contained in F. S. Regs., Part II. and the Staff Manual respectively. Title pages will be prepared in manuscript.

WAR DIARY or ~~INTELLIGENCE SUMMARY.~~

(*Erase heading not required.*)

SHEET No. 1.

2nd Bn. R.M.L.I.

Army Form C. 2118.

Place	Date	Hour	Summary of Events and Information	Remarks and references to Appendices
Forceville	April 1st 1918		Bn. cleaning up, refitting etc + inspections. Capt. G.A. NEWLING M.C. R.M. joined Bn. + assumed duties of Second in Command. O.O. No. 130 issued.	JCW. appendix I
"	" 2nd "		Bn. proceeds by march route to TOUTENCOURT.	JCW
TOUTENCOURT	" 3rd "		" " " " " " ENGELBELMER. MAJOR H.S. Clutterbuck R.M.L.I. joined + assumed command of Bn. Lt/Cmdr. J. Cook M.C. R.N.V.R. returned to ANSON Bn. O.O. No. 131 issued	JCW appendix II
ENGELBELMER	" 4th "		Bn. Salvage + working parties. LTS. Greenwood + Smith. R.W.K. joined Bn. 1 casualty.	JCW.
"	" 5th "		" " " " " 4 casualties	JCW.
"	" 6th "		O.O. No. 132 issued. Bn. moved into positions ~~on~~ N.W. Edge of AVELUY Wood. About 9.0 A.M. the Bn attacked the enemy position in the wood + succeeded in driving him out, inflicting casualties + capturing prisoners + 9 machine guns. 5 officers wounded (LTS. Proffitt, Braid, Greenwood, 2/LT. E. BING + Sub/LT. OLDHAM) 15 ORs killed, 55 wounded, 26 unaccounted for.	JCW. appendix III
AVELUY WOOD	" 7th "		27 ORs joined Bn. Bn. holding front line position. Relieved p.m. by ANSON Bn + moved to billets in FORCEVILLE. O.O. No. 133 issued.	appendix IV. JCW
Forceville	" 8th "		Bn cleaning up, refitting etc. 12 officers + 240 ORs (army reinforcements) joined Bn. Capt. E.L. ANDREWS + 65 R.M.L.I. reinforcements joined Bn.	JCW.
"	" 9th "		cleaning up, refitting etc. O.O. No. 134 issued. Relieved HOOD Bn in front line	appendix V
AVELUY WOOD	" 10th "		Bn in front line, consolidating etc. 1 casualty.	JCW
"	" 11th "		" " " " ", Relieved by 4th Bn. Bedford. Regt. + proceeded to FORCEVILLE.	JCW.
			O.O. No 135 issued.	appendix VI
FORCEVILLE	" 12th "		Bn cleaning up, baths refitting etc. 39 OR reinforcements joined Bn.	JCW. JCW

A7092 Wt. W128 9/M1293 750,000. 1/17. D. D & I. Ltd. Forms/C2118/14.

Instructions regarding War Diaries and Intelligence Summaries are contained in F. S. Regs., Part II. and the Staff Manual respectively. Title pages will be prepared in manuscript.

WAR DIARY
or
INTELLIGENCE SUMMARY.
(Erase heading not required.)

SHEET. No. 2.

2nd Bn. R.M.L.I.

Army Form C. 2118.

Place	Date	Hour	Summary of Events and Information	Remarks and references to Appendices
FORCEVILLE	APRIL	13th 1918	Bn. cleaning up, baths, refitting etc. Specialist training. O.O. No. 136 issued. Working party	appendix No. 4. JGW.
"	"	14th "	Bn. moved by march route to ARQUEVES.	JGW.
ARQUEVES	"	15th "	SPECIALIST TRAINING + WORKING PARTIES. LT. R. St. G. DOWNER. R.M. rejoined Bn.	JGW.
"	"	16th "	" " " "	JGW.
"	"	17th "	" + Bn. Training.	JGW.
"	"	18th "	" " "	JGW.
"	"	19th "	" Training + working parties. 11 reinforcements joined Bn.	JGW.
"	"	20th "	" + Bn. Training. MAJOR SANDILANDS. R.M.L.I. joined Bn. + assumed duties of Second in Command. CAPT. G. A. Hawkins. M.C. R.M. assumed duties of ADJUTANT.	JGW.
"	"	21st "	CHURCH PARADES.	JGW.
"	"	22nd "	SPECIALIST + Bn. TRAINING. 10 R.M. officers + 4 O.R. reinforcements joined Bn.	JGW.
"	"	23rd "	" TRAINING + WORKING PARTIES.	JGW.
"	"	24th "	" + Bn. TRAINING. 4 reinforcements joined Bn.	JGW.
"	"	25th "	" + " "	JGW.
"	"	26th "	" " " : Inspection by General. Hon. SIR J. H. G. BYNG. K.C.B., K.C.M.G., M.V.O.	JGW.
"	"	27th "	" Training + working parties.	JGW.
"	"	28th "	CHURCH PARADES. Bn. amalgamated with 1st Bn. R.M.L.I. under the name of 1st Bn. R.M.L.I.	JGW.

N. B. Chitterwell;
Lieut. Colonel R.M.L.I.
Comdg. 2nd Bn. R.M.L.I.

A7092 Wt. W128 9/M1293 750,000. 1/17. D. D & I. Ltd. Forms/C2118/14.

Secret | Copy No. 1

2nd Battalion Royal Marine Light Inf

Operation Orders No. 130

Reference Maps:
Sheet 57 d
LENS 11, ed 2

Bn. Hqrs.
1/4/18

1. The 2nd Bn R.M.L.I will move by march route to billets in Toutencourt, to-morrow, 2/4/18.

2. Stores: Blankets tightly rolled in bundles of ten (+ labelled) Lewis Guns and magazines, officers valises, mess, medical and Orderly Room gear will be dumped at the cooker at Bn Hqrs at 10 a.m. O.C. "B" Coy will detail a party of 1 N.C.O + 10 O.R's to report at Bn Hqrs at 10 a.m. for loading above stores

3. The Bn will parade in the orchard at 11 a.m. Dress: Battle order. Separate orders have been issued for 1st line transport. The Bn Sanitary Sergeant and 6 pioneers will remain behind after the departure of the Bn to clear up latrines etc.

4. Order of march:- The Bn. will march in the following order: Hqrs, A, B, C, D, Coys. maintaining a distance of 200 yds as far as Acheux when the Bn will close up. Usual halts will be observed. Head of column will pass the starting point, cross roads Forceville at 11.30 a.m.

5. Route: via Acheux - Lealvillers to Toutencourt

6. Advance parties:- Advance parties under the command of Lt. Spraggett consisting of 1 N.C.O per Coy and Hqrs will proceed to Toutencourt at 9.30 a.m.

7. O.C. Coys will report to the Officer Commanding at 10.30 a.m. at Bn Hqrs that the billets of their respective Coys are being vacated in a clean and sanitary condition.

8. Acknowledge.

J. Lee

Lieut and A/Adjutant
2nd Bn. R.M.L.I.

Issued at

No. 1 O.C and Retain
2 O.C "A" Coy
3 O.C. "B"
4 O.C. "C"
5 O.C. "D"
6 War Diary

Secret

Copy No 1

2nd Battalion Royal Marine L. I.
Operation Orders No 131

Reference Maps.
Sheet 57 d
LENS 11, ed 2.

Bn Hqrs
3-4-18.

1. Move: The Battalion will move to-day by march route to Englebelmer via Harponville - Varennes - Hedauville.

2. Advance Party: Lt Spraggett and 1 N.C.O per Coy. and Headquarters will report to the Adjutant at 8.30 a.m. at Bn. Hqrs.

3 Stores: Blankets in bundles of ten, and labelled, Lewis guns with all magazines, officers' valises and mess, medical and Orderly Room gear will be dumped at Bn Hqrs at 8.45 a.m. O.C. "C" Coy. will detail a party of 1 N.C.O. and 10 O.R's to report to the Bn Hqrs at 8.45 a.m. for loading the above stores.

4. Transport. Separate orders have been issued to the Transport Officer.

5. The Bn. will form up in column of route on the road outside Bn. Hqrs. at 9.30 a.m. Dress: Battle order. From Varennes forward move will be at a distance of 200 yds between Coys. The Bn will be met on arrival by the advance party at P.23 d 9090. The Bn sanitary Sergeant and 6 pioneers will remain behind after the departure of the Bn to clear up latrines etc. O.C. Companies will report to Officer commanding at 9 a.m. at Bn. Head Quarters that their respective companies have vacated billets in a clean and sanitary condition.

6. Acknowledge.

J. C. Lee
Lieut & A/Adjutant
2nd Bn. R.M.L.I.

Issued at 7.15 a.m.

No. 1 O.C. and Retain
2 O.C. "A" Coy.
3 O.C. "B" "
4 O.C. "C" "
5 O.C. "D"
6 War Diary

Secret

Copy No. 1

2nd Battalion Royal Marine L.I
Operation Orders No 132

Reference Maps
Sheet 57 d
LENS 11 ed 2

Bn. Hqrs
6 - 4 - 18

1. Move. The Battalion will move this morning by march route to the north western edge of Aveluy Wood concentrating on arrival at the Light Railway from Q 34 a 00. 00. to Q 34 a 20. 50.

2. Stores: Lewis Guns with all magazines will be carried by Lewis Gun Teams. Orderly room gear and surplus officers' mess gear to be dumped at Bn Hqrs.

3. The Bn will form up in column of route on the Englebelmer – Martinsart Road in the order Hqrs, A, B, C, D Coys. Head of column to be at Q 25. b. 50. 30 at 2.30 am. 50 yds distance will be maintained between companies

4. Route via Martinsart to position as indicated in para. 1

5. Acknowledge.

J. C. Lee

Lieut & A/Adjt
2nd Bn. R. M. L. I.

Issued at 12.20 am.

No. 1 O.C. and Retain
2 O.C. "A" Coys.
3 O.C. "B" "
4 O.C. "C" "
5 O.C. "D" "
6 War Diary

Secret

Copy No 1

2nd Battalion Royal Marine L. Inf.
Operation Orders No 133

Reference Maps
Sheet 57. d
LENS 11 ed. 2

Bn. Hqrs
1/4/18.

1. Relief. The Bn. will be relieved to-night in the front line by the ANSON Bn, and after relief Coys will concentrate at Q. 33. d. 90. 65 where they will be met by the O.C.

2. Method of Relief
A Coy 2nd Bn. R.M.L.I will relieve "A" Coy of the Anson Bn
B ———— " ———— ditto ———— " ————
C ———— " ———— ditto ———— " ————
D ———— " ———— ditto ———— " ————
Officers commanding Coys will detail one guide per platoon to report to Bn Hqrs at 8.30 pm.

3. Stores Medical stores, orderly room and signal gear will be dumped at the Bn. ration dump at 8 pm. Lewis guns and all magazines will be carried by Lewis gun crews to the cross roads at Englebelmer where they will be placed on limbers for conveyance to Forceville.

4. Special orders concerning relief and billeting have been issued to the T.O and Q.M. Coys will be met by guides at the cross roads Forceville

5. Acknowledge

J.C. Lee
Lieut & Adjutant
2nd Bn. R.M.L.I.

Issued at 4 pm

No. 1 O.C. and Return
2 O.C. "A" Coy
3 O.C. "B" "
4 O.C. "C" "
5 O.C. "D" "
6 War Diary
7 O.C. Anson Bn

Secret

Copy No 1

2nd Battalion Royal Marine L. Inf
Operation Orders No 134

Bn Hqrs
9.4.18

1. The Bn will relieve the Hood Bn to-night in the front line, extent of front to be held from Q. 35 central - northwards along railway bank to the northern grid line of Q. 35.

2. "A" Coy will occupy the front line "B" Coy in immediate support just inside Northern edge of AVELUY WOOD from Q 34 b 90.40 to Q. 35 a. 20. 80 "C" Coy along the Northern edge of AVELUY wood (just inside) in Q. 35 a + b. "D" Coy in shelters by the light railway from Q. 34. a. 10.40 to Q. 33. d. 90.80. Bn Hqrs will be in large mound at Q. 34 b. 30.90. R.A.P. will be located at about Q. 34. a 20.00 (on edge of wood).

3. Route: Southern corner of FORCEVILLE - overland due EAST to HEDAUVILLE - MAILLY-MAILLET Road, leaving ENGELBELMER on left - along MARTINSART Road - thence overland leaving MARTINSART on the right to Q. 34 a. 10.40 where guides from HOOD Bn will meet A Coy. The O.C. of B. C + D Coys will be provided with a Bn runner to act as guide.

4. Special instructions have been issued to T.O. + Q.M.

5. Bn will fall in by Coys outside billets at 6.10 pm. Dress: Battle order. Order of march, A H.Q. B. C + D Coys.

6. All billets will be left in a clean and sanitary condition. O.C. Coys will report to O.C at Bn HQ at 6.0 pm that their billets are clean.

7. Coys will report in position to Bn HQ by code word BISCUITS

8. Bn dump will be located at Q. 34 a. 10.00

9. Acknowledge

J. Shee

Lieut + A/ Adjutant
2nd Bn. R.M.L.I

Copies to
1 O.C. and Retain
2 O.C A Coy.
3 O.C B "
4 O.C C "
5 O.C D "

Secret

2nd Bn Royal Marine Light Infantry
Operation Order No 135

Copy No 1

Bn Hqrs
11/4/18

1. Relief — The Bn will be relieved to-night by the 4th Bn Bedfordshire Regt and on completion of relief will proceed to FORCEVILLE. Each Coy will be relieved by the corresponding Coy of the 4th Bn Bedfordshire Regt.

2. Method of Relief — B and C Coys will fall in ready to move off just outside the northern edge of AVELUY WOOD at 9 pm. A and D Coy will fall in at the Bn Ration Dump. When B and C Coys have been relieved they will close on "D" Coy and O Cs of each Coy will report personally "Relief complete" to the 2nd i/c at the Bn Ration Dump who will issue orders to them re moving off.

3. Guides — Each Coy will detail one guide per platoon to report at Bn H.Q at 8 pm where they will be joined by one Bn H.Q. runner per Coy. These guides will conduct the incoming units into their areas.

4. Lewis Guns — Lewis Guns and all magazines will be carried by crews to the cross roads at ENGELBELMER where they will be placed on limbers for conveyance to FORCEVILLE.

5. Stores —
(a) Medical stores, Orderly Room, Signal & mess gear will be dumped at the Bn Ration Dump by 8 pm.
(b) Every effort is to be made to send down to the ration dump by 8 pm all picks, shovels, & petrol tins in the area and every man is to leave the line with a complete set of equipment, rifle, bayonet, steel helmet, box respirator + 250 rounds of ammunition.
(c) Disposition maps, summaries of intelligence, arrangements, cooking, water and rations, & S.A.A will be turned over to the incoming unit. Receipts will be obtained and forwarded to these HQrs as soon as possible. Periscopes, Very pistols are not to be turned over to the incoming unit.

6. Special orders concerning the relief have been issued to O.C. A Coy, Q.M., T.O. + Cook Sergeant.

7. Companies will be met at the Cross Roads, FORCEVILLE by billeting N.C.O.

8. Acknowledge

J. [signature]

Lieut + A/ Adjutant
2nd Bn. R.M.L.I.

Issued at 1.10 pm

1 Captain
2 OC 4th Bn Bedfordshire Regt
3 OC "A" Coy
4 OC "B" "
5 OC "C" "
6 OC "D" "

Secret

Copy No 1

2nd Battalion Royal Marine L.I.
Operation Orders No 136

Reference Maps
Sheet 57. d
LENS 11 ed 2.

Bn Hqrs
13-4-18

1. Bn will move by march route to-morrow to billets at ARQUEVES via ACHEUX - LEALVILLERS - BELLE EGLISE. Separate orders have been issued to the Transport Officer.

2. Advance Party. The advance billeting party consisting of Lt Spraggett and 1 N.C.O. per Coy and Hqrs will report to the Adjutant at Bn Hqrs at 8.30 am. to-morrow.

3. Stores. Blankets, tightly rolled in bundles of ten, and labelled, Officers' valises, Lewis guns with all magazines, Orderly Room, Medical & Mess Gear will be dumped at Bn Hqrs at 10 am. O.C. D Coy. will detail 1 N.C.O and 10 O.Rs who will report to the Adjutant at 10.0am for loading the above stores.

4. The Bn will parade by Companies at 11 am. Dress:- marching order with steel helmets and will form up in the order: Hqrs, A. B. C & D Coys. 200 yds distance being maintained between Coys. Head of column to be at P.27. b. 45.85 at 11.25 a.m. Usual halts to be observed. The Bn will close up on the ACHEUX - LEALVILLERS Road. The Bn Pioneer and 6 pioneers will remain behind to clear up latrines etc.

5. Cook. Dinner will be served on arrival at ARQUEVES. O.C. Companies will report to the O.C at 10.45 am. at Bn Hqrs that their respective Coys have vacated billets in a clean and sanitary condition.

J. Shee

Issued at 7 pm

Lieut & Adjutant
2nd Bn. R.M.L.I.

No 1 O.C retains
2 O.C. A
3 O.C. B
4 O.C. C
5 O.C. D
6 War Diary